HUMAN RIGHTS:
THIRTY YEARS AFTER THE UNIVERSAL DECLARATION

HUMAN RIGHTS: THIRTY YEARS AFTER THE UNIVERSAL DECLARATION

COMMEMORATIVE VOLUME ON THE OCCASION OF THE THIRTIETH ANNIVERSARY OF THE UNIVERSAL DECLARATION OF HUMAN RIGHTS

edited by

DR. B.G. RAMCHARAN
Special Assistant to the Director,
United Nations Division of Human Rights

Published under the auspices of the International Forum on Human Rights

1979
MARTINUS NIJHOFF
THE HAGUE/BOSTON/LONDON

The distribution of this book is handled by the following team of publishers:

for the United States and Canada

Kluwer Boston, Inc.
160 Old Derby Street
Hingham, MA 02043
USA

for all other countries

Kluwer Academic Publishers Group
Distribution Center
P.O. Box 322
3300 AH Dordrecht
The Netherlands

Library of Congress Cataloging in Publication Data

Main entry under title:

Human rights.

'Published under the auspices of the International Forum on Human Rights.'
'The Universal declaration of human rights': p.
Includes index.
1. Civil rights (International law) – Addresses, essays, lectures. 2. United Nations – Civil rights – Addresses, essays, lectures. I. Ramcharan, B.G. II. International Forum on Human Rights. III. United Nations. General Assembly. Universal declaration of human rights. 1978.

K3240.6.H88   341.48'1   79-9932

ISBN 90 247 2145 8

PRINTED IN THE NETHERLANDS

CONTENTS

MESSAGE

SEAN MACBRIDE S.C.
Nobel Laureate

The thirty years which have elapsed since the proclamation of the Universal Declaration of Human Rights have witnessed significant progress in the elaboration of universally accepted standards on human rights, in the development of measures and methods for their implementation and in devising action for combating violations. However, there is no room for complacency because the world still witnesses today violations of human rights as widespread and massive as anything it has ever seen in the past. Perhaps some of the present generation of rulers were educated before the influence of the Universal Declaration began to be felt; more certainly remains to be done to instil the principles of the Declaration in the minds of people everywhere. Whatever the reasons, the human rights situation today remains a tragic one.

The thirtieth anniversary of the Universal Declaration is an occasion for a renewed *Call to Action* to people of goodwill everywhere to join in a determined endeavour to protect the rights of human beings everywhere. We should seek to mobilize all the forces at our disposal in this noble endeavour and strive, in the remaining years of the twentieth century to build a climate in which those who may be minded to disrespect human rights will immediately feel the ostracism and, if necessary, the sanctions of the international community.

The Universal Declaration remains the fundamental basis for our actions. As is happening presently in relation to the new international economic order, human needs, science and technology, the environment, communications and other areas, the human rights concept will continue to be enriched and enlarged, but the precepts of the universal Declaration are immutable and will remain valid forever: the right to life, freedom from torture, the right to be free from arbitrary arrest and detention and other such rights know no bounds of time.

On the occasion of the thirtieth anniversary of the Universal Declaration let the *Call to Action* go forth in the world to the end that every individual and every organ of society, keeping the Universal Declaration in mind,

shall strive not only by teaching and education but also by active partisan-
ship to promote respect for the rights and freedoms of human beings
everywhere and to bring about their realization.

Sean MacBride
10 December, 1978

FOREWORD: THE INTERNATIONAL PROTECTION OF HUMAN RIGHTS.
THIRTY YEARS AFTER THE UNIVERSAL DECLARATION*

MR. E. LUARD

There is nothing new in concern for human rights. For centuries this has been at the centre of political thinking and political aspirations. Demands for protection against the tyrannical acts of governments, for assurances against arbitrary arrest and inhumane punishments, for freedom of assembly and expression, for the rule of law, for the exercise of political rights through the universal franchise and the secret ballot, have been among the most insistent themes of all political activity in many countries. In many cases such aspirations took the form of an explicit demand for Bills of Rights or similar constitutional safeguards to protect those freedoms.

The importance of the system of human rights protection established over the last 35 years – in the United Nations Charter, and in particular in the Universal Declaration of Human Rights, the anniversary of which this volume commemorates – is that those same demands were now for the first time put forward, not as claims made by the citizens of one country against their own government, but addressed by the peoples of all nations to governments all over the world. The concern about the human condition, which had been expressed so often within each national state, was now internationalised.

This raised new and difficult problems. Governments are not always receptive to criticisms, even by their own subjects, of the treatment they accord their citizens. But they are still less receptive to complaints by the citizens of other countries about their activities relating to their own subjects within their own borders. They have been accustomed to feel such actions are of no concern to those elsewhere. And traditional international law justified them in refusing to admit the right of foreigners to interfere in any matters which they could claim to be within their own domestic jurisdiction.

Such arguments, however, are no longer acceptable today. Perhaps the fundamental reason is that the world has become smaller. We all know

* Parliamentary Under-Secretary of State.

much more about what happens elsewhere. We have closer contacts with those who live under the rule of other governments. Concern cannot be suddenly cut off at the nearest international frontier so that we can be our brother's keeper on one side but not on the other. We are all one of another today, internationally as well as nationally. And the human rights situation in any part of the world, it is now recognised, is a legitimate matter of international concern.

Even in the thirty years since the Universal Declaration was signed that recognition has become more widespread. Concern over human rights matters is probably more widely aroused today than in any previous time. No country today, it is generally believed, has the right to raise impenetrable barriers at their frontiers, behind which they can do what they please with their own citizens. Nor can any country make itself indifferent to criticism elsewhere. Every nation, however apparently impervious, is to some extent concerned at the judgements of their actions which are made in other states.

Many governments nevertheless maintain strong resistance against the judgements made elsewhere of their human rights performance. They at least profess to be uninfluenced by these. And of course they maintain that their performance in this field in any case leaves nothing to be desired. How then can international concern make itself felt most effectively?

First, a beginning can be made by setting out the *standards* which the international community demands of governments everywhere in this respect. Such standards were laid down for *individual* governments in those earlier Bills of Rights. They were laid down for *all* governments everywhere in the Universal Declaration of Human Rights. That process of standard-setting has been carried further in subsequent years in the drafting of Conventions and Declarations in various specialised fields – such as the elimination of racial discrimination, for example – during the years that followed the signing of the Declaration. This process reached its culmination in the signing and coming into force of the two Covenants on civil and political rights and on economic, social and cultural rights, perhaps the most comprehensive undertakings which governments have yet entered into in this field.

But over the last decade or two it has increasingly been felt that to set standards alone is not enough. This does nothing in itself to protect individual human rights if the standards laid down are then blatantly disregarded. A second need therefore, it is now increasingly recognised, is to establish machinery for *implementation:* that is, to ensure that the commitments entered into are in fact fulfilled. This need too has been increasinly understood by international bodies in recent years.

Effective measures of implementation of this kind were first established in the European system of human rights: through the European Commission and Court of Human Rights in Strasbourg. Within the UN system measures of this kind were introduced first (apart from the fairly developed machinery of this kind established by the ILO for supervising implementation of conventions affecting working conditions) in the provisions of the Convention on the Elimination of all Forms of Racial Discrimination, under which a committee was established to supervise the performance of governments in fulfilling their undertakings. Similarly the Covenant on Civil and Political Rights established a Human Rights Committee to examine its implementation. But possibly the most important advance was that made in ECOSOC Resolution 1503 (XLVIII), establishing new procedures for dealing with communications that reveal a consistent pattern of gross violations of human rights. The procedure is a long and cumbrous one. Discussion takes place only in private. But it does at least allow international debate and judgement on the most glaring violations of human rights which occur in any part of the world. At the same time there has been, over the last two or three years, an increasing readiness in the Commission to discuss such matters, under other procedures, in public sessions of the Commission as well.

It would be hard to say how much effect these procedures have had on the human rights situation in those countries which have actually been discussed. At the very least the governments concerned have been compelled to justify their acts to the outside world. Where some form of investigation has occurred (and this too is now being more frequently instituted) this serves to expose the situation, on the basis of objective evidence, to the public outside. In a few cases it may even cause the government concerned to seek to put its house in order and introduce reforms. There is no government in the world that is not to some extent concerned about its image within the international community generally. All wish to avoid condemnation if they can. Sometimes the only way to do this effectively may be to abolish the practices which have aroused concern.

Perhaps the most important way in which such discussions exert influence, at least over the longer term, is that they establish, slowly, a different international environment. They make clear the standard of conduct which the international community generally expects of governments. This then comes to influence, if only slowly, the thinking of all. It can be used by the population of the country concerned itself to demand reforms from their own government. And even the thinking of the erring governments themselves may eventually be slowly influenced.

If protection is to be made more effective than it is today there are further improvements in the machinery which could be made. Many observers feel that, to reflect the world-wide concern today felt on human rights questions, the United Nations Human Rights Commission should meet more frequently, and perhaps for longer periods. It should be more ready to undertake public debate on the human rights situation in individual countries, since it is the fear of public exposure which is the main inducement to reform. The Commission should be willing where necessary to propose on-the-spot examination of the situation in a country that is criticised: since the nation with nothing to hide should have no reason to resist this, it can be to some extent a means of testing the validity of the accusations made. For this purpose the Commission may need to appoint assessors, either individuals or committees, which can assemble independent evidence concerning the situation in particular states. There is scope for more regional bodies in this field which may have more influence with governments. There is need, many think, for more specialised activity as well: perhaps by separate bodies to protect rights in particular fields – the rights of prisoners, of mental patients, of conscientious objectors, of religious freedom, freedom of the press and so on. Above all, the Commission needs of course to show itself entirely free from political partiality in its approach to all such questions: so that the nature of the action taken, and of the judgements made, is related directly to the scale of the violations established, and not to whether or not the country accused is a popular scapegoat or is politically congenial to other member states.

These are only a few ways in which the effectiveness of the United Nations Commission on Human Rights and similar bodies could be increased. Other ideas are considered in the pages of this volume. One essential if work of this kind is to achieve its purpose is that it should secure adequate publicity and notice in the world as a whole. Since it is adverse publicity which is the main stimulus to governments to improve their performance in this field, no improvement in the procedures or machinery of human rights bodies can have much effect unless their judgements are also widely publicised in the world as a whole. It is a matter for some regret that the meetings and activities of the United Nations Commission on Human Rights (including the welcome improvements in its method of working introduced in the last few years) at present receive so little notice in the world's press and other media.

In the thirty years since the Universal Declaration was signed there has undoubtedly been an advance in the response to human rights violations of the international bodies responsible. We have gone beyond the stage of drafting high-sounding declarations; we are more willing to consider individual situations and pronounce judgements on them. Yet human rights are still being grievously violated in very many parts of the world. Let us hope that in the next thirty years we can strengthen the machinery still further so that the rights of individuals are more adequately safe-guarded in every nation of the world. This book may contribute a little to-wards that process.

Foreign and Commonwealth Office
London
April 1978

HUMAN RIGHTS:
THIRTY YEARS AFTER THE UNIVERSAL DECLARATION

INTRODUCTION

DR. B.G. RAMCHARAN

Thirty years ago, on 10 December 1948, the General Assembly adopted and proclaimed the Universal Declaration of Human Rights as a common standard of achievement for all peoples and all nations. This was the first step in the promulgation of an International Bill of Human Rights, a goal which was eventually realized in 1966 with the adoption of the International Covenant on Economic, Social and Cultural Rights, the International Covenant on Civil and Political Rights and the Optional Protocol thereto.[1] All three of these instruments finally entered into force in 1976.

At the very time as the Covenants became operational however, the concepts of human rights and fundamental freedoms evolved thus far were being tested for their contemporary relevance. Questions were also being posed as to the approaches which should be followed in order to bring about the implementation of human rights. The issues raised require careful study and examination if the Universal Declaration of Human Rights is to become a reality in the lives of human beings everywhere.

The International Forum on Human Rights, which was established in 1977 with the objective of promoting inter-disciplinary study and discussion of human rights issues, decided to invite leading scholars and practitioners in the field to address their minds to some of the issues facing the international community presently. This volume contains the fruits of their labours.

The present introduction will attempt to identify some of the main ideas and suggestions contained in the chapters which follow, with a view to seeing the extent to which they offer a programme of action for the future.

REAFFIRMATION OF THE UNIVERSAL DECLARATION

The thirty years which have passed since the adoption of the Universal Declaration have, according to Dr. van Boven, reaffirmed its validity as can

[1] For the texts of these instruments, see Appendix.

authoritative statement of human rights. He cites convincing evidence for
this view. The Universal Declaration, he adds, will continue to serve within
and outside the United Nations as "a common standard of achievement for
all peoples and all nations" and as "a common understanding of the
peoples of the world concerning the inalienable and inviolable rights of
all members of the human family". This view accords with that of the
General Assembly which, in its resolution 32/123 on the observance of the
thirtieth anniversary of the Universal Declaration, adopted without dissent
on 16 December 1977, confirmed that the Universal Declaration "has been
and rightly continues to be a fundamental source of inspiration for national and international efforts for the protection and promotion of human
rights and fundamental freedoms".

STATUS OF THE UNIVERSAL DECLARATION

Prof. Humphrey argues persuasively that there can now be no doubt that
the Universal Declaration possesses high moral and political authority. Not
only has it become an international standard by which the conduct of
governments is judged both within and outside the United Nations; it has
inspired a whole cluster of treaties – including the European Convention
for the Protection of Human Rights and Fundamental Freedoms; it is
reflected in many national constitutions, some of which reproduce its
provisions *verbatim* as well as in national legislation and in the decisions of
both national and international courts. He argues, further, that, in addition to their admitted moral and political authority, the justiciable provisions of the Declaration, including those enunciated in articles two to
twenty-one inclusive, have now acquired the force of law as part of the
customary law of nations.

REALITIES THAT FALL SHORT OF ASPIRATIONS

Notwithstanding the ideals of the Universal Declaration, many blemishes,
UNESCO points out, mar the picture that the actual situation presents.
Human rights are still not effectively assured in practice in most of the
world's countries. Clashes of interest, over-riding reasons of State, sudden,
sharp changes in the economy and in social relationships, the vicissitudes
of national and international policy, inter-group antagonisms, fluctuations
in power relationships, the pressures of egoism, intolerance or obscuran-

tism, the pretexts afforded by circumstances – all these are continually responsible for shameful retreats which may well produce indignation and alarm. It would be disastrous, it is urged, if, in the end, these retreats were to be met by the false wisdom or illusory realism of resigned acceptance.

Specific violations of human rights take many different forms in our present-day world: deliberate violations that State authorities, claiming to be the sole judges of their legitimacy, justify on the grounds of particular circumstances of political or social crisis, the need for the maintenance of order or the safeguarding of national unity; flagrant violations (although there is often an attempt to conceal these beneath a travesty of the very principles that are being trampled underfoot) such as those revealed in exceptional, localized situations – *apartheid,* vestiges or upsurges of colonialist or neo-colonialist oppression, foreign occupation; less obvious violations, embodied in the structures or the functioning of unjust societies which, under the veneer of formal democracy, engage in forms of oppression and exploitation that bear particularly heavily on underprivileged groups or on certain categories of individuals, including the great mass of women; interference with freedom of thought, conscience or religion, or with the possibility of seeking, receiving or spreading information or ideas; violations of which the community has more recently become conscious, such as those involved in the unjustified appropriation of natural and cultural resources or the despoiling of the environment or, again, those that may, for individuals and nations, attend the consequences of scientific and technological progress; violations arising from contempt for or rejection of cultural identity, or from the tensions present in multi-ethnic societies, and so on. The problem of the protection and application of human rights is immense, since it covers every aspect of the life of individuals and groups.

THE HEART OF THE MATTER

UNESCO emphasizes that while the full achievement of human rights presupposes patient efforts in the furtherance of development, the dissemination of knowledge and the equalization of opportunities for acquiring it, the humanizing of the environment and the background to life, the enhancement of cultures and communication between them and the promotion of a genuine mutual communication system among people, this does not mean that active measures for the protection, achievement and extension of human rights can be put off until tomorrow except at the cost of an intolerable abdication. It is one thing to take into account the fact that circumstances are difficult, the need for patient improvement of the conditions determining the life of every society and the extent and level of what it can achieve, the limited amount and precarious nature of the resources that can be mobilized for this purpose, and the need for a determined and prolonged effort to build a better and a juster world. It would be quite another to disregard the obligation, admitting of no compromise, to tackle without further ado all the clear denials of human rights which are already such a scandal. In the first case, what is involved is a question of degree – a more or less satisfactory position as regards the possible achievement of rights. In the second instance, a question of principle is at stake: the question of respect for man, which is indivisible. The difficulties of the times do not remove the scandal of inequality – rather the reverse; the requirements of public order and safety – not to mention the will to power – can neither justify nor excuse arbitrary arrest and the use of torture, any more than concern for growth – not to mention the lure of gain – can make the subjection and exploitation of human labour acceptable, or than the desire to build up an intellectual elite can warrant keeping the mass of the people in ignorance. Without prejudice to the persistent efforts needed to build a world more conducive to the full enjoyment of human rights, the protection, consolidation and extension of those same rights call urgently for resolute, specific, direct action.

A STRUCTURAL AND GLOBAL APPROACH

Dr. van Boven sees ambiguities in the present international human rights debate; this debate, he thinks, is to a certain extent, a dialogue of the deaf, because external factors and internal conditions are not taken in their mutual relationships and consequences. Wealthy and powerful nations can only make their domestic and foreign human rights policies credible and acceptable if they cease using their influence and powers to the detriment of peoples elsewhere and if they are ready to accept radical changes in the international order so as to promote greater justice, self-reliance and economic growth among and within poor nations. At the same time the rightful demand by many developing countries for a new international order, politically and economically, should go hand in hand with a commitment to work for a just economic, social and political order at national and local levels. A new international order can never be separated from the domestic orders.

It is admitted that contextual circumstances may, by themselves, be a threat to human rights or that they may constitute, as such, gross violations of human rights. They can provide an explanation why human rights are seriously at stake, but they can certainly not be adduced as a justification for the infringements of certain very basic rights and freedoms, such as the right to life, the right to be free form torture or from cruel, inhuman or degrading treatment or punishment, the right not to be held in slavery or in slavery-like conditions and the right to be free from arbitrary arrest or detention. Too often the violations of these very basic rights and freedoms are the result of abuse of power by selfish rulers, of grotesque arrogance of those who claim to be masters, of ill-conceived notions and practices of superiority, of racist ideologies. It is tempting and deceiving on the part of such abusers of powers to invoke structural causes and external factors in order to camouflage violations of human rights which they are consistently committing, thus adding immensely to the suffering which is already prevalent as a result of the contextual circumstances. He submits that a structural and global approach is definitely called for, if a human order is to be built up in which political freedom and social justice can prevail, and if a just and participatory society is to be constructed.

The call for a structural and global approach, however, cannot serve as an excuse for not devising, as a matter of urgency and immediacy, ways and means of improving the capacity of the United Nations to put a stop to violations of human rights wherever they may occur. In this connexion it is his view that a United Nations High Commissioner for Human Rights could be one of the "ways and means of improving the capacity of the United Nations to put a stop to violations of human rights wherever they may occur" and could be considered as a complementary device to the structural and global approach.

SYNTHESIS OF THE HUMAN RIGHTS CONCEPT

Professor Hector Gros Espiell, while cautioning against the imprecisions of classifying human rights approaches into those of "Western", "Socialist" and "Third World" countries, points out the main trends of the approaches followed by these three groups and concludes that the reciprocal and growing influences and relationships between the fundamental ideas of the predominant concepts existing in each of these groups, their permeability and the relativity of their limitations, reflect an optimistic outlook as to the continuity, acceleration and depth of the approximation and interpenetration process between the different concepts of human rights existing in the world today.

Even while recognizing the inevitable dissensions which arise as a consequence of the different ideological backgrounds, the different historical roots, the contrasting traditions and the diversity of political, economic and social outlooks, this process must, he feels, inevitably result in a progressive improvement in the world-wide position of human rights, if we bear in mind the essential factor of human unity and the necessary equality of all men, based on respect for their dignity.

Although the respect, promotion and protection of human rights presupposes an idea which is unalterable in essence due to the human dignity possessed by every individual, it cannot be doubted that the concept of human rights, their relationship with political society and with socio-economic factors, their limitations and forms of legal protection, will evolve and change with the course of time.

This evolution and this change has, during recent years, revealed a process directed towards coalescing the different concepts and accentuating the efficiency of procedures aimed at guaranteeing and protecting individual rights and freedoms. These ideas whose merits and positive values cannot be ignored, do not signify, however, a forgetfulness or denial of the sad reality existing in many countries of the world today, located in all areas.

Professor Gros Espiell feels that if the enormous and deplorable gap between poverty and opulence and between development and under-development could be diminished, and the misery and ignorance which characterize a majority of the peoples of the Third World could sensibly decrease, an acceleration in the process of the effective recognition of human rights, especially in these countries, could be expected. He immediately adds, however, that the negative circumstances of poverty, sickness and ignorance are not the only factors in determining and explaining violations of human rights. Present-day history and reality show many examples of cultured peoples and countries with a relatively high level of living which suffer from despotism and a flagrant violation of freedom. Nevertheless, in fighting poverty and ignorance, the international community is fighting for final victory in the cause of human rights.

Without prejudice to other actions which should be undertaken in the field of human rights at the present time so that progress can be made towards the goal of universal and effective respect, it is necessary, he feels, to persevere in the fight to affirm the existence of an ideal and of a concept common to all peoples, as listed in the Universal Declaration of Human

Rights and reiterated in the Proclamation of Teheran under which equal and inalienable rights are attributed to all members of the human family.

The acceptance of this ideal, of this common concept, is the essential basis for progress, looking at the question with universal vision, in the long, painful and difficult process towards the effective respect of man's freedoms and rights throughout the world.

In looking at the ground already covered, despite a feeling of sadness due to the deplorable situations which have existed and continue to exist, we cannot allow ourselves to give way to scepticism.

HUMAN RIGHTS AND FOREIGN POLICY

Regarding the role of human rights in the foreign policy of States, Prof. Fremond detects that a large proportion of governments seems to pay more attention to the protection of human rights abroad than at home and that, as a result, the defence of human rights has become an instrument of foreign policy. Dealing specifically with the policy of the Carter administration in the USA, he poses the question whether certain difficulties now being experienced in that policy should lead to a return to the ranks of the apostles of *Realpolitik,* for whom the protection of human rights must be left to States, and for whom any other approach could only aggravate tensions in the relations between States. This attitude, he asserts, is impractical in that it does not propose an alternative solution. He feels that critics of the Carter policy are passing judgement over a policy which is just beginning to show results. He detects in the policy a radical and deliberate change of stress: the protection of human rights is no longer but one among other concerns of foreign policy; it has become an objective. He thinks that "uncertain though the results, and contradictory though the commentaries may be, there can be no doubt that an interesting experiment is underway. A government disposing of great means is currently trying to promote the protection of human rights through diplomatic action. The enterprise is based on a realistic appraisal of the situation. It is clear that in our transnational system internal unrest is dangerous to international peace. A government which abuses its powers by limiting the fundamental freedoms of its citizens, by threatening the integrity of persons, by practising or tolerating torture, by permitting corruption and practices which aggravate social contradictions and, therefore, lead to explosive tension prevents the normalization of international relations. The protection of human rights has thus become one of the essential conditions for the preservation or the re-establishment of peace. It can clearly be seen that on this point the Carter administration, by making it one of the mainstays of its foreign policy, has shown the way which must be followed.''

STANDARD-SETTING

The editor of the present volume recalls that the General Assembly has recommended in its resolution 32/130 that the standard-setting work of the United Nations system in the field of human rights, and the universal acceptance and implementation of the relevant international instruments should be encouraged. He suggests that a balance needs to be struck between the implementation of existing standards and the elaboration of new standards. The emphasis should be placed on the former always mindful, though, that standard-setting is an inherent part of the process of implementing human rights. Human rights standards should be aimed at the establishment of a new human order alongside the new international economic order. Human rights standards should also be brought to bear upon efforts to establish a new international economic order so as to ensure that the human factor is never lost sight of.

There is need, it is argued, for better planning and more careful consideration of priorities in standard-setting activities because it is felt that the present system operates on too *ad hoc* a basis and that sometimes not enough groundwork is done before the standard-setting exercise is begun. Responsibility for planning is recommended to be entrusted to the Sub-Commission on Prevention of Discrimination and Protection of Minorities.

It is also urged that greater use should be made of more flexible forms of standard-setting, for example, recommendations, bodies of principles, model codes, and declarations, especially when standards are being elaborated to spell out rights already stated in principle in existing instruments.

The need is also perceived for the ongoing collection, analysis, systematisation and dissemination of procedural standards being developed in the application of implementation procedures as well as those contained in resolutions of human rights organs.

Regarding the future outlook for the adoption of international labour standards, Dr. Valticos finds that a huge area remains to be covered by international labour law, which will continue to make a major contribution to social policy in the world as long as it is able to anticipate and channel the new needs of societies in constant evolution.

UNIVERSALITY OF STANDARDS

Dr. Valticos reminds us that one of the main effects of the standards adopted in the United Nations system has been to underline the universal validity of human rights. Sometimes, however, he finds there has been a tendency to voice doubts as to the possibility of having universal standards in view of the diversity which exists between countries in the economic, social and political fields. Nothing, he pleads, could be more dangerous for the protection of human rights than this sceptical relativism. Reasoning of this kind would lead to a denial of the recognition by mankind of certain common values which transcend differences of race, faith, political structure, culture and economic development and which are based on the equality, freedom and solidarity of all men. It would be equivalent to dividing up the world with sealed partitions and admitting that there should be "sub-standards for sub-humans".

This does not mean that there is no room for regional instruments alongside the universal standards. Such instruments could supplement the existing universal standards on subjects of particular interest to a given region, or even open the way to subsequent universal action. It can also be useful to examine at the regional level the problems which arise in the implementation of universal standards in a given region. This has been done by the ILO since 1970.

The standards themselves, however, in a world which has to live as one and meet the universal aspirations of its peoples, must in their essentials be uniform. Recent consultations undertaken by the ILO resulted in a massive affirmation of this principle.

IMPLEMENTATION IN THE FUTURE

Mr. Luard feels that if protection is to be made more effective than it is today there are further improvements in the machinery which could be made. Many observers, he asserts, feel that, to reflect the world-wide concern today felt on human rights questions, the United Nations Human Rights Commission should meet more frequently, and perhaps for longer periods. It should be more ready to undertake public debate on the human rights situation in individual countries, since it is the fear of public exposure which is the main inducement to reform. The Commission should be willing, where necessary, to propose on-the-spot examination of the situation in a country that is criticised: since the nation with nothing to hide should have no reason to resist this, it can be to some extent a means of testing the validity of the accusations made. For this purpose the Commission may need to appoint assessors, either individuals, or committees, who can assemble independent evidence concerning the situation in particular States. There is scope for more regional bodies in this field, which may have more influence with governments. There is need for more specialised activity as well: perhaps by separate bodies to protect rights in particular fields – the rights of prisoners, of mental patients, of conscientious objectors, of religious freedom, freedom of the press and so on. Above all, the Commission needs to show itself entirely free from political partiality in its approach to all such questions: so that the nature of the action taken, and of the judgements made, is related directly to the scale of the violations established, and not to whether or not the country accused is a popular scapegoat or is politically congenial to other member States. One essential if work of this kind is to achieve its purpose is that it should secure adequate publicity and notice in the world as a whole. Since it is adverse publicity which is the main stimulus to governments to improve their performance in this field, no improvement in the procedures or machinery of human rights bodies can have much effect unless their judgements are also widely publicized in the world as a whole. It is a matter for some regret, he feels, that the meetings and activities of the United Nations Commission on Human Rights (including the welcome improvements in its method of working introduced in the last few years) at present receive so little notice in the world's press and other media.

Mr. Moskowitz, however, feels that is is not a question of creating new institutions or of refining old procedures, but one of perception and understanding; what is called for is an integrated approach that takes into account all important factors which bear upon the subject and seeks to resolve the internal and external contradictions blocking the evolution of international human rights.

But first, he says, we must rid ourselves of certain notions which encumber the United Nations human rights programme and contribute to its general disorientation. For example, in our eagerness to pass from standard-setting to implementation, or from word to deed, we have tended to overlook the broad area of promotion and its vast opportunities and possibilities for constructive achievement, in favour of a role for the United Nations in redressing violations of human rights outside the framework of the International Covenants on Human Rights. Whatever the immediate reasons which prompted some or all of us to force the world body into a role for which it was ill-equipped constitutionally, politically, as well as morally, it has become abundantly clear that international protection of human rights will not be achieved by reproach or condemnations, whether by majority vote or consensus. As Dr. van Boven, Director of the Human Rights Division of the United Nations, pointed out in his maiden speech at the opening of the thirty-fourth session of the Commission on Human Rights on 6 February 1978, the misconception that the Commission should deal with violations of human rights by either condemning a Government or by instituting an investigation may be one source of the Commission's difficulties in handling allegations of violations of human rights. The same applies to the General Assembly and other United Nations organs concerned. A careful examination of United Nations intervention in the racial situation in southern Africa, in the Middle East dispute and, more recently, also in Chile, shows, he asserts, that the world body has little to offer to the resolution of problems short of complete submission or capitulation. Moreover, these three cases of United Nations experience with situations involving allegations of gross violations of human rights, have been patently acts of political assertion and can hardly serve as models for the conciliation of disputes and the redressing of wrongs. Rather, they would indicate that the authority of the United Nations might be invoked to better advantage by the general acceptance of the undisputed and uninhibited right of every State Member to inveigh in every major organ of the Organisation against what it regards as grave injustices and to raise issues of gross violations of human rights without the encumbrance of formal procedures and without formal conclusions and recommendations.

Let us, he advises, leave the Covenants on Human Rights to work out their own historical dialectics and to contribute their just share to the growth of an international human rights jurisprudence as a reliable and predictable guardian of the liberties of man. For the rest, the most constructive work in which the United Nations might engage with great profit in the immediate future, is to turn its attention to a systematic examination of the conceptual political and practical problems which impede the realization, in whole or in part, of the Universal Declaration of Human Rights, with a view to removing such impediments. Surely, if the United Nations had been engaged in an examination of that kind, resolution A/32/130 could never have proved by assertion what it could not assert by fact. The resolution is only symptomatic of the intellectual chaos which pervades the international human rights field; there are no valid reasons

why in this the thirtieth year of the Universal Declaration that document,
which was conceived of the ages should have been shaken to its foundations. The great task before the United Nations is to restore intellectual discipline to its work in human rights, to draw clear distinctions between
fashionable fads and critical causes, and to cleanse the human rights programme of all cant and pretense. Only then can we hope for a rational approach that will permit the consolidation of the achievements of the past
and ensure progress in the future.

THE INTERNATIONAL COVENANTS

A forceful point mady by Dr. Valticos is that the true effectiveness of the
methods of implementing instruments on human rights will depend in large
part on the setting aside of political considerations so as to permit an objective, quasi-judicial examination of cases. While representative bodies
have an important role to play they must do this so as to contribute together to a fuller observance of human rights and not – and this concerns
governments especially – by showing mutual indulgence or engaging in a
form of diplomatic warfare.

On the new page which has been turned for the international protection
of human rights by the Covenants, what will matter – whatever the organisation concerned – will be not so much the procedural rules – although they
are of undeniable importance – as the spirit in which they are implemented.
This means that States – old as well as new – must recognize more and more
completely that the concepts of co-operation and interdependence and the
principles of community interest in human rights and the welfare of mankind are in the process of replacing the traditional concept of national sovereignty in its absolute and exclusive sense. It also means that the international organizations, and more particularly the bodies responsible for following up the implementation of the relevant international instruments,
must be able to carry out their functions with the combination of thoroughness, objectivity, common sense and diplomacy but firmness which is
necessary to the realization of these standards. The international community would have a heavy burden of responsibility to bear if it did not
prove equal to such a task.

The editor of the present volume finds that the first report of the Human
Rights Committee shows evidence of seriousness, independence, courage
and dedication. He notes that the Committee has underlined its independence by pointing out, in its first report, that it is not a subsidiary United

Nations body but a conventional organ established by the States parties to the Covenant. It recognizes that it is not a court but, rather, an expert body mindful of judicial, diplomatic, fact-finding and conciliation elements in its functions.

GENERAL PROTOCOL FOR PROMOTION AND PROTECTION OF HUMAN RIGHTS

Dr. Das draws attention to a certain want of focus, which, according to him, arises out of conflicts in the objectives of the Charter, their inter-dependency and a co-ordinated approach to them; out of absence of knowledge about, and the possibilities of, national action and co-operation; and out of failure to discuss flexible international machinery. After dealing with these, Dr. Das submits for discussion a draft protocol which could eventually be adopted by the General Assembly, providing a scheme whereby States may accept certain minimum undertakings and optionally adhere to greater commitments. He suggestst it be called a General Protocol for Promotion and Protection of Human Rights and Fundamental Freedoms, and could consist of various parts. Parts I and II might contain certain general provisions. Part III might deal with national reporting systems, and part IV with international reporting. All these parts with parts IX and X on reservations and declarations and final clauses, respectively, might be the minimum to which a State party to the protocol would commit itself. The other parts would all be optional subject to individual declarations under various conditions. These parts might include: part V, good offices and conciliation; part VI, communications from individuals, groups of individuals and non-governmental organizations; part VII, mediation; and part VIII, international court of human rights. While parts V to VIII would be tied to each other to some extent, flexibility lies in the ability to subscribe to all or any of them or to none of them. All of these parts would be open to separate declarations. A State party may be willing to subscribe to one part but not to another.

It would be left to the General Assembly to decide to apply the protocol to existing or future conventions, whether or not they include measures for their implementation, because it would allow States parties to various conventions to weigh and decide for themselves whether they wish to go beyond these measures and subscribe to more far-reaching obligations. This does not exclude discussion, decision or inclusion in conventions of appropriate provisions for their implementation. Besides conventions, the

General Assembly may open the protocol to implementing certain Declarations or parts of them which it would designate, since there may well be subjects on which a declaration need not be followed by a convention.

The proposed protocol could also be utilized with regard to specific Recommendations, which may be designated by the General Assembly relating to special subjects for which neither a convention nor a declaration may be most suitable, or when some particular objective of a limited scope is contemplated.

THE FUTURE ROLE OF ILO

After being in the vanguard, there is a danger, Dr. Valticos points out, of finding ony day that one has become a venerated ancestor and a somewhat outdated model. Is the ILO model still valid? An emphatic "affirmative reply is given". However, evolution is still possible in future supervision. For example, while the role of employers' and workers' organizations is already considerable – and indeed essential for the thoroughness of supervision – measures taken in recent years to inform and train them so as to better equip them to fulfil their functions in this area could be further developed. At the national level, more systematic co-operation could also be developed between these organizations and their countries' governments following the adoption in 1976 of Convention No. 144, which provides for tripartite consultations on matters affecting international labour standards.

But at the present stage of development of the supervisory procedures, major improvements, he thinks, no longer seem possible: the fundamental principle of complementary resort to independent bodies and tripartite bodies is firmly established and can hardly be called into question. In addition, two relatively recent trends will no doubt develop in the years to come: in the first place, the use of discreet methods of discussion between the governments concerned and the representatives of the Director-General in an attempt to overcome difficulties encountered; in the second place, in serious cases – and possibly in cases in which the discreet attempts at settlement have failed – resort to the formal procedures of complaint and representation, the number of which has for a series of reasons substantially increased in the course of the last ten years.

STRATEGIES FOR FUTURE REGIONAL ACTION

The editor of the present volume advances a policy for future regional action encompassing: (a) The establishment of further regional commissions; (b) the establishment of arrangements at sub-regional levels; (c) the establishment of less formal, more consultative arrangements such as standing conferences or consultative committees; (d) the establishment of human rights committees or task forces in existing regional political, economic or social organizations; (e) the establishment of human rights desks, task forces or committees in the Secretariats of existing regional organizations; (f) the assignment of a role in the promotion of human rights and in the dissemination of information thereon by the United Nations regional economic and social commissions; (g) the establishment of regional institutes on human rights; (h) the holding of more regional seminars and training courses on human rights; (i) encouraging and assisting non-governmental organizations such as regional bar associations, trade unions and church organizations to contribute to the promotion of human rights. The major non-governmental organizations should aim at appointing regional field officers for human rights; (j) the appointment of United Nations field officers for human rights in the various regions of the world.

THE ROLE OF TRANSNATIONAL GROUPS

Prof. Cassese traces the activities of certain "progressive" transnational groups and concludes that they usefully complement the activity of the United Nations in the field of human rights. These groups, he finds, are aware of the fact that they have come into being in part because of the greater awareness of human dignity diffused from 1948 to the present by the United Nations. It is their intent to act in a way that is supplementary and complementary with respect to the activity of the United Nations. They start from the assumption that it is necessary to fight on more than one front and more than one level in order to effectively carry human rights and the rights of peoples into effect. The groups in question therefore intend to support and help the United Nations in fields in which the latter cannot explicate an effective action because of the governmental conditioning to which it is subjected. At the same time, however, these groups try to strengthen and enhance the more progressive United Nations Member States, in order to stimulate a more incisive action for human rights, mainly by investigating more deeply the socio-economic causes of

situations which deviate from the respect of human rights and by seeking to
abandon nationalistic or group outlooks.

PART ONE:

THE CONTRIBUTION OF THE UNIVERSAL DECLARATION

CHAPTER I

THE UNIVERSAL DECLARATION OF ·HUMAN RIGHTS: ITS HISTORY, IMPACT AND JURIDICAL CHARACTER

PROF. JOHN P. HUMPHREY*

A. HISTORY OF THE UNIVERSAL DECLARATION

The catalyst to which we owe the Universal Declaration of Human Rights and indeed much of the new international law of human rights which has so radically changed the theory and practice of the law of nations[1] was the gross violations of human rights that were committed in and by certain countries during and immediately before the Second World War. For it was these atrocities that fostered the climate of world opinion which made it possible for the San Francisco Conference to make the promotion of respect for human rights and fundamental freedoms "for all without distinction as to race, sex, language or religion" one of the pillars on which the United Nations was erected and a stated purpose of the Organization.[2] It was on these foundations that the new international law of human rights was built.

There are seven specific references in the Charter to human rights and freedoms but nowhere does it catalogue or define them. A few delegations to the Conference, including the Chilean, Cuban and Panamian delegations sponsored provisions which would have had the Charter guarantee the protection of specified rights; and Panama even urged the incorporation of a bill of rights; but none of these proposals were accepted. Largely as a result of an energetic lobby conducted by certain American nongovernmental organizations,[3] however, the Conference did include in the Charter an article 68 by which the Economic and Social Council was instructed to set up a commission for the promotion of human rights; and although there was no mention in the article of such a mandate it was

---

* Former Director of the United Nations Division of Human Rights.
[1] See Humphrey, "The International Law of Human Rights in the Middle Twentieth Century" in Bos (ed.) *The Present State of International Law* (Kloner, 1973) p. 75 *et seq.*
[2] Article I of the Chapter.
[3] See Humphrey, "The U.N. Charter and the Universal Declaration of Human Rights" in Luard (ed.) *The International Protection of Human Rights* (London, 1967) p. 40 *et seq.*

generally understood that this commission would draft an international bill of rights.[4]

One of the first acts of the Economic and Social Council was to set up this commission with an explicit mandate to prepare, amongst other things, a draft bill.[5] Before, however, the new Commission on Human Rights could act on this mandate, an attempt was made by Panama in the General Assembly to have the draft which it had sponsored at San Francisco adopted as a resolution of the Assembly. Had it succeeded the history of the human rights programme in the United Nations would have been different; but the attempt was defeated, largely by the efforts of Eleanor Roosevelt, a member of the United States delegation, whom everyone expected would become the first chairman of the Human Rights Commission.

The most important business of the Commission when it met under Mrs. Roosevelt's chairmanship in its first regular session on 27 January, 1947, was to make arrangements for the drafting of the bill. No decision had yet been taken as to its form. There were several possibilities which were discussed in a Secretariat working paper; it could be drafted as a resolution of the General Assembly – in effect a declaration – but this would only have the force of a recommendation and would not be binding in international law; it could be a multilateral convention binding on all states which ratified it (an option which, the Secretariat prophetically added, might involve delays) or there could be an amendment to the Charter which if adopted would make the bill part of the fundamental law of the United Nations, in effect the solution that had been rejected at San Francisco. Although the Australian and Indian delegations strongly advocated a convention, the great majority of the governments represented at this first session of the Commission favoured a declaration, and it was in that form that the first draft, the so-called Secretariat Outline,[6] was prepared. It was only at its second session that the Commission decided to draft a bill in three parts: a declaration, a multilateral convention (soon known as the Covenant and later as the Covenants after the General Assembly decided that there would

[4] In the speech with which he closed the Conference President Truman said that "under the Charter we have good reason to expect the framing of an international bill of rights acceptable to all the nations involved." United States Department of State Bulletin, vol. xiii, no. 314, p. 5.

[5] ECOSOC Resolution 1/5 of 16 February, 1946. It may be noted that the council did not adopt the recommendation of the United Nations Preparatory Commission that the work of the commission also be directed to "any matters within the field of human rights considered likely to impair the general welfare or friendly relations between nations".

[6] U.N. Document E/CN/AC.1/3. This draft is reproduced as Annex A of document E/CN.4/21 and also in the Yearbook on Human Rights for 1947 (United Nations, Lake Success, 1949) at p. 484.

be two conventions) and measures of implementation.

The Commission made no attempt at its first session to draft the declaration, but it did appoint a committee consisting of its chairman (Mrs. Roosevelt of the United States), its vice-chairman (P.C. Chang of China) and its rapporteur (Charles Malik of the Lebanon) to prepare a first draft. This Committee of three held only one meeting– a tea-party really in Mrs. Roosevelt's Washington Square apartment on the Sunday following the adjournment of the Commission – and soon found itself without a mandate. Nor did it draft any articles, partly because Chang and Malik – two of the most brilliant men ever to sit on the Human Rights Commission and who would later be among the principal architects of the International Bill of Rights – were poles apart philosophically and could seldom agree on anything; but the committee did ask the Director of the Human Rights Division in the Secretariat to prepare a draft declaration. He eventually did so but not until after the Commission's arrangements were upset by the Economic and Social Council when somewhat tardily the Soviet Union realized that these arrangements effectively excluded it from any role in the early drafting process. The issue was resolved when on 24 March Mrs. Roosevelt informed the president of the Council that she was appointing a new drafting committee of eight members of the Commission: Australia, Chile, China, France, the Lebanon, the United States, the United Kingdom and the Soviet Union. Strictly speaking she had no legal right to change a decision of the Commission in a matter on which it had been explicit; but her solution was realistic and politically acceptable and it was approved by the Council which also instructed the Secretariat to prepare a 'documented outline' of the Bill, a confirmation in effect of the mandate it had received from the committee of three except that whereas that committee had asked for a draft declaration the Council was now calling for a documented outline which could have been interpreted as meaning a simple list of rights. In fact the so-called Outline was a draft declaration.[7] This draft, which was based on a number of drafts that had been prepared by a number of individuals and organizations,[8] contained forty-eight short

[7] The work of the Secretariat was later described by the late Nobel laureate, René Cassin, as not being capable of use in oral debate. See his *La Pensée et l'Action*. He uses substantially the same language in an article, *Quelques souvenirs sur la Déclaration universelle de 1948, Revue de Droit contemporain* (15e année, no. 1/1968) p. 3 *et seq*. *"C'est pourquoi"*, he writes, *"je fus chargé par mes collègues de rédiger, sous ma seule responsabilité, un premier avant-projet"*. This statement is patently wrong as the record shows. See *infra*. Nowhere does Cassin mention that there existed a Secretariat draft.

[8] They included a draft by Gustavo Gutierrez (which had probably inspired the draft Declaration of the Duties and Rights of the Individual which Cuba sponsored at San Francisco) and others by H.G. Wells, Professor (as he then was) Hersch Lauterpacht, the Reverend Wilfrid Parsons, S.J., Rollin McNitt and by a committee presided over by Lord Sankey after a

articles in which both civil and political and economic and social rights were catalogued and defined. With two exceptions all the texts on which the Director worked came from English-speaking sources and all of them from the democratic West; but the documentation which the Secretariat later brought together in support of his draft included texts extracted from the constitutions of many countries.

The new drafting committee of eight met at Lake Success from 9 to 25 June. After a long debate during which the Secretariat draft declaration was discussed and compared with a draft convention sponsored by the United Kingdom,[9] the representative of the Soviet Union, Professor Koretsky – a future judge of the International Court of Justice – suggested that a working group consisting of the representatives of France, the Lebanon and the United Kingdom be asked to collate the opinions that had been expressed. He wanted this working group to report back to the Drafting Committee a few days before the next session of the full Commission. Koretsky's motion was interpreted as a delaying tactic, but the working group was nevertheless appointed with a mandate to report back forthwith 'a logical rearrangement' of the articles of the Secretariat draft and how they should be redrafted in the light of the committee's discussions and divided between a manifesto and a convention. The working group met immediately and asked the representative of France, René Cassin, to prepare a new draft based on those articles of the Secretariat draft which he considered appropriate for a declaration. He did this over the week-end with the help of Emile Giraud, an officer in the Division of Human Rights.

Cassin's draft[10] reproduced the Secretariat draft in most of its essentials and style. Scme of his articles were no more than a new French version of the official United Nations translation of the English original. He also changed the order of some of the articles, combined in one article principles the Secretariat draft had expressed in two and divided some of them

public debate conducted in Britain by the *Daily Herald.* Still others came from the American Law Institute (the text sponsored by Panama at San Francisco and in the General Assembly), the American Association for the United Nations, the American Jewish Congress, the World Government Association, the *Institut de droit international* and the editors of *Free World;* and the American Bar Association provided an enumeration of subjects.

[9] See U.N. Document E/CN.4/21 Annex B/R.25. The United Kingdom draft convention had little if any influence on the final outcome. It had, however, been prepared with skill and imagination and had it been pushed more energetically might have become a solid basis for the Covenant on Civil and Political Rights. It did not contain any mention of economic, social and cultural rights.

[10] This draft in Cassin's handwriting was displayed, at the request of the French government, at United Nations Headquarters on the occasion of the tenth anniversary of the adoption of the Universal Declaration; and a photographic reproduction of the same manuscript is reproduced in his book, *La Pensée et l'Action,* already cited.

into two or more articles; and he left out some of the articles because, in his opinion, they could be more appropriately included in a convention. Many of his changes and in particular his changed order did not survive the test of time.

One of the very few new ideas in Cassin's draft was in his article twenty-eight which said that "the protection of human rights requires a public force" a truism which the Drafting Committee did not retain. Other articles enunciated principles which were more philosophical than legal, principles not included in the Secretariat draft which had avoided assertions that did not enunciate justiciable rights. His first article which read: "All men are brothers. Being endowed wtith reason, members of one family, they are free and possess equal dignity and rights" created so much difficulty at the Commission's second session that Ambassador Bogomolov was prompted to ask why the Declaration should be filled with solemn affirmations lacking in sense. It also led to difficulties with the Commission on the Status of Women which objected to its language. But the greatest harm that resulted from the introduction of unnecessary philosophical concepts was the needless controversy and useless debate which they invited, particularly in the General Assembly.

With the help of the Commission on the Status of Women, the Commission's two sub-commissions on freedom of information and the prevention of discrimination, the 1948 Geneva Conference on Freedom of Information, the Specialized Agencies and non-governmental organizations, the Human Rights Commission and its Drafting Committee continued to work on the Declaration until the late Spring of 1948. Its work on the two covenants, as they later became, would not be completed until 1954; but on 18 June, 1948, at the end of its third session the Commission adopted its draft of the Declaration with twelve of its members voting in favour. Byelorussia, the Soviet Union, the Ukraine and Yugoslavia – anticipating the stand they would later take in the General Assembly – all abstained from voting. The draft declaration was therefore ready for consideration by the Assembly at its third session.

Although the Economic and Social Council through which the Commission's text was transmitted to the General Assembly had so many human rights items on the agenda of its seventh session, including the draft convention on genocide and the Final Act of the Information Conference, that exceptionally it set up a special committee to deal with them, the Council made no changes in the text of the Declaration which when it reached the Assembly was sent to the Third Committee. In the light of the many difficulties which then arose, it was fortunate that the chairman of this committee was Charles Malik who as rapporteur of the Commission was familiar with all the details of the legislative history of the draft. It was a tribute to the work of the Commission that many of the governments represented in the Assembly would have accepted the text as it stood; but in the event the Third Committee devoted eighty-one long meetings to it and dealt with one hundred and sixty-eight resolutions containing amendments. In the circumstances it is remarkable that the text finally adopted was so much like the Commission's text.

Several delegations, including those of New Zealand and the Soviet Union, tried for different reasons to postpone the adoption of the Declaration. The New Zealanders were opposed to adopting any declaration until the Covenant was ready: "If the Declaration were adopted first", its representative argued, "there was less likelihood that the Covenant would be adopted at all".[11] Had this advice been followed the adoption of the Declaration could have been postponed indefinitely; for it was only in 1966, eighteen years later, that the Assembly approved the Covenants and opened them for signature. Since in the meantime the United Nations human rights programme became a vehicle for political controversy, it is quite unlikely that at any time after, say 1949, the Declaration could have been adopted with its present content. It is inconceivable, for example, that at any later date there would have been no mention in it of the controversial principle of the self-determination of peoples which soon became a hot issue in the United Nations.[12]

Another unsuccessful challenge to the Commission's text was the well organized attempt, under the leadership of Cuba, to replace it in most of its essentials by the text of the American Declaration of the Rights and Duties of Man which the Organization of American States had adopted at Bogota earlier in the year – no small threat when it is remembered that twenty of the then fifty-nine member states of the United Nations were Latin American.

Although the Third Committee was ostensibly a non-political forum, the atmosphere in which it worked was charged by the Cold War and by irrelevant recriminations coming from both sides; but the Committee worked hard and by United Nations standards efficiently. Some of the most controversial issues came up in connection with matters that should never have been discussed. One pregnant source of controversy was the article, already mentioned, that Cassin had fathered in the Commission's

[11] A/C3/S.R. 89 at p. 4.
[12] The Soviet Union did try to have a reference to the principle inserted in the document even in 1948.

Drafting Committee which now read: "All human beings are born free and equal in dignity and rights. They are endowed by nature with reason and conscience and should act towards one another in a spirit of brotherhood". A motion to transfer the article to the preamble was defeated after an emotional debate, probably because the South Africans had tried to amend it in a way which in the charged atmosphere was interpreted as an attempt to weaken it. But the most controversial issue to which the article gave rise was whether it should contain some reference to the Deity. In the event the words "by nature" were deleted.

Attempts to postpone the adoption of the Declaration were, as already indicated, defeated. It was, however only in the night of 6 December that the Third Committee finished its task and forwarded its report to the plenary session of the Assembly, just in time for that body to adopt the Declaration in the night of 10 December,[13] only two days before the end of the session. There were no dissenting votes but the six communist countries which were then members of the United Nations, Saudi Arabia and South Africa all abstained.

This is not the place to review the legislative history of the Declaration[14] or even to analyse its thirty articles. Some of the articles could have been better formulated and the document suffers from the inclusion in it of certain assertions which do not enunciate justiciable rights; but having regard to the very great number of people who in one way or another contributed to the text it is a remarkably well drafted document. There were some important omissions including the failure to include any article on the protection of minorities[15] and to recognize any right of petition even at the national level – a right so fundamental that it is recognized even by some authoritarian countries – let alone by the United Nations.[16]

Remembering that the final arbiters of the text were governments it is perhaps just as well that no serious attempt was made to catalogue or define those duties which are correlative to human rights; but the principle that everyone owes duties to the community is recognized in article 29. This important article also stipulates the conditions under which limitations may be legitimately placed on the exercise of human rights and freedoms, the only permitted limitations being such "as are determined by law solely

---

[13] G.A. A/811.

[14] On the legislative history, see Albert Verdoodt, *La Naissance et Signification de la Déclaration universelle des droits de l'homme* (Louvain, 1964).

[15] See Humphrey, "The Sub-Commission on the Prevention of Discrimination and the Protection of Minorities", *American Journal of International Law,* vol. 62 (1968) p. 869 *et seq.*

[16] Humphrey, "The Right of Petition in the United Nations", *Human Rights Journal,* vol. iv, p. 463 *et seq.*

for the purpose of securing due recognition and respect for the rights and freedoms of others and of meeting the just requirements of morality, public order and the general welfare in a democratic society".[17] The reference here to public order can be compared with advantage to the use in the Covenant on Civil and Political Rights of the expression "public order (ordre public)" which insofar as that instrument is concerned in any event introduces the nebulous and dangerous concept of public order in civil law jurisdictions.

The Declaration gives pride of place to the traditional civil and political rights which are catalogued and defined in its first twenty-one articles. There then follows, after an "umbrella article", a list and definitions of economic, social and cultural rights which, in 1948, were still controversial in many countries; witness the principal reason that motivated the division of the Covenant into two parts. It was indeed the inclusion of these rights in the Declaration which was one of the reasons for its great historical importance.

B. IMPACT AND JURIDICAL CHARACTER OF THE UNIVERSAL DECLARATION

The adoption of the Declaration was recognized as a great achievement and it immediately took on a moral and political authority not possessed by any other contemporary international instrument with the exception of the Charter itself. One of the very few dissenting voices was that of Sir Hersch Lauterpacht who in a book published shortly after the adoption of the Declaration went so far as to question even its moral authority.[18] Had this great lawyer, who was also a dedicated if impatient partisan of human rights, lived longer, he would have recognized not only the great moral authority of the Declaration but, it is submitted, its now binding character as part of the law of nations. There can now in any event, thirty years after its adoption, be no doubt, that the Declaration does possess both moral and political authority. Not only has it become an international standard by which the conduct of governments is judged both within and outside the

---

[17] The author of the present essay has attempted in an essay in a book to be published sometime in 1978 to discover the meaning of this article.

[18] "The moral authority and influence of an international instrument of this nature must be in direct proportion to the degree of sacrifice of the sovereignty of states which it involves . . . The Declaration does not import to imply any sacrifice of the sovereignty of the state on the altar of the inalienable rights of man and, through them, of the peace of the world." International Law and Human Rights (London, 1950) p. 419.

United Nations (it has been invoked so many times that it would require a major effort of research simply to list them); it has inspired a whole cluster of treaties – including the very important European Convention for the Protection of Human Rights and Fundamental Freedoms[19] – it is reflected in many national constitutions, some of which reproduce its provisions *verbatim* as well as in international legislation and in the decisions of both national and international courts.[20] The thesis to which the remainder of this essay will be devoted is that, in addition to their admitted moral and political authority, the justiciable provisions of the Declaration, including certainly, those enunciated in articles two to twenty-one inclusive,[21] have now acquired the force of law as part of the customary law of nations.

Law as that term is understood by lawyers acquires its normative binding force from the source or authority from which it emanates. In the case of international law this is ultimately the will of the international community, which has been traditionally expressed either directly by customary rules or indirectly by treaties which are themselves binding by virtue of the customary rule, *pacta sunt servanda*. To these two traditional sources the Statute of the International Court of Justice has added a third, "the general principles of law recognized by civilized nations". The fact therefore that the Declaration is not a treaty is not a reason for denying that it has the quality of law. A very good case can be made for the proposition that, as suggested by the French delegation at the 1948 session of the General Assembly many if not all principles set forth in the Declaration are "general principles of law"[22] a proposition ample evidence for which can be found in the documentation prepared by the United Nations Secretariat for the Drafting Committee of the Human Rights Commission in 1947. But if that is so (and it most probably is) those principles would be part of international law by virtue of their recognition by the legal systems of "civilized nations" and not because they are proclaimed by the Universal Declaration. The question, important as it may be, is not therefore an appropriate one for further examination in an inquiry into the juridical

---

[19] See the preamble to this Convention.

[20] See Egon Schwelb, "The Influence of the Universal Declaration of Human Rights on International and National Law", Proceedings of the American Society of International Law (1959) p. 217 *et seq.*; and "United Nations Action in the Field of Human Rights", U.N. Publication ST/HR/2 Sales number E 74 V. The latter very useful Secretariat document is now being brought up to date.

[21] Some of the articles set forth, as already indicated, philosophical assertions. Most of the rights proclaimed in articles 22 to 28, but not all of them, are programme rights the implementation of which can only be progressive.

[22] See Sir Humphrey Waldock, 106 *Recueil des Cours* (1962) p. 198: "certain fundamental rights are general principles of law recognized by civilized nations and have been frequently applied by international tribunals in cases concerning the treatment of foreigners."

character of the Declaration itself. If the Declaration as such now has the force of law it must be because it has acquired the force of customary law.

There is no agreement as to the meaning or character of custom in international law.[23] Professor A. d'Amato has gone so far indeed as to argue that the concept as traditionally understood must now be replaced by the concept of consensus.[24] The terms "custom" and "customary law" are no more than convenient terms for describing a particular juridical phenomenon; what is important is the phenomenon and not the tag. But tempting as it is to try to discover the real meaning of the phenomenon in the light of some of the theories that are now being put forward as to its real nature and to apply the findings to the Declaration, the case for its binding character will be stronger if these tags are given their traditional (one is tempted to say customary) meaning.

Traditionally and in the still dominant theory "custom", as the tag implies, is usage or practice which is accepted as law, a definition that has behind it the authority of both the Statute of the International Court of Justice[25] and of the Court itself.[26] Usage implies an element of time; but, whereas it was once thought that usage had to be of long standing, it would now seem that although time is still an element the necessary duration need not be long.[27] As Tanaka J. wrote in his dissenting opinion in the Continental Shelf cases, "the speedy tempo of present international life promoted by highly developed communication . . . has diminished the importance of the time factor and made possible the acceleration of the formation of customary international law. What required a hundred years in former days may now require less than ten years".[28] The point need not be laboured here because the Universal Declaration is already thirty years old and the practice that will presently be referred to stretches over the whole of that period.

[23] The much quoted observation made by Professor Jules Basdevant in 1936 is still true: *les idées des juristes sur le caractère de la coutume n'ont atteint ni à l'unité ni à la clarté"*. Règles générales de la paix, *Recueil des Cours* 1936 – IV p. 508.

[24] The Concept of Custom in International Law (Cornell University Press, 1971). For a criticism of this theory see H.W.A. Thirlway, *International Law and Codification* (Leiden, 1972) p. 49 *et seq.*

[25] Article 38 1 (b).

[26] See in particular the Continental Shelf cases, I.C.J. Reports, 1969, p. 3 at p. 44.

[27] Josef L. Kunz, "The Nature of Customary Law", *American Journal of International Law*, vol. 47 (1947) p. 666: "international law contains no rules as to how many times or for how long a time this practice must be repeated".

G. Schwarzenberger, *Manual of International Law* (London, 1967) p. 32: "It is not, however, necessary to prove that the practice has been followed for any particular period of time."

Even Thirlway, *op. cit.,* who otherwise takes a very conservative view of the nature of custom, admits that "in the circumstances of today" customary law can "change and develop very much more rapidly than was the case in the smaller and in a sense less active international community of the last century".

[28] Continental Shelf cases, *op. cit.,* 1977. Quoted by Thirlway.

What is the nature of the practice required? According to the author of a recent prize-winning monograph,[29] "the substance of the practice required is that states have done, or abstained from doing, certain things in the international field". "The occasion of an act of state contributing to the formation of custom must always", he says, "be some specific dispute or potential dispute . . . . The mere assertion *in abstracto* of the existence of a legal right or legal rule is not an act of state practice". However, the author gives no authority for his statement, and it is submitted that he is merely describing the kind of state practice that contributed to the formation of customary law when there were few if any alternative means.[30] In the world of the late twentieth century states have more ways, particularly as a result of their participation in many international organizations including the United Nations, through which to express their juridical opinion as to the existence of this or that customary rule.[31] The practice of states in international organizations such as the United Nations and its specialized agencies is just as much evidence of "general practice accepted as law" as the positions they take in disputes or potential disputes. What more authoritative way can there be for a state to express its opinion as to the existence of a customary rule than by the officially recorded votes of their authorized representatives, authorized it may be noted by the state organ, i.e. the Ministry of Foreign Affairs, most competent to bind the state internationally? There is growing support for the proposition that the collective acts of international organizations are evidence in themselves of the development of customary rules[32] and there seems to be no good reason in prin-

[29] Thirlway, *op. cit.,* at p. 58.

[30] The statement isn't even true of primitive national law. See Sir Paul Vinogradoff, *Common Sense in Law* (second edition, London, 1946) at p. 117: "the first thing to be noticed is that legal customs often arise independently of any litigation by the growth of definite views as to rights and duties."

[31] Cf. Richard A. Falk, *The Status of Law in International Society* (Princeton, 1970) at p. 154: "So long as international society was highly decentralized it was necessary to rest all law-making procedures on state practice, but with the growth of the organized international community it certainly seems increasingly plausible to allow the collective acts of the competent international institutions to serve as evidence of 'general practice accepted as law'." Falk, it will be noted, goes further than the thesis defended in this essay which is that the conduct of states as evidenced by their votes in international organizations is proof of state practice, not that the collective acts of such institutions is evidence of the formation of customary law. And see Kunz, *op. cit.,* at p. 667, who includes international decisions and the practice of international organizations as evidence of the development of customary rules. And Rosalyn Higgins, *The Development of International Law through the Political Organs of the United Nations* (London, 1963) at p. 2 where after pointing out that the practice of states includes "their international dealings as manifested by their diplomatic actions and public pronouncements", goes on to say that "with the development of international organizations, the votes and views of states have come to have legal significance as evidence of customary law". See finally G.I. Tunkin, *Droit international public, problèmes théoriques* (Paris, 1965) p. 101 *et seq.*

[32] Cf. the opinion of Professor Falk referred to in the previous footnote.

ciple why this should not be so. As Professor Virally suggests, "since international institutions are themselves subjects of international law, it is clear that their practice can contribute to the creation of custom".[33] The thesis being defended in this essay however is the less radical one that resolutions adopted by international conferences are evidence of *state* practice, not that the collective acts of such conferences are in themselves evidence of the development of customary rules.

What does the practice of states as proved by their votes officially recorded at international conferences show? Nothing could be clearer than that the Declaration was never meant to be binding as part of international law nor could it be simply by virtue of its having been adopted as a resolution of the General Assembly, the decisions of which have the force of recommendations only, except of course, resolutions relating to internal or house-keeping matters. It must be remembered that when it was adopted the Declaration was intended to be only one part of a tri-partite Bill one part of which was to be a multilateral treaty or Covenant. If the Declaration were to be binding why would it be necessary also to have a multilateral convention covering substantially the same ground? It was hardly necessary, therefore, for a number of delegations to stress, when explaining their votes, that the document was not binding. There were some delegations, it is true, which saw some sparks of juridical validity in the Declaration. These included the South Africans who presciently warned the Assembly that although not a treaty the Declaration would nevertheless impose certain obligations on states since it would undoubtedly be regarded as an authoritative interpretation of the rights and freedoms mentioned but not defined by the Charter. Although unlike the South Africans they nevertheless voted for the Declaration, the Chinese and French took a similar position. Referring to the Charter commitment to observe human rights, the Chinese said that the Declaration "stated these rights explicitly"; and the French after saying that the document could be considered an authoritative interpretation of the Charter went on to suggest that the norms set forth in it could also be considered "general principles of law" and therefore a source of law under the Statute of the International Court of Justice. Another delegation that detected elements of juridical obligation in the Declaration was the Chilean which said that "violation by any

---

[33] Max Sørensen (ed.) *Manual of International Law* (London, 1969) p. 139. In its Advisory Opinion relating to the Treaty of Lausanne and the frontier between Turkey and Iraq, the Permanent Court of International Justice invoked the unanimity rule as being "in accordance with the unvarying tradition of all diplomatic meetings or conferences". Publications of the Court, Series B., no. 12 at p. 30.

state of the rights enumerated in the Declaration would mean violation of the principles of the United Nations",[34] a statement which was undoubtedly motivated by the dispute mentioned below between Chile and the Soviet Union regarding the refusal of the Government of the latter country to allow the wife of a Chilean diplomat to leave the Soviet Union with her husband. These first official *dicta* were the beginning of a now developed practice of regarding the Declaration as an authoritative and therefore binding interpretation of the Charter.

To say that the Declaration is now part of the customary law of nations is, as already indicated, not to say that it is binding by virtue of the fact that it was adopted as a resolution of the General Assembly. As Sir Hersch Lauterpacht put it in the book already mentioned it was (and still is) "idle to attempt to kindle sparks of legal vitality in the Universal Declaration of Human Rights by regarding it as a recommendation of the General Assembly and by inquiry into its legal effects as such".[35] If the Declaration is now part of the law of nations and therefore binding on all states whether they voted for it or not, this is not because it was adopted by the Assembly, important as that may have been, but for other reasons including subsequent events and the emergence of a juridical consensus evidenced by the practice of states that the Declaration is now, whatever the intention of its authors may have been in 1948, binding as part of the law of nations.[36]

No scholar has yet attempted to review all the cases where the Declaration has been invoked either within or outside the United Nations with a view to determining whether they provide evidence of practice accepted as law and hence juridical consensus. That attempt will not be made here; but mention will be made of a few cases – all of them except one from United Nations practice – which, it is submitted, show that the Declaration has in fact been accepted as law.

The Declaration was less than five months old when, on 25 April, 1949, the General Assembly invoked two of its articles – article 13 on the right of everyone to leave any country including his own and article 16 on the right to marry without any limitation due to race, nationality or religion – in a resolution stating that "measures which prevent or coerce the wives of citizens of other nationalities from leaving their country of origin with their husbands or to join them abroad are not in conformity with the Charter"

---

[34] A/C.3/S.R.91 at p. 97.

[35] *Op. cit.,* p. 412.

[36] Reference may be made here to the dissenting opinion of Tanaka J. in the South West Africa cases, Second Phase, where he said that although not binding in itself, the Universal Declaration constituted evidence of the interpretation and application of the relevant Charter provisions. I.C.J. Reports 1966, pp. 288 and 293.

and recommended that the Soviet Union withdraw measures of that nature.[37] The resolution does not say in so many words that the Declaration is binding; but it does say after invoking the two articles in question that the measures adopted by the Soviet Union were not in conformity with the Charter. Since the Charter neither catalogues nor defines human rights, the logical and inescapable conclusion is that the states which voted for the resolution were using the Declaration to interpret the Charter. This was the first of many times that the General Assembly used the Declaration – as certain delegations said in 1948 it should be used – as an authentic interpretation of the Charter.[38]

Further evidence of the growth of the practice is to be found in the Declaration on the Granting of Independence to Colonial Countries and Peoples which the General Assembly adopted in 1960.[39] This Declaration, which was adopted by eighty-nine votes (including the votes of all the states except South Africa which abstained in the voting on the Universal Declaration in 1948) to none with nine abstentions, provides in its seventh and final paragraph that "all states shall observe faithfully and strictly the provisions of . . . the Universal Declaration of Human Rights". Like that Declaration, the Declaration on the Granting of Independence is not binding by virtue of its having been adopted by the General Assembly; its peremptory terms are however evidence of the practice and juridical consensus of states. The fact that the powers responsible for the administration of the colonial territories in question all abstained from voting undoubtedly affects the quality of the evidence. It may be noted, however, that Professor Tunkin, the distinguished Soviet international lawyer (who was at the time the legal counsel of the Soviet Foreign Office) has nevertheless said that the 1960 declaration is itself part of customary law.[40] His arguments can be applied with much greater force to the Universal Declaration of Human Rights.

The objection that the most interested states abstained from voting cannot be raised against the probative value of the Declaration on the Elimination of All Forms of Racial Discrimination which the General Assembly

---

[37] G.A. Resolution 285 (III).

[38] See Sir Humphrey Waldock, 106 *Recueil des Cours* (1962) p. 199 where he says that the Declaration may be referred to "for indications of the content of the human rights envisaged in the Charter". He went further in a lecture to the British Institute of International and Comparative Law where he mentioned the "constant and widespread recognition of the principles of the Universal Declaration" which "clothes it, in my opinion, in the character of customary law". International and Comparative Law Quarterly, Supplementary Publication no. II, 1965, p. 15. And see Goodrich and Hambro, *The Charter of the United Nations* (Revised second edition, Boston, 1949) p. 547.

[39] G.A. Resolution 1514 (XV) of 14 December 1960.

[40] *Op. cit.,* and see my discussion of the question in Luard (ed.) *op. cit.* pp. 51-52.

unanimously adopted on 20 November, 1963. In terms only slightly different from those used in the 1960 Declaration, article 11 of this Declaration says that "every state shall promote respect for and observance of human rights and fundamental freedoms in accordance with the Charter of the United Nations and shall fully and faithfully observe the provisions of . . . the Universal Declaration of Human Rights".[41] In voting for such a provision states must be taken as meaning what they say. They cannot on one occasion say that the Declaration is to be fully and faithfully observed and on another that it is not binding. The provision is also pertinent for another reason; for it is obviously another example of the use of the Universal Declaration to interpret the Charter.

In the same year, on 4 December, 1963, the Security Council adopted a resolution which speaks of *apartheid* as being "in violation" of South Africa's "obligations as a member of the United Nations and of the Provisions of the Universal Declaration of Human Rights".[42] Here again the Security Council was obviously using the Declaration to interpret the Charter. Because of its limited membership resolutions of the Security Council, however authoritative in other respects, are not as good evidence of state practice as are those of an Assembly the membership of which is now practically universal. Reference may therefore be made to the resolution of 27 October 1966 by which the General Assembly terminated the mandate of South Africa over South West Africa (Namibia) on the ground that the mandate had "been conducted in a manner contrary to the mandate, the Charter of the United Nations and the Universal Declaration of Human Rights".[43] That the General Assembly was again using the Declaration to interpret the Charter is clear enough. When, however, the International Court of Justice upheld in 1971 the right of the United Nations to terminate the mandate over South West Africa, it did not have to base its opinion on the Declaration although Judge Fuad Ammoun very nearly did so in his separate opinion.[44] For although the Charter does not catalogue or define human rights it does stipulate that they shall be enjoyed "by all without distinction as to race, sex, language or religion".[45] Therefore, in the words of the Court, "to establish instead, and to enforce, distinctions, exclusions, restrictions and limitations based on grounds of race, colour, descent or national or ethnic origin which constitute a

---

[41] G.A. Resolution 1904 (XVIII) of 20 November, 1963.
[42] Resolution S/5471.
[43] Resolution 2145 (XXI). Portugal and South Africa voted against and France, Malawi and the United Kingdom abstained.
[44] I.C.J. Reports, 1971, p. 16 *et seq.* For Judge Ammoun's separate opinion see p. 76 *et seq.*
[45] E.g. Articles 1 and 55.

denial of fundamental human rights is a flagrant violation of the purposes
and principles of the Charter".[46]

The Advisory Opinion of the Court in the Namibia case is, therefore, of
little help in proving the proposition that the Universal Declaration is now
part of the law of nations. This cannot be said of the Proclamation of
Teheran which was unanimously approved on 13 May, 1968, by the International Conference on Human Rights, an inter-governmental conference
convened by the United Nations at which 84 states were represented.
Article 2 of this proclamation which was later endorsed by the General Assembly in its resolution of 19 December 1968, says that the Universal Declaration of Human Rights "constitutes an obligation for the members of
the international community".[47] Still more recent evidence of the now
binding character of the Declaration can be found in the Final Act of the
Helsinki Conference on Security and Cooperation in Europe of 1975, section VII of which says, *inter alia,* that "in the field of human rights and
fundamental freedoms, the participating states will act in conformity with
the purposes and principles of the Charter of the United Nations and with
the Universal Declaration of Human Rights". Again the same consistent
association of the Declaration with the Charter and the same underlying
assumption that the latter must be interpreted by reference to the former.
That the participating states were treating the Declaration as giving rise to
legally binding obligations appears most clearly from the ensuing sentence
where they say that "they will *also fulfil their obligations* as set forth in the
international declarations and agreements in this field, including *inter alia*
the International Covenants on Human Rights, by which they may be
bound".[48] The fact that the Final Act may itself not be binding is for
present purposes irrelevant; for what we are looking for is evidence of state
practice and *opinio juris.*

This review of state practice relating to the Universal Declaration does
not pretend to be exhaustive. Enough has been said, however, to conclude
that if governments mean what they say – and it must be assumed that they
do mean what their officially authorized representatives say on their behalf
– then the Declaration is to be "faithfully and strictly" observed (words of
the Declaration on the Granting of Independence to Colonial Countries
and Peoples), that it is to be "fully and faithfully" observed (words of the
Declaration on the Elimination of all Forms of Racial Discrimination) that

[46] See p. 57, para. 131 of the Advisory Opinion.

[47] Final Act of the International Conference on Human Rights, Teheran, 22 April – 13 May,
1968. A/Conf. 32/41 p. 4.

[48] Italics added.

states shall "act in conformity" with it (words of the Helsinki Agreement) and that it therefore "constitutes an obligation for the members of the international community" (words of the Teheran Conference) – which is to say that it is binding on states as part of the law of nations. There is indeed a kind of inescapable logic in this conclusion. For it is the only instrument universally applicable to all states which catalogues and defines the human rights and fundamental freedoms which, it is now generally recognized, the Charter binds states to respect although it does not define or list them. By the development of a new customary rule the Universal Declaration of Human Rights has become an authentic interpretation of the Charter.

The importance of the Conclusion can hardly be exaggerated. The conventional wisdom of certain jurists is to say that, while the Declaration may have great moral and political authority, it is merely, as its preamble says, "a common standard of achievement" and has no binding legal force; the Covenants on the other hand are binding on all states that ratify them. It is unlikely, however, that the Covenants will ever be universally ratified; but if, by the development of a new rule of customary international law, the Declaration has become an authentic interpretation of the human rights provisions of the Charter, then its provisions, like those of the Charter itself, bind all member states. If, in addition to becoming an authentic interpretation of the Charter the Declaration has become part of the customary law irrespective of the Charter, it is also binding on all states whether they are members of the United Nations or not. This would mean, amongst other things, that if, for example, a country were expelled from the Organization under article six of the Charter, that country would nevertheless continue to be bound by the Declaration. In countries, moreover, in which the customary law of nations is part of the law of the land, the Declaration could be invoked before and applied by national courts.

The question of the juridical character of the Universal Declaration is not, therefore, an idle academic exercise. If the thesis set forth in this essay that it has become part of the customary law of nations is correct then its adoption by the United Nations on 10 December, 1948, was a far greater achievement than its authors could ever have imagined.

PART TWO:

HUMAN RIGHTS TODAY

CHAPTER II

THE EVOLVING CONCEPT OF HUMAN RIGHTS:
WESTERN, SOCIALIST AND THIRD WORLD APPROACHES

PROF. H. GROS ESPIELL*

I

1. In the 30 years which have elapsed since the General Assembly of the United Nations adopted and solemnly proclaimed the Universal Declaration of Human Rights on December 10, 1948, there have been political, economic, social and cultural changes which have unquestionably made an impression on the concept of human rights, on the question of their protection and guarantee by national and international law, on their effectiveness and on the actual respect held for them in today's world.

In fact, it is difficult to find a period in the history of mankind when the question of human rights has had a greater and more general significance in theory and practice than during the period from 1948 to date. There have been times when the matter held capital importance in a given State or region, but never has the question of human rights been the object of such wide general attention as nowadays. Furthermore, this matter has never held such interest for the masses and the peoples of practically the whole world as it has during these years.

The universalization of the question of human rights, a characteristic phenomenon of our era never heretofore seen in its present form, has been associated also with the legal and political internationalization of this theme, since human rights are no longer a question which attracts the attention of mankind solely from a historical, philosophical and doctrinal viewpoint, but have become, both politically and legally, a matter of interest to the international community as a whole. From both a legal and political point of view it has evolved from being an exclusive or almost exclusive question of national law – belonging to a nation's internal jurisdiction - into an international reality, and beyond all theories, into an object wherein coexist, in different degree, internal and international regulations, the obligations of States, and the attributes of international agencies,

*Secretary-General of OPANAL.

derived from the norms and principles of present international law in accordance with the varying political criteria of different applicable standards.[1] There is no doubt that today the question of human rights is regulated at least partially by international law. Therefore, it would be both absurd and a denial, not only of law, but of prevailing international reality, to uphold that it constitutes a domain entirely restricted and inherent to a nation's internal jurisdiction.

2. The phenomenon of universal and international acceptance of the question of human rights is obviously an unfinished process whose future is an open one.

The roots and precedents go back to former times, referred to in this work,[2] but its beginning was undoubtedly at the end of the Second World War, when the Charter of the United Nations entered into force. The ideas enunciated in the Charter on the rights of man and the universality of the international community were consecrated in the Universal Declaration of Human rights three years later.[3] This text, however, based as it was on the idea of the necessary and inevitable universality of human rights,[4] could only give a real and practical sense to this universality when, as a

---

[1] In regard to this matter which was considered essential for the progress of the protection of human rights, but that has been overcome by international reality: L. Preuss, Article 2, paragraph 7 of the Charter of the United Nations and matters of domestic jurisdiction, *Recueil des Cours, Académie de Droit International,* 1949, t. 74; Hans Kelsen, *The Law of the United Nations,* N.Y., 1950, p. 774; Ph. Jessup, *A Modern Law of Nations,* N.Y., 1950, p. 2; H. Lauterpacht, *International Law and Human Rights;* Human Rights under the Charter of the United Nations, Effect of the Clause of Domestic Jurisdiction, pp. 166-213, Archon Books, 1968; Carlos García Bauer, *Los derechos humanos, preocupación universal,* Guatemala, 1960, pp. 51-69; F. Ermacora, Human Rights and Domestic Jurisdiction, (Article 2.7 of the Charter), *Académie de Droit International, Recueil des Cours,* 1968, II; A. Verdross, La Compétence Nationale, dans le cadre de l'Organisation des Nations Unies et l'Indépendance des Etats, *Revue Générale de Droit International Public,* 1965, No. 2, pp. 8-9; S. Glaser, Les Droits de l'Homme à la lumière du Droit International Public, *Mélanges offerts à Henry Rollin,* pp. 112-115, Pedone, Paris 1964; A. Movchán, Problems of human rights in contemporary international law, *El Derecho Internacional Contemporáneo,* Moscow, 1973, pp. 273-275; Christian Daubie, Protection Internationale des Droits de l'Homme et souveraineté des Etats; Un antagonisme inéluctable, *Annales de Droit, Revue trimestrielle de Droit Belge,* t. XXXIV, 1974.

[2] On the farthest backgrounds see: H. Lauterpacht, *International Law and Human Rights,* Section II, The Law of Nations and the rights of man, Archon Books, 1968, pp. 73-127; on the nearest backgrounds, since postwar of 1918: René Cassin, Le texte de la Déclaration Universelle, *Lumen Vitae,* Vol. XXIII, No. 4, Bruxelles, 1968; also see: I. Szabo, Fondements historiques et développement des droits de l'homme, *Les dimensions internationales des Droits de l'Homme, Manuel Unesco des Droits de l'Homme, provisional edition,* Strasbourg, 1976, pp. 12-56.

[3] On the text of the Universal Declaration and its process of elaboration, in a practically contemporary appreciation of its adoption by the General Assembly: René Cassin, La Déclaration Universelle et la mise en oeuvre des droits de l'homme, *Recueil des Cours, Académie de Droit International,* 1951.

[4] On the question of the universality of the Universal Declaration, René Cassin, *op. cit.,* Chap. III, 2, paragraphs 30-33.

result of the process of political decolonisation and recognition of the right to the self-determination of peoples, the rights of human beings ceased to be the heritage solely of those men who inhabited the countries then independent – many of them colonial powers which denied independence to the peoples they exploited, and ignored the rights of the individuals who made up those peoples – and became the heritage of all men, without distinction or discrimination of race. For this reason the end of political colonialism – whose aftermath was that all men, whichever nation or people they belonged to, are genuinely entitled to the rights and freedoms of the human being – has been an element necessary to the achieving of a true universalization of the question of human rights.

There is, certainly, a long road to pursue in this process and many groups in the world population to whom the question of human rights is practically unknown, not only inasmuch as they are not endowed with the rights which are, theoretically at least, the heritage of all men, but because they have not yet acquired any intellectual conscience of the existence of such rights. The advance of the process towards universal acceptance is inevitable.[5] The period from 1948 to date best shows that what lies ahead will be achieved successfully.

3. The advancement of universal acceptance of the program of human rights runs parallel to the progress reached thus far in their concept and substance.

The old individualistic conception of human rights which endowed them with only a political and civil nature, was in both theory and practice already obsolete by 1948. To the few precedents existing under national law before the First World War, some contributions were added as a result of the Soviet Revolution in 1918, the Mexican Revolution and of many Constitutions promulgated after the end of the war which, together with contributions from important sectors of political and legal thought, gave rise to different ways of thinking,[6] demonstrated that human rights

[5] We cannot forget in this process of universalization of human rights, the role fulfilled in the last years by the Catholic Church. It is necessary to quote specially the *Encyclical Pacem in Terris* (1963), whose chapter on the rights of the human being, starts from the principle that "every human being is a person, that is, nature with intelligence and free will and therefore from that same nature rise directly, at the same time, rights and duties which, being inviolable, are also absolutely inalienable".

[6] G. Gurvitch, *La Déclaration des Droits Sociaux,* New York, 1944; J. Maritain, *Les droits de l'homme et la loi naturelle,* New York, 1943. It is interesting to reread today the works gathered in 1947 by UNESCO on the question of the possibility of the adoption of a Universal Declaration in: *Human Rights, Comments and Interpretations. A Symposium;* among those who especially refer to this matter, were: Jacques Maritain, Harold Laski, Benedetto Croce, Sergius Hessen and Boris Tchechko. Also see: Héctor Gros Espiell, *Economic, Social and Cultural Rights: Concept and Evolution in National and International Law,* 1972, International Institute of Human Rights, *Selected Readings on the International and Comparative Law*

constitute an integral complex, interdependent and indivisible, notwithstanding deep discrepancies as regards their respective nature and legal
jurisprudence[7] which of necessity comprise political and civil as well as
economic, social and cultural rights.[8]

The reality of each of these rights will be secured only by their integral
recognition, as otherwise, if the cultural, social and economic aspects are
not effective, the political and civil rights will be reduced to a mere statement of form. Likewise, without the reality of political and civil rights and
without the effectiveness of freedom – as understood in its broadest sense –
economic and social rights have no real sense nor significance. This idea of
essential integrality, interdependence and indivisibility of the concept and
reality of human rights, in a way implicit in the Charter of the United
Nations, was gathered, amplified and organized in 1948 in the Universal
Declaration of Human Rights, and was once again reaffirmed in the International Covenants on Human Rights adopted by the General Assembly in
1966 and in force since 1976, in the Proclamation of Teheran of 1968 and
in the Resolution of the General Assembly adopted in 1977, in connection
with criteria and means to improve the effective enjoyment of human
rights and fundamental freedoms.[9]

of Human Rights, 1974; I. Szabo, op. cit., pp. 24-27; V. Kartachkin, Economic, Social and
Cultural Rights, Les Dimensions Internationales des Droits de l'Homme, Manuel Unesco,
op. cit.
    [7] Paul Oriane, De la Juridicité des droits économiques et sociaux reconnus dans la Déclara-
tion Universelle, Annales de Droit, Revue Trimestrielle de Droit Belge, t. XXXIV, 1974.
    [8] On the recognition of the economic, social and cultural rights in Article 22 of the Univer-
sal Declaration and the difficult process which led to its adoption: R. Cassin, Le texte de la
Déclaration Universelle, op. cit., pp. 607-609. Regarding the present situation of the economic, social and cultural rights, see the extensive and documented study of M. Ganji, The
Realization of Economic, Social and Cultural Rights: Problems, Policies Progress, United
Nations, S.75.XIV.2, 1975.
    [9] Paragraph 1 of GA resolution, 32/130 adopted by 126 votes in favour, none against and
11 abstentions (ten countries from Western Europe and the United States), reads in its first
three operative paragraphs:
"Decides that the approach to the future work within the United Nations system with respect
to human rights questions should take into account the following concepts:
    (a) All human rights and fundamental freedoms are indivisible and interdependent; equal
attention and urgent consideration should be given to the implementation, promotion and
protection of both civil and political, and economic, social and cultural rights;
    (b) "The full realization of civil and political rights without the enjoyment of economic,
social and cultural rights is impossible; the achievement of lasting progress in the implementation of human rights is dependent upon sound and effective national and international policies of economic and social development", as recognized by the Proclamation of Teheran of
1968;
    (c) All human rights and fundamental freedoms of the human person and of peoples are
inalienable; . . . ".
Also see the resolution of the 54th International Labour Conference, on Trade Union Rights
and their relationship with Civil Liberties, adopted with no opposition in 1970.

It can thus be affirmed that the overall scope of the idea of human rights, which can be termed horizontal and which is aimed at universal recognition, is parallel to the vertical or conceptual scope of its contents.

4. One of the most interesting confirmations of the progress achieved over the past 30 years in the matter of human rights is that shown by the current acceptance by all States of the principles, criteria and ideas affirmed in the Universal Declaration of 1948. What, at the moment the Declaration was adopted, was the result of the will of 48 States with no opposing votes and 8 abstentions resulting from reticence and forebearance in the drafting of the Declaration, is nowadays accepted by all Members of the international community without theoretical restrictions or restraint. In addition to numerous other resolutions of the United Nations under which this obligation was affirmed, the Proclamation of Teheran, unanimously adopted by more than 120 States in 1968, solemnly declared in its paragraph 2 that the Universal Declaration of Human Rights "constitutes an obligation for the members of the international community".[10]

5. The provisions of the Universal Declaration are admitted today as obligatory, both in the sense that they are considered general principles of international law, and as an interpretation of the Charter expressly and repeatedly accepted by the international community by means of resolutions of the General Assembly of the United Nations as a spokesman for mankind proclaiming these rights and freedoms.[11] The Universal Declaration of Human Rights has been transformed from a moral standard to a document under which definitive rights and duties are imposed on States.

---

[10] A meticulous analysis of this process at the United Nations has been done by Marc Schreiber (Réflexions à l'occasion de la commémoration du vingt-cinquième anniversaire de l'adoption de la Déclaration Universelle des Droits de l'Homme, *Annales de Droit, Revue Trimestrielle de Droit Belge,* t. XXXI, 1-2 Bruxelles, 1974). Also see: Marc Schreiber, La pratique récente des Nations Unies dans le domaine de la protection des droits de l'homme, *Académie de Droit International, Recueil des Cours,* Vol. II, 1975, pp. 311-322.

[11] The supported approaches until 1960, in which the idea predominated to deny juridical value to the Declaration, are gathered in Carlos García Bauer, *op. cit.,* pp. 79-90. For the subsequent thesis see the excellent study on the question made by Louis B. Sohn, La Declaración Universal de Derechos Humanos, Un ideal común? La posición de la Declaración Universal en el Derecho Internacional, *Revista de la Comisión Internacional de Juristas,* 1967, Vol. VII, No. 2, p. 20. Also, R.J. Dupuy, Droit Déclaratoire et Droit Programmatoire, de la Coutume sauvage à la "Soft-Law", *Société Française pour le Droit International,* Colloque de Toulouse, 1974; Heinz Guradze, Are Human Rights Resolutions of the United Nations General Assembly law-making? *Revue des Droits de l'Homme,* Vol. IV, 2-3, Paris, 1971, p. 453; Jorge Castañeda, *Valor jurídico de las Resoluciones de las Naciones Unidas,* El Colegio de México, 1967, pp. 177-181, 200 and 202; *Legal effects of United Nations Resolutions,* Columbia University Press, 1969, Valeur juridique des résolutions des Nations Unies, *Académie de Droit International, Recueil des Cours,* 1970, Vol. 129, and Frank C. Newman, Interpreting the Human Rights Clauses of the UN Charter, *Revue des Droits de l'Homme,* Vol. V. No. 2-3, Paris 1972, pp. 288-289.

It has gone farther by affirming – we believe in all justice – that it constitutes an inalienable rule of general international law, a case of *jus cogens* characteristic of our era, and that there is an obligation to respect human rights in all circumstances.[12] Respect for, and the validity of, the foregoing are linked with the idea of an "international public order" which also carries important connotations.[13]

6. The Universal Declaration was based in the need to affirm "a common understanding of these rights and freedoms", and to achieve "a common standard for all peoples and nations".[14]

To arrive at a concept consecrating a common standard of mankind for human rights beyond theoretical and practical differences on the nature of man's rights and freedoms, was perhaps the most important achievement of the Universal Declaration. This achievement led afterwards to the wording of two International Pacts which opened enormous horizons regarding the promotion, defense and protection of human rights, notwithstanding a world divided by ideologies and by numerous political,

[12] On the obligation to respect human rights as *jus cogens* and the Vienna Convention on the Law of Treaties, see: Roberto Ago, *El hecho internacionalmente ilícito de Estado como fuente de responsabilidad internacional,* A/CN.4/291/add. 2, 1976, paragraphs 28 and 79 and Article 18, 3c, of the Draft on responsibility of States, adopted in 1976 by the Internatio-nal Law Commission; Manuel Pérez González, Los Gobiernos y el *jus cogens:* Las normas imperativas del Derecho Internacional en la Sexta Comisión, Estudios de Derecho Interna-cional Público y Privado, Homenaje al Profesor Luis Sela Sempil, Oviedo 1970, p. 133; José Antonio Pastor Ridruejo, *La determinación del contenido del jus cogens,* I.H.L.A.D.I., Madrid, 1972. In our report on the *"Aplicación de las resoluciones de las Naciones Unidas relativas al derecho a la libre determinación de los pueblos sometidos a dominación colonial y extranjera",* document E/CN.4/Sub. 2/390, there is a reference to this question and the quotation of an extensive bibliography (paragraphs 61-71). The International Court of Justice in its judgement in the case of *Barcelona Traction,* said that the principles and the rules concerning fundamental rights of the human person create obligations with respect to the international community as a whole. The importance of these rights has the effect that all States may be considered as having a juridical interest that these rights be protected; "that is why these obligations are obligations *erga omnes"* (Cour Internationale de Justice, Arrêt de février 1970, p. 32). On the interpretation of this paragraph and its relation with *jus cogens:* Adolfo Miaja de la Muela, *Aportación de la sentencia del Tribunal de La Haya en el caso Barcelona Traction a la Jurisprudencia Internacional,* Universidad de Valladolid, 1970, pp. 72-77. Another interesting reference is in the advisory opinion on *Namibia* (1971). See also: E. Schwelb, The International Court of Justice and the Human Rights Clauses of the Charter, *American Journal of International Law,* Vol. 66, 1972, and Frank C. Newman, *op. cit.,* p. 283.

[13] W.J. Ganshof Van der Meersch, L'Ordre Public et les Droits de l'Homme, *J.T.,* 30/XI/68, p. 666; Charles De Visscher, Positivisme et *jus cogens, Revue Générale de Droit International Public,* 1971, No. 1; R. Monaco, Cours Général de Droit International Public, *Académie de Droit International, Recueil des Cours,* 1968, Vol. 125, pp. 202-212.

[14] *La Declaración Universal de Derechos Humanos, Un ideal común,* United Nations, 63.I.13; Theo C. Van Boven, Partners in the promotion and protection of human rights, *Essays on International Law and relations in honour of A.J.P. Tammes, Netherlands International Law Review,* Vol. XXIV, 1/2, 1977; François Rigaux, Vers une conception écu-ménique des droits de l'homme, *Annales de Droit, Revue Trimestrielle de Droit Belge,* Vol. XXXIV, 1974.

social and economic systems, which have of necessity different criteria as to the nature and essence of human rights.

7. None of the foregoing implies either ignorance of the long road still to be covered in order that universal acceptance of the idea of human rights can be achieved, nor – what is even more serious, more tragic and more distressing – the deep abyss between, on one side, the theoretical principles, legal formulae, and the solemn political proclamations and, on the other, the reality of a world in which basic human rights are denied or ignored with tremendous intensity and frequency.

These violations come not only from the nations themselves, but may arise, and do arise in reality, from very different sources. The phenomenon of terrorism, although often the direct consequence of State and/or governmental actions, is exercised on other occasions by individuals acting not under the orders of a State or Government, which is a factual and serious example showing that individual rights and freedoms are subject to attack from different sources. Its protection and guaranty must take this question into consideration, since it is not possible to handle the question as though a State, through its Government, was necessarily the only source of violations of human rights. However, it cannot be ignored that the State, which should be the first to guarantee the rights of man, and which in some cases does,[15] still constitutes even today the main and most serious source of violations of the freedom and the rights of the individual.

All comment on the positive process carried out since 1948 must not eradicate memory of the setbacks which have taken place in some areas, areas which were, not long ago, an example of respect for the dignity and rights of man but today give a dreary and disheartening panorama.

However, this recognition of existing realities should not cause us to deny or disregard the steps forward, the importance of the progress achieved during the last 30 years in universalizing the promotion, guaranty and respect for human rights. What has still to be done is an enormous and difficult task. It is a task for which we have to be conscious of the impossibility of totally achieving the desired objective and reaching the optimum result, since the violation of law is inherent to human society, and

---

[15] In fact the modern democratic State should be, and is in some cases, the firmest defense and guarantee of human rights against the attacks coming from other sources. President G. Pompidou said in this regard, on April 29, 1970: "Le temps n'est plus où, dans un pays tel que le nôtre, l'autorité de l'Etat pouvait apparaître comme une menace pour la liberté du citoyen. Elle en constitue, au contraire aujourd'hui, plus que jamais la force. N'est pas seulement indispensable à la Nation pour assurer son avenir et sa sécurité, mais aussi à l'individu pour assurer la liberté" (Héctor Gros Espiell, *El Predominio del Poder Ejecutivo en América Latina*, UNAM, México 1977, p. 20).

freedom constitutes a goal which can never be entirely accomplished or secured.

The consciousness of past achievements combined with present-day reality form a spur which assures that history will continue to follow in the steps of freedom.

II

8. It is not simple, and may not even be scientifically correct, to advance ideas connected with the evolution of the concept of human rights during these 30 years by classifying the groups of countries as listed in the title of this work. For example, the ambiguity of the term "Third World" complicates to a high degree all analysis of the evolution of human rights classified under this term. The different criteria encountered nowadays in connection with the expression "Third World"[16] and the nations contained therein, combined with the fact that so-called socialist countries may coexist shoulder to shoulder with free economy nations[17] reveal that entire regions coming under a western concept of laws and politics (such as in the case of Latin America among others), belong to the Third World, and show the problems resulting from use of this classification in the light of the present-day concept of human rights.

However, bearing such difficulties in mind, together with the problems to which they give rise, we may for the purposes of this work try to put some ideas and reflections in order (while at the same time taking into consideration the imperfections and deficiencies of dividing and classifying the world), and establish the pertinent consequences in the cases analyzed.[18]

[16] We should take into account, for instance, the radical opposition between the Soviet concept and the Chinese concept on the integration and nature of each one of the Three World. In this regard see the extensive study published in Renmin Riba on November 1st, 1977, *La teorial del Presidente Mao sobre los Tres Mundos constituye una gran contribución al marxismo-leninismo,* Ediciones de lenguas extranjeras, Pekin, 1977, and the speech of the Minister for Foreign Affairs of China, Huang-Hua in the General Assembly of the United Nations, on September 29, 1977 *(Pekin Informa,* No. 41, 12/XI/77, pp. 31-40).

[17] Not only States of Africa and Asia which call themselves as such, but also, for instance, Yugoslavia which has been and is anessential part of the group of countries of the Third World, Romania which has submitted to the UNCTAD her wish to belong to the group of socialist countries of Eastern Europe and at the same time to the developing countries, and Cuba which is part of the COMECON and which has actively associated with the countries of the Third World. The case of China is also very important, because she has a theory of Three Worlds where there are no political or ideological formulae to be included in one of these "worlds", but other considerations, as she considers herself as part of the Third World.

[18] A similar classification for the study of human rights was accepted in the work of François Rigaux (Vers une conception œcuménique . . ., *op. cit.,* p. 7).

It is also necessary to point out the practical impossibility of attempting to cover the situation in a few pages, due to its immense and complex nature. As we have already stated, we only intend to make reflections, which will of necessity be partial and incomplete.

III

9. The expression "western approach" shall as far as human rights are concerned, be understood in a broader sense than that including only Western Europe, due to its geographical lack of precision and its relative irreality.

Under this heading can be included both the United States and Canada, which come within the so-called Western Hemisphere, and have been nourished with political and ideological thought in the so-called western tradition; and Israel may also be included in this group not only because of its present political location, but also because of its people's background.

Also, and here the matter becomes more complex, Latin America comes under western criteria although economically it is included among the developing countries, and may also be conceived as a part of the Third World. Notwithstanding the fact that its economic and social structures are different from those of the so-called Western countries, and despite the large percentage of native and mixed blood, these nations have, in the question of human rights, followed a western concept, and an ideology which stemmed from the great Spanish legal tradition of equality, liberty and human dignity – a remarkable tradition despite its clouding and denial by the anti-Spanish "Black Legend" – as well as from French revolutionary thought and many precepts of the U.S. Constitution.[19] This western concept in the question of human rights presently reveals in Latin America – regrettably and with anguish – some examples of backwardness and rejection of traditional thought which, by their very nature, must of necessity be temporary and transitory.

The existence in Latin America of some States which accept the Marxist-Leninist conception, such as the case of Cuba and perhaps one other, naturally excludes these countries at present from the possibility of integration with the predominant western concept of human rights in this continent.

[19] Héctor Gros Espiell, *La Organización Internacional del Trabajo y los derechos del hombre en la América Latina,* UNAM, México, 1977.

Furthermore, countries such as Australia and New Zealand must be included within the western concept of human rights, although they are geographically located in another hemisphere. These are fully-developed nations, outside the Third World, where a population of European origin holds absolute predominance.

Another very interesting example is Japan, located in the Far East, which has an ancient and strong philosophical tradition of its own, and is nowadays accepted from a certain point of view as falling within the Western Group, inasmuch as it is a highly developed country which follows the free market economy system. Aside from the foregoing there is, added to the question of human rights, the circumstance that, commencing with the Peace Treaty signed with the United States and other Powers, and the adoption of its new Constitution, Japan has become closer to the western field of thought both politically and in its concept of human rights. It is therefore, a paradox in that an eastern country, with the legacy of a great culture and strong traditions, must be placed outside the geographic sphere in which it is located and the historical framework in which it was developed due to political and economic circumstances, and classified of necessity as regards human rights within the western field of thought, despite the inevitable differences and apparent absurdity of such action.

It is not possible, on the other hand, to consider the South African Republic as within the group of nations accepting the western concept of rights and freedoms. On the contrary, the applied doctrine of apartheid constitutes a monstrous and sickening violation of human rights and is completely incompatible with true western ideology, although it may be considered as derived from certain criteria which originated in Western Europe.

It is, in fact, not possible to forget that it was in Europe – and this is not the only quotable example – where nazism was born and developed, founded on the radical denial of human rights. This political theory and its terrible results revealed, once more, that no region of the world can credit itself with absolute superiority in the affirmation and preservation of ideas upon which the rights and freedoms of man are based.

10. There have been, and are, in this western concept several criteria and different doctrinal positions on the nature and basis of human rights from *jus naturalis,* in its different forms to positivism, which seems today to be in decadence, and from viewpoints based on philosophical idealism to those resulting from currents of materialism. However, in its predominant aspect, it may be asserted that the concept known as "western" affirms the existence of rights and freedoms inherent to man's nature and to his status

as an individual which rise above the State and above all political organizations, imprescriptible and irrefutable. These rights are essentially attributes of the human being, and not the result of being a citizen of a State.[20]

The predominant legal theory of the Western countries has also affirmed and maintained, strongly and continuously, that the human being is a subject of International Law.[21]

It is not possible to understand the so-called western concept of human rights without first taking into consideration the fact that the idea inherent in these rights is based on our dealing with political structures organized on the traditional democratic formula. This formula accepts political and ideological pluralism and the multi-party system, which of necessity presuppose electoral confrontations in periodical elections, whereas all currents of political opinion can meet without discrimination of any kind, either personal or ideological.

11. The last 30 years have witnessed the end of the old individualistic conception of human rights in the field of western thought. They have stopped adhering merely to civil and political freedoms, and the need has been accepted to recognize and guarantee the effectiveness of economic, social and cultural rights, not only for their own sake, but because without them, civil rights have no material basis and are lifeless formulae without reality. Today, all the so-called Western countries have renounced this individualistic and formal ideology although in different degrees and ratios, despite the fact that discrepancies still exist concerning the essence of economic, social and cultural rights, the nature of same and the formulae required to guarantee their protection.[22]

12. The growth of the State, the overwhelming bureaucratic complex and the weakness of the actual power of the individuals to make their rights valid have motivated the foundation of new institutions for the defense and protection of human rights in many of these countries, such as the Scandinavian *ombudsman*. Institutions such as these are characteristic of the concern of many Western countries to solve the new problems which the protection of human rights raises in national law in a practical manner. It is interesting to note that formulae of this type have recently influenced several

---

[20] Gregorio Peces Barba, *Derechos Fundamentales, Teoría General,* Madrid, 1973, pp. 53-58, for a summary of the different "western" theories on human rights. With a different approach: J. Castán Tobeñas, *Los derechos del hombre,* Madrid, 1969, pp. 40-77.

[21] René Cassin, l'homme sujet de Droit International et la protection des droits de l'homme dans la société universelle, *Mélanges Georges Scelle,* Paris, 1950.

[22] Paul Oriane, De la Juridicité des Droits économiques et sociaux reconnus dans la Déclaration Universelle, *Annales de Droit, op. cit.,* Vol. XXXIV, 1974.

countries of the Third World,[23] which illustrates the fruitful interchange of different systems and concepts in the field of human rights.

13. Included among the Western Group of countries is Western Europe, where the international protection of human rights has followed an important process of regional development which presently constitutes an example and a motivation to other parts of the world.[24]

The Statutes of the Council of Europe of May 5, 1948 affirmed as its purpose "the defense of individual freedom, political freedom and the pre-eminence of law".

The Convention for the Safeguard of Human Rights and Fundamental Freedoms, signed in Rome on November 4, 1950, established a conventional system for the international defense and guarantee of human rights and fundamental freedoms based on a Commission and European Court of Human Rights, and on the recognition of a common patrimony of ideals and political traditions with regard to freedom and the preeminence of law.

The European Social Charter of 1961 completed the conceptual determination of human rights in Western Europe, including promotion of the necessary respect for social and economic rights.

The admittance of Portugal and Spain to the Council of Europe in 1977, the signature by these countries of the two International Covenants on Human Rights and ratification of these by Spain, together with solution of the problem which brought about Greece's temporary separation from the Council of Europe, and ratification by Spain of ILO Agreements No. 87 and 98, and the negotiations for admittance of these three countries to the European Economic Community have resulted in the whole of Western Europe now being practically and politically integrated in the same concept of human rights and fundamental freedoms.[25]

The effective operation of the European regional system has served as an added example for the possibility of associating local and international systems for the protection of human rights in the present-day world. In this regard, universalism and regionalism are not individual or conflicting formulae, but regimes to be combined and harmonized for the advantage of each in accordance with their different circumstances, so that the goal of an international guarantee for the rights and freedoms of human beings may be better achieved.[26]

[23] T.O. Elías, *Human Rights and the Developing Countries,* International Institute of Human Rights, Strasbourg, 1977.

[24] To quote just one work, among the enormous bibliography in this regard, K. Vasak, Le Conseil de l'Europe, *Manuel Unesco, op. cit.*

[25] Antonio Truyol y Serra, *Los Derechos Humanos,* Madrid, 1977. Epílogo, p. 174.

[26] Héctor Gros Espiell, Le Système Interaméricain comme régime régional de protection

14. The fact that the so-called Western countries coexist in Europe with a group of socialist Eastern European States naturally following a different approach in the matter of human rights from those of their neighbours, has given rise to very specific problems.

It is of interest to note that the common standard and concept proclaimed by the Universal Declaration of Human Rights have permitted positive progress through general acceptance of the need to protect and guarantee human rights in Europe. These are advances on the road towards an international recognition of human rights covering the entire continent of Europe, together with documents such as the Resolution on the Freedom of Trade Unions and Professions Associations in Europe, adopted at the Second European Regional Conference of ILO (Geneva, January, 1974) and the Final Act of the Conference on Security and Cooperation in Europe (Helsinki, 1975).[27]

internationale des Droits de l'homme, *Académie de Droit International, Recueil des Cours,* 1975, pp. 7-12; K. Vasak, Problemas relativos a la Constitución de Comisiones de Derechos Humanos, *Veinte años de Evolución de los Derechos Humanos,* UNAM, México 1974, p. 575; Roger Pinto, Régionalisme et universalisme dans la protection des droits de l'homme, *Nobel Symposium,* Stockholm 1968, p. 177.

[27] Paragraph 1 of the resolution on trade union liberty and professional associations in Europe (Second European Regional Conference of ILO, Geneva, January 1974).

Chapter VII of the Declaration of Principles to guide "The relations among the participant States", of the Conference on Security and Co-operation in Europe, Helsinki, 1975, in its Final Act reads:

"The participating States will respect human rights and fundamental freedoms, including the freedom of thought, conscience, religion or belief, for all without distinction as to race, sex, language or religion.

They will promote and encourage the effective exercise of civil, political, economic, social, cultural and other rights and freedoms all of which derive from the inherent dignity of the human person and are essential for his free and full development. Within this framework the participating States will recognize and respect the freedom of the individual to profess and practise, alone or in community with others, religion or belief acting in accordance with the dictates of his own conscience.

The participating States on whose territory national minorities exist will respect the right of persons belonging to such minorities to equality before the law, will afford them full opportunity for the actual enjoyment of human rights and fundamental freedoms and will, in this manner, protect legitimate interests in this sphere.

The participating States recognize the universal significance of human rights and fundamental freedoms, respect for which is an essential factor for the peace, justice and well-being necessary to ensure the development of friendly relations and co-operation among themselves as among all States.

They will constantly respect these rights and freedoms in their mutual relations and will endeavour jointly and separately, including in co-operation with the United Nations, to promote universal and effective respect for them. They confirm the right of the individual to know and act upon his rights and duties in this field. In the field of human rights and fundamental freedoms, the participating States will act in conformity with the purposes and principles of the Charter of the United Nations and with the Universal Declaration of Human Rights. They will also fulfil their obligations as set forth in the international declarations and agreements in this field, including inter alia the International Covenants of Human Rights, by which they may be bound."

These two documents demonstrate, once more, the practical possibility of an agreement covering the listing of human rights and the protection thereof, notwithstanding the present discrepancies of theory and doctrine in the conception of the common standard proclaimed by the Universal Declaration. While not ignoring the sad plight of human rights in many countries, it is not utopian to think that this agreement will have practical, positive and progressive results, even though the process may be neither fast nor immediate.

Thus, the fact that important political parties are acting in Western Europe (aside from the social-democratic parties) which parties, both socialist and communist, are ideologically the result of a Marxist-Leninist doctrine, is a circumstance of undoubted importance which cannot be ignored if one is to understand the position of human rights in the West. The phenomenon of euro-communism as connected with human rights has an undeniable significance which we will refer to again later when we reach current social conceptions.[28]

15. The evolution of approaches to human rights in Latin America is the result of the ambivalent situation in this continent: in theory pertaining to the West, and in reality to a continent in a process of development with tremendous economic and social problems.

Legally speaking, the American Declaration of Human Rights of 1948, the American International Charter of Social Guaranties of 1948, the Bogota Charter of the same year which formed the foundation of the Inter-American System, the Inter-American Commission of Human Rights founded in 1959, the Protocol of Buenos Aires of 1967 reforming the Bogota Charter and the San Jose Convention (which recently entered into force), constitute highly important stages based on international resolutions, similar in form to those of Western Europe and inspired by similar ideas.

But, Latin America has in fact seen the abyss existing between these rights and actuality, between the liberties proclaimed therein and the reality of poverty and exploitation. The present confused situation arising from the above contradictions and from many other factors which it is not possible to examine here, undoubtedly reveals a deep crisis in the question of human rights in Latin America. But it is possible to assert that this crisis is circumstantial and transitory and that Latin America will come to the defence of its traditional conception of human rights, nourishing this with the necessary economic and social elements which can only be authentic if

[28] A. Truyol y Serra, *Los Derechos Humanos, op. cit.*, p. 164, 1965.

based on development and in the changing of obsolete structures which have hindered progress and justice.

IV

16. In expressing judgement on development in the concept of human rights occurring over the last thirty years in the socialist countries, we must clarify that we intend solely to make certain general observations, which are of necessity incomplete and partial. In these references we must include not only data connected with some socialist countries of Eastern Europe, but also Cuba and Yugoslavia – which are part of the Third World and non-aligned countries – together with China, which, in its theory of three worlds, includes first the Soviet Union and the United States, and itself forms part of the Third World. References shall be made to other socialist countries of Africa and Asia when dealing with the evolution of human rights in the Third World, but at present we will concentrate our attention solely on the above-mentioned socialist countries whose organization is based on expressed acceptance of the Marxist theory, despite the existence of well known exceptions to this rule.

It should also be clarified that we cannot study the important question of the evolution of this concept in the thought and present political action of the socialist and communist parties of Western Europe, and we will limit ourselves to a marginal reference only.

17. Before we turn to details which show evolution in the concept of human rights in the socialist field during recent years, it should be repeated that the Marxist school of thought – born in the West within the philosophical tradition of Western Europe – implies a theory of human rights with different characteristics and based on different elements from those accepted in what is generally known as the Western concept. This diversity, which we will not discuss since it is well known,[29] did not how-ever hinder the reaching of an agreement in 1948 (at that time very diffi-

[29] B. Tchechko, The concept of human rights in the USSR, according to official texts, *Human Rights, Comments and Interpretations, a Symposium,* UNESCO, 1949; V. Kartachkin, Coopération des pays socialistes dans le domaine du Droit International, *Manuel Unesco, op. cit.:* A. Movchán, Problemas de los derechos del hombre en el Derecho Internacional Contemporáneo, *El Derecho Internacional Contemporáneo,* Moscow, 1973, p. 275; Jovan Djordjevic, Human Rights and Freedom in the Contemporary World, *Review of International Affairs,* No. 650, Belgrad, 1977; I. Szabo, Fondements historiques et développement des droits de l'homme, *Manual Unesco, op. cit.,* and the studies gathered in the collective works *Socialist concept of Human Rights,* Budapest, 1966, and *La République Populaire de Bulgarie et les Droits de l'Homme,* Association Bulgare de Droit International, Bucarest, 1971.

cult), which resulted in an ideal and a common conception being proclaimed in the Universal Declaration of Human Rights. This basic
coincidence – maintaining the difference of the various theories on the
basis of human rights, their nature and other questions linked with their
legal aspect – has been affirmed and developed as a result of later evolution. It has thus been possible to achieve coincidences of special significance, such as that registered when the two International Covenants on
Human Rights were approved by the General Assembly of the United
Nations by a vote in which both the Western and socialist nations joined,
and also in the ratification of these Covenants by many socialist and many
Western countries, as well as in documents such as those already
mentioned in paragraph 14 above, specifically the Final Act of the Conference of Helsinki.

18. As regards international protection of the rights of man, the
majority of the socialist countries have ratified the two International
Covenants on Human Rights. This attitude has been very important since it
has, in a way, made its entry into force in 1976 possible but none of them
have either signed or ratified the Optional Protocol to the Covenant on
Civil and Political Rights. The regime established under this Protocol in
connection with the possibility of individual complaints is not, even today,
admitted by the legal theory of the socialist countries, the doctrine and
international practice of which continue to affirm that the individual is not
a subject of international law. The acceptance of international instruments
such as the Covenants on Human Rights does not mean that these rights
are directly conferred on individuals by international law. The above texts
are limited to the imposition of obligations on States as to their duty to
respect the rights and freedoms listed therein. [30]

There is in these countries no system of regional protection of human
rights such as the one in force in Europe, or that of Latin America resulting
from the action of the Inter-American Commission, or the one planned for
this continent under the Convention of San Jose.

International co-operation in this matter among the socialist countries
comes from a different doctrinal concept, and is carried out by means of
bilateral or multilateral co-operation agreements, with formulae
completely different from those inspired by the European or American sys-

---

[30] V. Kartachkin, *op. cit.,* A. Movchán, *op. cit.;* on the Soviet position before the ratification of the two International Pacts of Human Rights: John Carey, Implementing Human
Rights Conventions, The Soviet view, *Kentucky Law Journal,* Vol. 115, and Kent L. Tedin,
The development of Soviet attitude toward implementing human rights under the UN Charter, *Revue des Droits de l'Homme,* Vol. V, 2-3, 1972, p. 399.

tems for the regional protection of human rights.[31]

19. The Constitutions of the socialist countries of Eastern Europe have upheld and developed the characteristic elements of the Marxist theory as regards the rights of their citizens.

We will not refer to the general rules on the rights of citizens under these Constitutions which naturally deny, among other things, the right to private ownership of production resources, and state that these rights, which cannot be exercised against the socialist State, can only exist within the scope of the specific situation regulated by socialist law, and cannot be conceived as prior or superior to the State, or inherent to the quality of the human being.

We will point out only that the majority of the more recent Constitutions of these countries maintain the traditional formula of incorporating declarations related to the rights and duties of the citizens and not to the rights and freedoms of men in general or of the inhabitants, i.e. of all individuals within the territory of the State.[32] This peculiarity continues to be a distinctive element of the socialist concept of human rights, as opposed to what is generally known as the western concept. It is also the formula accepted by the Constitution of the People's Republic of China.[33] However, there have been some examples lately which alter this traditional formula to a certain degree. Thus, the new Soviet Constitution of 1977, under article 37, guarantees foreign citizens and persons without citizenship in the USRR the rights and freedoms provided by law, including the right to appeal to Tribunals and other organs of the State in order to defend their personal, patrimonial and family rights. In other words, although the law recognizes the rights of foreigners and the Constitution allows them the right to appeal to Tribunals and other organs of the State, they do not possess the civil rights attributed under the Constitution to Soviet citizens who are, of course, the only recipients and logical holders of political rights. This text of the new Soviet Constitution is a step forward as opposed to the 1936 Constitution, which refers only to the rights of citizens (Chapter X, Arts. 118-133).

---

[31] V. Kartachkin, *op. cit.*

[32] Constitution of the Democratic Republic of Germany of April 6, 1968, supplemented and amended on October 7, 1974 (Part II, Chapter I, Rights and fundamental duties of citizens); Constitution of the Socialist Republic of Rumania of December 27, 1974, modified on March 28, 1975 (Title II, Rights and fundamental duties of citizens); Constitution of the Socialist Republic of Albania of December 28; 1977, First Part, Chapter II, Rights and fundamental duties of citizens.

[33] Constitution of the People's Republic of China of January 17, 1975, Chapter III, Rights and fundamental duties of citizens.

The 1976 Constitution of the Republic of Cuba under Chapters V (Equality) and VI (Fundamental rights, duties and guaranties) refers to the right of citizens to equality (Arts. 30-43) and, although many rights are granted only to citizens, in some cases certain rights are recognized for all individuals, persons or inhabitants depending on the case (Arts. 44-65).

The Czechoslovak Constitution of 1960, modified in 1970 under Constitutional Acts 143 and 144, although referring in general to the rights of citizens (Chapter II), speaks also in certain cases of the rights of workers (Arts. 22-23) and, more important, guarantees the inviolability of the individual (Art. 30).

A deeper alteration of the traditional concept of the socialist Constitutions is contained in the Yugoslav Constitution of 1974. This text dedicated its Chapter III to the "Freedoms, rights and duties of man and citizen". Some of the declared rights, among them naturally political rights, hold citizens solely as subjects, and the recipients of other rights are the "workers", the "persons" or "men".[34]

This shows that an interesting process is being initiated or evolved which aims towards a wider recognition of individual rights – even though, naturally, within the scope of the Marxist-Leninist conception – and which is not limited only to citizens of the socialist countries.

20. The growing importance of the question of human rights in the socialist countries is evident. It is shown, among other possible examples, in the phenomenon of "dissidents" in the Soviet Union and in the case of the 1977 Declaration in Czechoslovakia which followed several years after the "spring" of Prague in 1968, with a different approach held not only by socialist parties nourished by the Marxist theory of Western Europe, the positions of which are officially supported by the socialist countries of Eastern Europe,[35] but also accepted by some communist parties of the Western European countries, many of which expressly and implicity accept in proclaiming the so-called "euro-communism" unorthodox formulae in matters of human rights as regards criteria originally accepted in legal theory and political practice of the communist countries.[36]

---

[34] Alejsander Fera, Libertades y derechos del hombre y del ciudadano según la Constitución de la R.S.F.J., *Política Internacional,* No. 655, Belgrad, 20/I/1977.

[35] See, for instance, the thought of the French Socialist Party, with reference to the question of human rights, in the collective work *Liberté, Libertés,* Gallimard, Paris, 1976.

[36] See, for instance, the analysis of the question of human rights in the book of Santiago Carrillo, *Eurocomunismo y Estado,* Barcelona 1977, pp. 17, 201 and 202, wherein is included expressly a revaluation of the so-called "formal liberties" and the necessary respect for them, signifying "to the democratic liberties and human rights as a 'historical and irreversible achievement of the human progress'".

Without analyzing these phenomena, there is no doubt about their interest and their possible future influence on changes in the concept of the legal aspect of human rights, the political scope over which these rights and freedoms may have influence, and their protection by national and by international law.

V

21. An analysis of the evolution of the human rights concept in the Third World raises problems of particular complexity. It is not only extremely difficult if not impossible, to arrive at a concept of the Third World which is unanimously acceptable and which may also clarify its relations with the non-aligned group and with countries in the process of development,[37] implying a clear idea as to countries forming the Third World (as already referred to in paragraphs 8,9 and 16) but is should also be borne in mind that there is no common theoretical conception of human rights among the countries of the Third World. In fact, there are States which accept the Marxist-Leninist conception, there are so-called socialist countries with different types of socialism which cannot be strictly integrated to Marxist doctrine, and there are countries which accept philosophies, ideologies or historical traditions implying particular and specific conceptions with regard to human rights.[38] There are, finally, other countries which, even though they totally or partially share the above ideological or philosophical conceptions, have organized themselves socially, economically and politically on models of the western capitalist type.

Moreover, in many of the countries of the Third World located in Africa and Asia, the incidence of constitutional models of countries which acted as colonial powers have left profound marks in greater or lesser degree, depending on the case, which have obviously influenced the legal aspect of the question of human rights.[39] The same can be said of the influence over

[37] G. de Lacharrière, La catégorie des pays en voie de développement, *Société Française pour le Droit International,* Colloque d'Aix en Provence, 1973; Eugenio Anguiano, México, El Tercer Mundo, Racionalización de una posición, *Foro Internacional,* No. 69, Vol. XVIII, julio-septiembre 1977, Vol. I.

[38] See, for instance, the works of Chung-Shu, Hamayun Kabir and S.V. Puntambeka, on the Chinese, Islamic and Hindu concepts on human rights in the already quoted *Symposium of UNESCO,* 1949 and the analysis of human rights in Africa by K.M. Baye, L'Organisation de l'Unité Africaine, *Manuel Unesco, op. cit.*

[39] For instance, as regards the Francophonic countries of Africa, Monique Lions, Los derechos del individuo en las Constituciones del Africa Francofónica, *Veinte años de Evolución de los Derechos Humanos,* UNAM, México, 1974, pp. 491-501. On the question of the

many other countries of the Third World of the constitutional models of
the communist countries.

Finally, there is the case of Latin America in which – with the exception of
Cuba and the less clear and defined situation of Guyana – the so-called
western concept has been accepted since the European influence has been
deeper and more radical than in the other developing countries, at least as
regards the governing class. With the exception of the Caribbean States, the
independence of Latin America took place in the XIXth century with a
chronological process which began long before the decolonisation of the
twentieth century (the origin of the majority of the Third World States of
Africa and Asia) and this had and continues to have repercussions on the
question of human rights throughout the Continent.

22. But if it is impossible to affirm the existence of a common concept
for human rights in the countries of the Third World, it is evident that their
characteristic, social and economic situation evidences the need for similar
approaches to the matter of human rights, even when accepting the
tremendous differences which apply to almost all the countries involved.

Underdevelopment combined with foreign and neocolonialist exploitation, poverty, illness and illiteracy undoubtedly impose a common
approach to the matter. Hence the connection between the problem of
human rights in the Third World, and efforts to re-establish a new international economic order.[40] Economic and social realities of the Third World
force us to give *de facto* preeminence to their recognition and application
or, at the least, to the invocation of economic, social and cultural rights
and to the idea that economic development should have priority over the
guarantee of civil and political rights. This should not interfere with the
immediate efforts of the State to solve the problems arising from the
priorities imposed during the normal course of social and economic
progress.[41]

A great majority of Third World countries affirm that the solving of the
essential problems of food, health, housing, clothing and education holds
priority over the question of 'formal' rights, which are an unknown factor

countries of Africa and Asia of English language: T.O. Elías, *Human Rights and developing
countries,* International Institute of Human Rights, Strasbourg, 1977; T.O. Elías, The new
Constitution of Nigeria and the protection of human rights and fundamental freedoms, *The
Juridical Review,* 1960, Vol. II; M. Moskowitz, *Human Rights and World Order,* New York,
1953.

[40] B. Ramcharan, *Human Rights in the Third World,* Background Paper, Division of
Human Rights, 1977.

[41] S.S. Ramphal, speech in the "Oxford University Africa Society" on March 8, 1977,
Commonwealth Record of Recueil Events, January-March, 1977, No. 21, pp. 12-14.

and one practically without interest to the ignorant and hungry masses which inhabit many of these countries.[42]

23. We should add, to this statement, that it is not possible to understand the question of human rights in the Third World without bearing in mind the consequences arising from the lack of stable and efficient administrative and institutional structures due to political instability, from the traditional lack of respect for constitutional methods and from the existence in many of the Third World countries (with a few exceptions, such as, for instance, India) of a sole political party, with the corresponding absence of periodic and free elections.

24. The developing countries of Africa en Asia, with a few exceptions, did not participate in the elaboration of the Universal Declaration of Human Rights. However, they took part in the preparation of the Covenants and in the deliberations thereon, and above all, in the Third Committee of the General Assembly of 1966, where they clearly expressed the concept contained under the preceding paragraph as to the priority to be given to economic and social development.[43] This also took place during the International Conference of Human Rights in Teheran in 1968.[44]

While the Pacts were being drafted these nations, along with the socialist countries opposed any formula including under the Covenant on Civil and Political Rights any system of individual accusations or communications which could make international protection of these rights effective. The decision to elaborate an Optional Protocol, finally adopted – but approved by the General Assembly with an inferior majority than that which adopted the two International Covenants of Human rights was a solution to the impasse supported by various underdeveloped countries, especially of the Afro-Asian block,[45] and was not at the time believed to be feasible since the possibility of its entry into force on a short-term basis was not thought possible. This prediction was contradicted by the number of ratifications obtained in accordance with the Protocol's Article 9, which brought about its entry into effect on March 23, 1976. Of the Afro-Asian block, only Madagascar and Mauritius initially ratified the Protocol (on the other hand there were 6 Latin American ratifications: Barbados, Colombia, Costa

[42] Héctor Cuadra, El desarrollo económico y los derechos humanos, *Proyección Internacional de los Derechos Humanos,* UNAM, México 1970, pp. 120-142.

[43] B. Ramcharan, *op. cit.,* p. 10, which quotes, as an example, the speech of the Representative of Guinea in the General Assembly on December 16, 1966, day of the adoption of the Pacts.

[44] Proclamation of Teheran, paragraphs 12, 13 and 14.

[45] Egon Schwelb, Civil and Political Rights: The International measures of implementation, *American Journal of International Law,* Vol. 62, No. 4, 1968, pp. 831 and 861.

Rica, Ecuador, Jamaica and Uruguay, and 4 European: Denmark, Finland, Norway and Sweden).

25. Overestimation of the role of the State, and belief in the need for it to take action without hindrance in order to achieve economic and social progress, which influenced the approach of the majority of the Third World countries against the traditional school of western thought (which considers the State as the greater violator of human rights and considers it necessary to regulate and control its actions, even by international means, in order to guarantee and protect these rights), has evolved slightly during recent years. If it has not changed in essence, it has progressed and affirmed itself in the developing countries. There are examples which reveal the idea that the recognition, guarantee, protection and effectiveness of civil and political rights are necessary for social and economic progress, that the question of human rights is of prime importance for development and that all categories of rights are conditioned and implied in a reciprocal manner.

26. We must point out that the contribution of the developing countries, especially the new States of Africa and Asia, to the recognition of the right to self-determination of peoples (a condition essential to make all other human rights feasible), together with the fight against apartheid, racism and all forms of racial discrimination, has been a determining although not exclusive factor, for acceptance by the international community of instruments such as the Convention for the elimination of all forms of racial discrimination and the Declaration on the Granting of Independence to colonial peoples, adopted by resolution 1514 (XV) of the General Assembly, which have given a new and necessary meaning and a factual and militant reality to the fight for human rights and universal, sincere and non-discriminatory respect for the same.[46]

27. If in many countries of the Third World deplorable examples of the violation of human rights are confirmed even today, it is not less true that against these cases (explicable but not justified in many instances by poverty, underdevelopment, ignorance and inexperience) there are many other examples of a real respect for human rights in the Third World. Furthermore, mankind has known and continues to know violations which are equally serious and perhaps less explicable in other regions.

28. While in Latin America there is a regional system for the international protection of human rights which shows great hope for future development, there is as yet nothing similar in Africa or in Asia. However, there is an Arab Regional Commission for Human Rights which has

---

[46] T.O. Elías, *op. cit.,* B. Ramcharan, *op. cit.*

planned interesting future activities and has prepared a draft Declaration of an Arab Charter for Human rights.[47] Examples could be quoted, together with some activities and certain plans, in the Organization of African Unity.[48] But the truth is that nothing of capital importance has as yet been achieved, so we must leave the question open to the future.

In these cases, as in that of Latin America, we believe that an efficient regional or subregional system for the protection of human rights should be established to incorporate and add the universal to the regional system, thus permitting co-ordination of the advantages of universalism with those of regionalism in an effort to achieve an effective protection of human rights taking into consideration the nature and conditions of each region.

29. The United Nations has given particular attention to the problem of human rights in the underdeveloped countries. The Commission on Human Rights has not only adopted resolutions of great importance to clarify the question[49] (which regrettably we cannot examine due to the brevity of this work) but has also, through a series of seminars dedicated to these problems, allowed the making of important conceptual definitions which have opened the way for later evolution, based on the understanding of the present situation in the Third World countries which will allow progressive improvement as regards the recognition of all human rights, and the promotion, protection and guaranty of same.[50]

VI

30. The overall and individual analysis of recent developments in the concept of human rights both in the West, the socialist countries and the countries of the Third World reveals that the complexity of the question impedes the reaching of definite, clear and precise conclusions as to the

[47] B. Boutros Ghali, La Ligue des Etats Arabes et les Droits de l'Homme, *Manuel Unesco, op. cit.*

[48] K. M'Baye, Les droits de l'homme en Afrique, *Manuel Unesco, op. cit.;* B. Ndiaje, La place des droits de l'homme dans l'Organisation de l'Unité Africaine, *Manuel Unesco, op. cit.;* K. Vasak, Problemas relativos a la Constitución de Comisiones de Derechos Humanos, especialmente en Africa, *Veinte Años de Evolución de los Derechos Humanos,* UNAM, México, 1974, p. 575.

[49] For instance, among others, Resolutions 4 (XXXIII) and 5 (XXXIII) of the Human Rights Commission.

[50] Human Rights in Developing Countries, Afghanistan, 1964; Senegal, 1966; Special problems relating to human rights in developing countries, Cyprus, 1969; The Establishment of Regional Commissions on Human Rights with special reference to Africa, United Arab Republic, 1969; The realization of Economic and Social Rights with particular reference to Developing Countries, Zambia 1970; The Study of new ways and means for promoting Human Rights with special attention to the problems and needs of Africa, Tanzania 1973.

existence, nature and limitations of these three concepts and on the countries comprising each of these categories.

Although it is possible in general terms to accept a classification bearing this triple division in mind we must conclude that this can only be relative in the absence of absolute criteria on the countries comprising each of these three groups. The reciprocal and growing influences and relationships between the fundamental ideas of the predominant concepts existing in each of the groups, and the permeability and relativity of their limitations, reflect an optimistic outlook as to the continuity, acceleration and depth of the approximation and interpenetration process between the different concepts of human rights existing in the world today.

Even while recognizing the inevitable dissensions which arise as a consequence of the different ideological backgrounds, the different historical roots, the contrasting traditions and the diversity of political, economic and social outlooks, this process must inevitably result in a progressive improvement in the world-wide position of human rights, if we bear in mind the essential factor of human unity and the necessary equality of all men, based on respect for their dignity.

Although the respect, promotion and protection of human rights presuppose an idea which is unalterable in essence due to the human dignity possessed by every individual, it cannot be doubted that the concept of human rights, of their relationship with political society and with socio-economic factors, their limitations and forms of legal protection, will evolve and change with the course of time.

This evolution and this change have, during recent years, revealed a process directed towards coalescing the different concepts and accentuating the efficiency of procedures aimed at guaranteeing and protecting individual rights and freedoms. These ideas whose merit and positive values are impossible to ignore, do not signify a forgetfulness or denial of the sad reality existing in many countries of the world today, located in all areas.

31. If the enormous and deplorable gap between poverty and opulence and between development and underdevelopment could be diminished, and the misery and ignorance which characterize a majority of the peoples of the Third World sensibly decrease, an acceleration in the process of the effective recognition of human rights, especially in these countries, could be looked for. We have to bear in mind, however, that the negative circumstances of poverty, sickness and ignorance are not the only factors in determining and explaining the violation of human rights. Present-day history and reality show many examples of cultured peoples and countries

with a relatively high level of living which suffer from despotism and a flagrant violation of freedom. But, even while recognizing this phenomenon, the analysis of which will take us far, we must admit in general terms, that, in fighting poverty and ignorance, we are fighting for final victory in the cause of human rights.

32. Today, without prejudice to many other actions which should be undertaken in the field of human rights so that progress can be made towards the goal of universal and effective respect, it is necessary to persevere in the fight to affirm the existence of an ideal and of a concept common to all peoples, as listed in the Universal Declaration of Human Rights and reiterated in the Proclamation of Teheran under which equal and inalienable rights are attributed to all members of the human family.[51]

The acceptance of this ideal, of this common concept, is the essential basis for progress, looking at the question with universal vision, in the long, painful and difficult process towards the effective respect of man's freedoms and rights throughout the world.

In looking at the ground already covered, despite a feeling of sadness due to the deplorable situations which have existed and continue to exist, we cannot allow ourselves to give way to scepticism. If the question of human rights is analyzed with a broad historic perspective, we must share the conclusions of René Cassin in 1968: "if the effective attempts against the fundamental freedoms of man have not significantly diminished, the fact in itself that resignation without hope, the wall of silence and the absence of any possible way of recourse are in clear retreat, if not on the way to complete disappearance, opens encouraging perspectives to mankind which we cannot allow to be dimmed at any price".

---

[51] In my speech given in the General Assembly as Representative of Uruguay on September 16, 1966, at the moment of the adoption of the International Pacts, I declared: "The Declaration, adopted with no votes against, 48 in favour and 8 abstentions, recognized, and this is comforting, that it is based in a 'common conception of these rights and freedoms'. That is, it presupposes that in spite of the different political, economical and social systems which divide the world, there is a universal idea of the rights of man, founded in the 'recognition of the intrinsic dignity and equal and inalienable rights of all members of the human family'."

CHAPTER III

HUMAN RIGHTS AND FOREIGN POLICY

PROF. JACQUES FREYMOND*

We have been told that, since the beginning of 1977 and President Carter's arrival at the White House, the protection of Human rights has taken on an international dimension.

This is to forget centuries of history during which governments, parties and factions, churches and sects, over and above their great speculations regarding the destiny, genius and weaknesses of man, his capacity for good and evil, the contrast between his aspirations and his achievements, have invoked the rights of man so as to legitimize a cause or, consciously or unconsciously, to justify a policy. It is to forget, closer to us, the revolutions of the XVIIth century, the American revolution, the revolution of 1789, the history of Europe in the XIXth century, carried by great national, liberal and social currents, that of the American people, illustrated by Jefferson, Lincoln, Wilson. It is to forget the arguments found in the ongoing confrontation between self-determination, legitimacy, security, and equilibrium. It is to forget the great struggles over intervention and non-intervention, the sincere or hypocritical denunciations of atrocities committed by others, of the exploitation of peoples and classes by the strong, the critique of imperialism, or rather of imperialisms of every variety. It is also to forget the great humanitarian spirit expressed after Solferino in the international movement of the Red Cross which, much earlier than is generally believed, devoted itself to the protection of the rights of man within existing societies. And let us not imagine, either, that this fundamental debate regarding the rights – and duties – of man in the society in which he lives was only the concern of Westerners. Every attempt to gain some perspective on the problem reveals to whoever wants to escape the prison of ethnocentrism the existence of many currents, all of which, through various institutions and forms of behavior, reflect the same concern for the definition of conditions in which humanity should have the right to live. This definition is not in itself a guarantee. It has never been

* Director of the Geneva Graduate Institute of International Studies.

one, nor has it ever prevented the persistence of social, religious and racial discrimination, nor the exploitation of man due to structures, modes of production or security considerations.

It must therefore be stressed, in an era tragically marked by the ignorance of historical perspective, that the reaffirmation of the need to protect the rights of man is not the result of the second World War and its Hitlerian phenomena, but of a struggle of centuries, between the forces striving after an ideal and the various forms of resistance which are born of human weakness, and resulting contradictions and tensions within societies.

One must, of course, recognize the fact that the United Nations Charter, with its articles 55 and 56, the Universal Declaration of Human Rights of 1948, the International Covenant on Economic, Social and Cultural Rights, The International Covenant on Civil and Political Rights and the Optional Protocol thereto, all three of which were adopted by the General Assembly of the United Nations on December 16, 1966, constitute an important stage in the fight to ensure the effective protection of human rights. The role of the European Convention for the protection of human rights and fundamental freedoms of 1950 must also be recognized, as well as the American Human Rights Convention.

The question to be asked is the following: what is the significance, and above all the efficacy of these international conventions for the protection of human rights? The universal answer will be that their application is a question of condition and of patience, that some societies are better able to ensure application of the terms of the Universal Declaration of Human Rights, whereas some others still need to go through an adaptive phase. We will not disagree. If the history of human societies in past centuries is to be made relevant to us today, it is precisely so as to give us a sense of relativity. But that need not prevent us from observing that in point of fact the impact of the decisions taken at the UN has been small. The International Covenant on Civil and Political rights, adopted in December 1966, took ten years to obtain the number of ratifications necessary for its implementation. Some Western countries showed themselves surprisingly reticent. So it was that Switzerland, whose citizens like to give lessons of civility to the whole world, held back even though the Covenant like the additional Protocol, are open to the signature of any State adhering to the Statute of the International Court of Justice. As for the clauses of the Covenant and the additional Protocol, the least that may be said is that they are marked by the all too obvious concern for the protection of the sovereignty of States, to the point of compromising the protection of human rights.

It would be a mistake to focus exclusively on the clauses of the International Covenant on Civil and Political Rights while ignoring one aspect of the provisions of the Universal Declaration of Human Rights concerning the condition of men in society, their economic rights, health, and education. Gillian Walker, in an interview with *Le Monde,*[1] recalled that "All of the activities of the UN relate to human rights, and it cannot be accused of total imperviousness in this area. Within the Organization, many people give themselves over wholeheartedly to the rights of children, refugees, etc. Its Human Rights Commission employs some forty people, but its work remains unknown". The statement is perfectly valid, and it would be a great injustice to reject as useless the considerable effort undertaken by the various organizations belonging to the United Nations system for the improvement of the conditions of human life the world over.

The statement is also useful in that it focuses our attention on the differences which exist in the hierarchy of human rights.

The Americans, as well as most of the countries – or at least the governments – of the West, place the accent on political rights. President Carter refers to Jefferson's definition and to the Declaration of Independence: "Life, liberty and the pursuit of happiness".[2] Carter then explains:

In most ways, there is no such thing as a 'typical American'.

In ancestry, religion, color, accent, cultural background – even country of birth – we are as varied as humanity itself. But if any one thing does unite us, it is a common belief in certain basic human rights.

In the eight months I have been in office, I have sought to weave a due regard for those rights into the fabric of our foreign policy. One of the incidental effects of this necessarily somewhat experimental effort has been a nationwide – indeed worldwide – debate on the nature of human rights and how best they may be advanced. Defining human rights is a hazardous business. There is the danger of leaving out something essential; there is the equal danger of including things which, however desirable they may be, are not rights at all. The best definition I know – and certainly the most succinct – is the phrase Jefferson used in the Declaration of Independence: Life, liberty, and the pursuit of happiness.

The most basic of these is life – the right to the integritiy of the person. This is the right of each individual to live unmolested and free of arbitrary execution, torture, or imprisonment.

There can't be any argument about this right among people of good will, no matter what their political ideology may be.

It is the irreducible basis of the social contract, and a regime that systematically and repeatedly violates it ultimately forfeits its own legitimacy.

Jefferson's second 'inalienable right', liberty, encompasses the civil freedoms

---

[1] I briefly dealt with this problem in an article entitled "Droits de l'homme et conflits internes", in *Annales d'études internationales,* Geneva, 1977, pp. 11-28 (published by the Alumni Association of The Graduate Institute of International Studies).

[2] From an article by President Carter published in the *Baltimore Sun* on September 19, 1977.

enshrined in many great documents, from our own Bill of Rights to the first half of the United Nations' Universal Declaration of Rights. The most important of these freedoms is freedom of conscience, with its corollaries, freedom of speech and freedom of the press.

The third right is the pursuit of happiness, and it is a mark of Jefferson's particular genius that he phrased it in just this way, instead of using the rather cold formulation of his day, 'the pursuit of property'. In a modern context, most of us would understand the pursuit of happiness to include the right to a basic standard of material existence – to food, shelter, health care, and education. In international law, this third right – which is not so much a freedom as it is a matter of social and economic justice – finds expression in the second half of the Universal Declaration. If defining human rights is difficult, finding ways to advance them is even more so. Human rights cannot be the only goal of our foreign policy – not in a world in which peace is literally a matter of survival. We are circumscribed by the fact that a choice that moves us towards one of our goals may move us farther away from another, and by the limits of our power. In this imperfect world, the results of our actions will usually be mixed, even when our motives are not.

Through public discussion and private persuasion, some progress has been made. But we cannot expect quick or easy results in the struggle for human rights, a struggle which has been going on for many centuries.

In the end, the best way we can advance the cause of human rights abroad is to do all we can to advance it at home. There is no comparison between the human rights situation in totalitarian countries and in our own. The systematic destruction of liberty by an all-powerful state has never been part of the American story.

Nevertheless, it is worth remembering that as recently as 15 years ago, American citizens were still being deprived of the right to vote on account of color. And even today, Jefferson's third freedom is still imperfectly fulfilled as far as many Americans are concerned.

The struggle goes on here at home. And if that remains true of the United States, whose democratic freedoms have a history that stretches across two centuries, it is truer still of the world, many parts of which have never known those freedoms. In the long run, I am optimistic. Changes will not come quickly, but they will surely come. History moves slowly and fitfully; but as long as we are true to ourselves, history, where human rights are concerned, is on our side.''

This expression of President Carter's point of view is reflected in the statements of his main advisers. For example Cyrus Vance, in a speech given before the University of Georgia Law School on April 30, made even clearer the concept of a human rights hierarchy: "First, there is the right to be free from governmental violation of the integrity of the person; second, there is the right to the fulfilment of such vital needs as food, shelter, health care and education; third, there is the right to enjoy civil and political liberties". Let us note in passing that Vance places the right to happiness second. But what is even more important is the fact that the UN and international debates place the Jeffersonian right to happiness first for the simple reason that misery has little concern for freedom. When they speak of the right to exist, the representatives of the developing countries, whether they are government officials, union members, or intellectuals, instinctively place the greatest stress on basic human needs. Death or suffering is not mainly perceived by them in the shape of summary execution or torture, but as famine, misery, malnutrition, or the inadequacy of sanitary and living conditions. The debate regarding the application of measures aimed at the protection of human rights is therefore dominated and distorted by a misunderstanding which is due as much to differences in living conditions as to ideological cleavages. And, to tell the truth, it is not easy to imagine how to get beyond that misunderstanding.

In addition to the question of priorities there is the resistance of States in the name of sovereignty. The governments of States, even the most democratic and liberal, are highly sensitive to any foreign interference in their internal affairs. Any international, bilateral and especially multilateral agreement may, by means of extensive interpretations of one or the other of its provisions – or of ambiguous terminology – be used to camouflage a manoeuver intended to weaken one of the contracting parties from within. This is a problem well known to historians of diplomacy and international lawyers, and which has become more complex and difficult to resolve due to the growth of multilateral diplomacy and the increased number of official languages. The desire to associate in global and comprehensive accord a number of States spread out over the entire planet and subjected to varying historical perspectives and social conditions, has led to the drafting of texts which can be interpreted in contradictory manners or which mean absolutely nothing and which, in either case, lead to political stalemate. This has paradoxically transformed the international system into a transnational one, inasmuch as societies interpenetrate one another, governmental accords, whose growth coincides with felt needs, tend to become empty and inoperative, precisely when they deal with delicate political questions. They project the image of a type of cooperation which everyone seems to yearn for and at the same time fears.

The history of the Helsinki accords provides a good demonstration of the impasse into which governments have manoeuvered one another. A reading of the texts containing the conclusions of the all too famous Third Basket made it clear to whoever was action oriented – that is to say, desired to see the measures implemented – that these were incoherent and poorly drafted provisions because they had been devised in different languages and from different perspectives. The accords of the Third Basket amount to what, in musical language, one might call a potpourri, conceived and composed in such a way as to play down differences in styles. By wanting to cover all possible subjects, the negotiators failed to deal with any in a satisfactory manner. The description of problems was mixed up with the timed outline of possible solutions. As a result, Helsinki appears to public opinion as nothing more than a diplomatic farce, a great deception without an identifiable deceiver. Is it not significant that the Belgrade Conference ended with a general declaration which makes no mention of human rights? Things have gotten to the point where the very mention of this subject is seen as intervention in the internal affairs of States. The Soviet government, pressed by its Western partners and especially by the representatives of the new American administration, decided to stall. This cannot be considered surprising. In negotiations concerning human rights, the Soviet representatives have always insisted on the need for States to assume the responsibility for ensuring the protection of human rights as they wish. This is a point regarding which the Soviet position has not changed. Belgrade is therefore not an exception in terms of substance. What was remarkable was the tone, which contrasts with the apparent general mood of détente.

The Soviet government is not alone in its categorical and simultaneously logical and absurd defense of the sovereignty of States. The diplomatic Conference for the reaffirmation and development of humanitarian law also came up against the obstacle of sovereignty, the resistance of governments to the principle of international control. If the delegations parted in an atmosphere of calm, leaving behind a protocol on international armed conflicts which had been ably emasculated, it was because the style of the Conference commanded moderation. But, in a certain sense, the failure in Geneva of those who had hoped for the reaffirmation and development of international law to include the victims of "internal unrest" among the categories to be protected, is very serious, more fraught with consequences for humanity than the impasse of the Belgrade negotiations. It is also more indicative of the dominant frame of mind around the world, since the quasi-general complicity of governments was required in order to keep "internal unrest" out of the area of application of the additional protocols. A complicity which was made possible by the indifference of public opinion and, even more serious, the silence of international non-governmental organisations which are not known for their unwillingness to speak up. How does one explain the fact that Amnesty International, the International Commission of Jurists and other organizations which have committed themselves to the struggle for the protection of human rights, let pass this opportunity, by means of the Geneva rights, to pave the way for possible monitoring of the condition of political prisoners? How come the very voices which denounce mistreatment and torture of prisoners with the greatest vigor and wish to fill a gap in the system of protection of human rights by even proposing a new convention against torture never made use of the various possibilities provided in the course of successive preparatory conferences prior to the opening of the Geneva Conference? I asked this question on several occasions and I ask it once again so as to emphasize the absence of an answer and the significance of such conscious or unconscious escapism.

The failure of Geneva and the complex provisions of international protocols on the protection of civil and political rights reveal that the interests of the State take priority over human rights.

This leads us to ask questions about the place and the role of those rights in the foreign policy of States. In answer one might note, based on one's observation of the world political scene, that a large proportion of governments seems to pay more attention to the protection of human rights abroad than at home and that, as a result, the defence of human rights has become an instrument of foreign policy.

It is an instrument of the foreign policy of States, but also of affinity groups of an ethnic, religious, ideological or political nature seeking the conquest of power. These groups of all types always struggle, or so they claim, for the protection of the rights of man against oppressors who occupy governmental positions. If they have recourse to violence, blackmail, terrorism, it is – or such is their argument – because they have no alternative. And so, for the past several years, there has unfolded a spiral of violence and counter-violence which everyone attempts to explain but whose dynamics no one can slow down, for a very good reason: when everyone feels entitled to act as law enforcer, there is no law, because, whoever or wherever you may be, you become judge as well as claimant.

Between those who have power and embody the authority of the State and those who want to conquer it, the struggle is unequal, or so one thinks but this is in fact less and less true. As for the means of combat, they tend to become more similar, whether in the area of armaments or in that of propaganda techniques. And this means that, exposed as he is to campaigns of propaganda for diverse and opposing causes, overwhelmed by the flood of denunciations and quantified violence, the man in the street can no longer have an opinion regarding the true condition of those about whom he is being informed. From all sides, he is being told that the rights of man are violated, in Chile, Argentina, Uganda, Ethiopia, the Middle East and many other places. He may read the successive declarations and resolutions, at the UN or in international conferences, always voted by crushing majorities which are often automatic or carefully prepared. But more and more he wonders deep within himself what are the rights and who is the Man in question. This leads him to let himself, consciously or unconsciously, slide towards a state of hibernation.

This is why the great sense of indignation which has been on the rise for years, caused by the more and more frequent and systematic recourse to violent means which destroy men physically and degrade them psychologically and morally, is only expressed through protests that have no impact, an anger lacking in political effect and leading to resignation through impotence. Terrible things, it is said, are happening in such and such a country. How is this known? How reliable are the reports? And who is committing the abuses or the atrocities: the police or its adversaries or, most probably, both?

Should the consciousness of this failure lead us to join the ranks of the apostles of *Realpolitik,* for whom the protection of human rights must be left to the States, and for whom any other approach could only aggravate tensions in the relations between States, and generalize confusion? This is the approach recommended by critics of the policy adopted by the Carter administration in the area of human rights.

But this attitude is impractical in that it does not propose an alternative solution. *Realpolitik* as practised over the past decades has resulted in failure. It was during the Nixon administration, when Kissinger had sovereign control over the foreign policy of the United States, that violations of human rights increased drastically. Not that those men bear total responsibility or that their predecessors should be totally absolved. If, during its struggle with the KGB, the CIA came to adopt methods which must finally result in the destruction of legal norms without which the international system cannot function, it is because governments in power practised a policy of *"benign neglect"* towards human rights. It must therefore be stated quite simply that critics of the Carter administration would do better to remember that the difficult situation which the latter must face is a result of their failure. They are also passing judgment over policies which are just beginning to show results.

What is in fact the Carter policy? Let us note first of all that the new administration to a great extent bases its premises on the publications and the activities of the State Department in matters concerning humanitarian law and human rights. It has been years since the House of Representatives conducted hearings on the state of human rights in certain countries receiving technical aid from the United States. In April 1977,[3] the State Department turned over to the Committee on International Relations of the House of Representatives its first report containing information from official and diplomatic sources regarding constitutional and legal provisions and the actual policy practised by governments. These brief official reports also contain information published by international non-governmental organizations such as Amnesty International, the International Commission of Jurists, and Freedom House.

This 137 page report was followed by a second, more elaborate one, published in February 1978,[4] containing a useful analysis of the evolution of the situation since the publication of the 1977 report. These publications, the idea for which, we stress again, did not come from the Carter administration, are a significant contribution to the identification of problems. Sober in style for obvious diplomatic reasons, they provide a general overview which intelligently evaluates often overdramatized reports coming from private sources. The characteristic of the new administration's policy can be seen through a radical and deliberate change of stress: the protection of human rights is no longer but one among other concerns of American policy, it has become an objective. It is no longer considered satisfactory to speak of it and to denounce abuses as a function of circumstances and interests. The administration, in its characteristically systematic fashion, has mobilized itself so as to obtain results. It is not only the President who speaks, but also officials whose speeches – and this is another striking feature of this administration – are based on the same model: the respect for human rights will serve as a criterion in determining relations with all countries and regimes whatever may be the state of existing relations with them. There will be no linkage between disarmament negotiations with the Soviet Union and the opinion which will be expressed regarding the conditions of opponents in Soviet Russia. Each problem will be dealt with on its own terms. Care will be taken to avoid hypocrisy, by adopting measures for the improvement of the conditions of American citizens themselves, not only through the encouragement given civil rights advocates, but through the lessening of restrictions on the freedom to travel, for example to Cuba. In the area of foreign policy, American actions are regular, systematic, but, depending on circumstances, sometimes public and sometimes discreet.

[3] April 25, 1977.
[4] February 3, 1978, Country Reports on Human Rights Practices, to the Committee on International Relations, U.S. House of Representatives and Committee on Foreign Relations, U.S. Senate, 426 p.

This approach is not purely rhetorical. It is translated into fact, first of all at the institutional level: by the creation of a Bureau of Human Rights and Humanitarian Affairs within the Department of State, by the nomination of full-time human rights officers in each of the Bureaus of the Department, by the instruction given ambassadors and chiefs of mission personally to carry out policies concerning human rights, by the setting up of an Inter-Agency Committee on Human Rights and Foreign Assistance whose mandate is to examine all negotiations regarding such matters as economic cooperation or the credit grants on the basis of a given government's human rights policy at home.

These institutional measures have been coupled with more spectacular decisions such as the signature of the American Convention on Human Rights and the International Covenant on Civil and Political Rights. In various international conferences and during UN sessions, as well as at the bilateral level, the US government has adopted positions which are both energetic and clear, sometimes going so far as to take economic and financial measures.[5]

It remains to be seen what will be the results. Here is where the controversy breaks out.

Let us first of all point to the positive aspects of current results: there is no doubt as to the fact that the Carter administration has to a certain

---

[5] In a report presented on October 25, 1977, to one of the House Sub-Committees, Mark L. Schneider, Deputy Assistant Secretary for Human Rights, stated the following:

"Third, we have undertaken diplomatic initiatives in innumerable countries urging the release of political prisoners, an end to states of siege which suspend constitutional due process protections, a return to the rule of law and the democratic process, an end to torture, and the enhancement of all human rights.

Fourth, we have halted or reduced security assistance programs and withheld commercial licenses for military equipment for armed forces in several countries which have engaged in serious human rights violations. No country can assume that it has a blank check to obtain arms from the United States, but especially those with serious human rights violations.

Fifth, we have examined our bilateral economic assistance programs with an eye toward ensuring that they go to benefit people and not to strengthen the hold of repressive governments. We are hopeful of increasing the level of our assistance to the development of the world's poorest countries and its poorest people. But as Secretary Vance said at Grenada: 'our cooperation in economic development must not be mocked by consistent patterns of gross violation of human rights'. This review involves overall budget levels to countries, decisions on the kinds of assistance that can be provided, and decisions not to go forward with certain programs. In some instances, it has meant a decrease in assistance to particular countries. Specifically, with regard to our bilateral programs, we have carried out demarches to a number of governments raising human rights concerns and delayed or reduced programs to others. Sixth, we have taken initiatives in the international financial institutions to promote the cause of human rights. We have opposed or sought the reconsideration of loans to governments engaged in serious violations, although again we have attempted to give special consideration to loans going to benefit the needy. We have carried out demarches to more than a score of governments regarding human rights concerns in relation to loans within the international financial institutions. In addition, we have abstained on seven loans. We also have told countries that we would oppose the loans if they were brought up for a vote."

extent managed to modify the image of the US and its policy in the UN and the Third World. US policy is no longer automatically identified with that of dictatorial or doubtful regimes. Even more, it is even perceived, through the initiatives of the likes of Andrew Young, as straightforwardly liberal, which implies risk-taking sometimes even considered excessive.

Furthermore, it is admitted that the accent placed on the problem by the entire administration and by US diplomats, and the activism of members of US delegations during meetings of the Human Rights Commission and other international conferences where the matter comes up for discussion, have had positive effects. The intransigence of the US has led some governments to control a bit more tightly their prisons as well as their law-enforcement agencies. It has often encouraged not only those who have valid reasons for protesting, but those who back them, particularly the organizations whose mission is the mobilization of opinion. The protection of human rights has become a basic theme and even one of the goals of international politics. Whoever has dealt with humanitarian problems over the last twenty years must recognize that there has been a profound trans-formation, almost a reversal, of the situation, due to the direct and steady intervention of a country whose power everyone recognizes.

The critics point out that US pressure is exercised in an irregular manner, that some countries have been spared whereas others have been publicly admonished. This is to forget that some of the representations have been made discreetly, thus enabling the governments in question to take heed without losing face. Another, more serious criticism is that American inter-vention has led to a hardening on the part of the governments concerned, whether in Latin America, South Africa, or the Soviet Union. One should, however, try to agree on what is meant by a "hardening". In a country like Argentina, for example, the government does not seem to control the situa-tion. It is difficult to speak of a hardening in reaction to US intervention when in fact violence is the result of an internal struggle between factions bent on destroying one another. The South African hardening is accom-panied by attempts to make the policy of separate development more credible, and it would be useful to examine more closely the causes of the government's dilemma and the critical arguments of those very people, who, among the white population, voted for it. As for the display of ill humor on the part of the USSR and the blocking which took place in Belgrade, it would be a mistake to see them as more than a tactical manoeuver intended to make Carter back down by taking advantage of the confusion of interests created in the US by contradictory and temporary coalitions which are blocking his initiatives and paralysing his policy.

The condition of those labeled dissidents and who are, in fact, "protesters" has, we are told, been made more difficult by American intervention: this remains to be proved. The profound movement of protest continues and it is certain that the very interest taken by the government of a large State in the fate of those who struggle to obtain the application of the provisions of the UN Charter, the Universal Declaration of Human Rights, and the International Covenant on Civil and Political Rights in their own country, constitutes an act of encouragement. Nothing proves that the protesters would have received better treatment if the US government had ignored their struggle.

Is it even arguable that it has the *right* to ignore it? The question may seem surprising, but it is in fact the logical consequence of the provisions of the UN Charter and other agreements just referred to. The States having signed the Charter committed themselves to respecting its provisions and, therefore, to applying them on their territory. Those who signed another Charter, Charter 77, which caused so much emotion in Western public opinion and so much concern in Prague, were only asking their government to respect and enforce respect by its administration of the International Covenant on Civil and Political Rights which it has just ratified and published. They did not only demand a right, they did their civic duty when they asked their government to honor a commitment which it had made to the Czechoslovak people and the international community. It is therefore normal and even necessary for signatories of the Charter to remind a fellow-member of its duties. But this prodding of a government should of course be done under conditions which promise success. This has not been the case. The new policy of the US government was not understood, nor is it really supported. Western governments, after having observed a prudent silence, went so far as to make more and more guarded and critical comments based on a superficial analysis of the content of official US documents and once again demonstrated their basic incapacity for long-term thinking. Even worse, the reactions of Giscard d'Estaing and Helmut Schmidt seemed to indicate that they both adhered to the Kissinger linkage policy which subordinated the protection of human rights to the conclusion of a SALT II accord which he was, incidentally, unable to obtain.

American solitude in an action of such fundamental interest was further aggravated by the clumsiness of the mass media which dramatize everything in a distorting manner. Charter 77 was the object of many commentaries before it was even read. It was transformed into a war machine directed against the Czechoslovak government when it was in fact a very moderate document, containing clearly constructed and reasoned arguments. Likewise, it is as a result of the clumsy questions asked at Carter's first press conferences that linkage was reintroduced and the idea widely propagated that Carter's human rights policy was an anti-Soviet tool.

Uncertain though the results, and contradictory though the commentaries may be, there can be no doubt that an interesting experiment is underway. A government disposing of great means is currently trying to promote the protection of human rights through diplomatic action. The enterprise is based on a realistic appraisal of the situation. It is clear that in our transnational system internal unrest is dangerous to international peace. A government which abuses its powers by limiting the fundamental freedoms of its citizens, by threatening the integritiy of persons, by practising or tolerating torture, by permitting corruption and practices which aggravate social contradictions and, therefore, lead to explosive tension prevents the normalization of international relations. The protection of human rights has thus become one of the essential conditions for the preservation or the reestablishment of peace. It can clearly be seen that on this point the Carter administration, by making it one of the mainstays of its foreign policy, has shown the way which must be followed.

It is, however, obvious that a single government, no matter how influential, cannot win a battle which, given the advanced state of degeneration of international relations, will be long and difficult. It is therefore important to follow its example and its continuing efforts, and that, at the UN and in regional groupings, the still-dominant stage of declarations of principle and humanitarian rhetoric be overcome, so as to concentrate on a global humanitarian strategy which coordinates the policies of governments and international governmental and non-governmental agencies. Ties have been progressively established and forms of collaboration have emerged here and there. Another step must be taken in the elaboration of an overall policy, one which combines information, the mobilization of opinion and the international media in a non-discriminatory fashion.

It is also important to subject armed groups which have recourse to violence to the same critical examination, so as to distinguish gangsterism and destructive nihilism from authentic opposition to arbitrary behavior by those in power. The mass media must be associated with this overall strategy by subjecting the information they furnish to a rigorous critique.

This grouping of forces is a necessity. As long as there are only isolated and case-to-case initiatives, there is little chance of obtaining more than partial successes. The action undertaken by the Carter administration, by a government, will collapse, and thus justify the skepticism of the proponents of *Realpolitik*. And, above all, colective action will make it possible to correct certain excesses, improve policies and tactics, and bring about a reexamination of simplistic solutions such as the absurdity of majority rule, that the government of a country with a federalist tradition chooses as its criterion for solutions to be adopted in countries where the imperative aim to bring about the coexistence in mutual respect of various ethnic groups and races. To take only one example, it is not majority rule which must be proposed for the replacement of apartheid, but a federalist solution, fundamentally different from the caricature of "separate development".

The protection of human rights is ultimately not the affair of a government but of the international community. Only a commonly coordinated policy will make it possible to obtain results. The United States has shown the way. Supportive action must now be undertaken through the development, the enlargement and the refinement of its action. This presents an organizational problem which may be resolved if governments, international governmental and non-governmental organizations agree to implement a policy free of the double burden which has heretofore paralyzed them: indignation and skepticism.

PART THREE:

THE FUTURE

CHAPTER IV

UNITED NATIONS POLICIES AND STRATEGIES: GLOBAL PERSPECTIVES?

DR. THEO C. VAN BOVEN*

1. With the increased attention for human rights and fundamental free-doms, the international human rights discussion takes on wider dimensions and is gaining in depth. No doubt, this discussion is largely influenced by ideological assumptions and political perceptions. Traditional concepts are reaffirmed by some and by the same token challenged by others. New concepts are developed, calling for a global and structural human rights approach. Emphasis is put on the rights of collectivities, on the conditions of the masses, on structural relationships rather than on the rights of individuals. It is rediscovered that the notions of liberty and equality can-not obtain their full meaning unless they are linked up with the notion of solidarity. This intensified human rights discussion may reflect a growing concern for the fate and well-being of peoples and persons. It may indicate that wide circles are actively seeking ways and means with a view to achieving more political freedom and social justice. On the other hand the motivations may not be that lofty and arguments may be put forward in the discussion in order to conceal serious deficiencies in the human rights record.

2. It is too facile to put the blame for serious violations of human rights on the outside world, on the other person, on the other nation. External factors cannot be overlooked but too often such matters as international conspiracy, the threat of outside aggression, unfavourable conditions on the international economic market are invoked as justifications or explanations for consistent and gross violations of human rights. One can-not escape the impression that rulers of certain nations are focussing on external factors as determining human rights conditions in order to shift the responsibility from their domestic scene to foreign neighbours in the vicinity or faraway lands. It is, however, also true that nations which can perhaps claim a fairly good domestic human rights record cause, as a result of their economic, political and military policies vis-à-vis other countries

---

* Director of the Division of Human Rights of the United Nations. The views expressed in this paper are those of the author in his purely personal capacity.

and the world at large, adverse consequences on the human rights situation elsewhere. Such policies can be manifested in many ways, e.g. assistance to racist and colonialist régimes,[1] or more generally assistance to oppressive powers, but also in drawing undue profits from the present international economic order which operates to the self-interest of the rich nations and at the detriment of the poor peoples.

3. The present international human rights debate is so ambiguous and to a certain extent a "dialogue des sourds" because external factors and internal conditions are not taken in their mutual relationships and consequences. Wealthy and powerful nations can only make their domestic and foreign human rights policies credible and acceptable if they cease using their influence and powers to the detriment of peoples elsewhere and if they are ready to accept changes in the international order so as to promote greater justice, self-reliance and economic growth among and within poor nations. At the same time the rightful demand by many developing countries for a new international order, politically and economically, should go hand in hand with a commitment to work for a just economic, social and political order at national and local levels. A new international order can never be separated from the domestic orders. Inasmuch as the international community and its members as represented in the United Nations, should be committed to work for a new international economic and political order, based on the purposes and principles of the United Nations Charter,[2] the nations are equally obliged to take joint and separate action in order to promote universal respect for human rights and fundamental freedoms and to work for a human order within their borders.[3] This idea was well expressed in the preamble of the International Development Strategy for the Second United Nations Development Decade, by which "Governments . . . pledge themselves, individually and collectively, to pursue policies designed to create a more just and rational world economic and social order in which equality of opportunities should be as much a prerogative of nations as of individuals within a nation".[4] The same notion, though not from the point of view of the nation but with the individual person as the principal subject, is inherent in article 28 of the Universal Declaration of Human Rights which states: "Everyone is entitled to a social and international order in which the rights and freedoms set

---

[1] See Ahmed M. Khalifa, The Adverse Consequence for the Enjoyment of Human Rights of Political, Military, Economic and Other Forms of Assistance given to Colonial and Racist Régimes in southern Africa, doc. E/CN.4/Sub.2/283.
[2] Articles 1 and 2 of the UN Charter.
[3] See Articles 55 and 56 of the UN Charter.
[4] General Assembly resolution 2626 (XXV), para. 12 of 24 October 1970.

forth in this Declaration can be fully realized.''

4. In the current human rights debate as carried on in United Nations fora and elsewhere, the very concept of human rights and fundamental freedoms is subject to re-examination and re-orientation. While hardly anybody would question the validity of a statement as contained in the preambles of both International Covenants on Human Rights to the effect that ''in accordance with the Universal Declaration of Human Rights, the ideal of free human beings enjoying freedom from fear and want can only be achieved if conditions are created whereby everyone may enjoy his civil and political rights, as well as his economic, social and cultural rights'', the practical implications and consequences of this statement give rise to many questions. By way of illustration two quite different views, expressed by two American Human Rights activists, may be cited. One view comes from a member of the Board of Trustees of ''Freedom House'' who has been carrying out periodically a comparative survey of freedom in order to monitor the status of freedom in the nations of the world. In the survey, freedom is defined in terms of civil and political rights, as these rights have been traditionally understood in the constitutional democratic States. The surveyor put it as follows: ''Essentially our model is that of Western constitutional democracy, and we are asking to what extent the countries of the world accord with this model. To many readers this has seemed a paternalistic or ethnocentric viewpoint, but we believe that the freedoms attained by Western democracies are desired by peoples everywhere.''[5]

5. Quite a different view is expressed by the Chairman of the Board of Trustees of the ''Institute for Policy Studies'' in a speech delivered at the first annual Letelier-Moffit Human Rights Award Ceremony on September 19, 1977. He suggested that there are three fatal flaws in the predominantly Western approach of putting strong emphasis on political and civil rights but of being virtually silent on vital human needs. ''The first is the failure to recognize that an infinitely larger number of the world's people are suffering – actually suffering – from 'consistent patterns of gross violations' of their fundamental rights to work, food, health, shelter and education – their rights, in short, to live their lives instead of struggling for their existence – than from violations of their rights to freedom from torture, arbitrary detention and censorship of the press. The second flaw is the failure to admit – since it is hardly possible not to recognize – that the economic policies and activities of the rich countries, in their relations with the poor countries, are playing a major role in perpetuating, if not

[5] Raymond D. Gastil, ''Comparative Survey of Freedom V,'' in: *Freedom at issue,* January-February 1975, no. 29, page 3.

deepening, their poverty. And the third flaw is the failure to understand the complex relationship between economic and political rights. One consequence of this is an assumption which is wholly unsupported, and indeed, controverted by historical evidence: that the securing of political and civil rights, which is sometimes referred to as Western-style democracy, will somehow, as if by magic, lead the Third World out of underdevelopment."[6]

6. It is indeed true that too often the structural causes of injustice are overlooked and that many people are looking exclusively at violations of human rights without being concerned with the causes which are at the bottom of human rights violations. Inasmuch as the United Nations deals with consistent patterns of gross violations of human rights on the basis of the various procedures which were established for this purpose, human rights can never be isolated from the contextual circumstances. The human rights conditions of the black peoples in southern Africa are intimately related to the *apartheid* policy in the area. The human rights situation in the Israeli occupied territories is conditioned by the fact of occupation itself. Human rights in Chile are determined by the policies and practices of the government of that country. In all these situations the United Nations has not hesitated to pronounce itself on the very facts of *apartheid*, occupation and a repressive system of military rule. In other situations, which were taken up by United Nations human rights organs in a less conspicuous manner, in private procedures, it is not so clear to what extent structural conditions or contextual circumstances were taken into account. But it is certainly in the minds of those who are familiar and concerned with living conditions in many developing countries that proverty, illiteracy, ignorance, hunger, disease, political instability, foreign intervention have such an effect that these countries find themselves virtually in a permanent state of political or economic emergency.[7]

7. These contextual circumstances are by themselves a threat to human rights or, more directly, they may constitute, as such, gross violations of human rights. They can provide an explanation why human rights are seriously at stake, but they can certainly not be adduced as a justification for the infringements of certain very basic rights and freedoms, such as the right to life, the right to be free from torture or from cruel, inhuman or degrading treatment or punishment, the right not to be held in slavery or in

---

[6] Peter Weiss, *Human Rights and Vital Needs, Transnational Institute, Washington, D.C.;* Amsterdam, pages 6-7.
[7] See also Kéba M'Baye, "Les réalités du monde noir et les droits de l'homme," *Revue des droits de l'homme,* (1969), pages 382-394.

slavery-like conditions and the right to be free from arbitrary arrest or detention.[8] Too often the violations of these very basic rights and freedoms are the result of abuse of power by selfish rulers, of grotesque arrogance of those who claim to be masters, of ill-conceived notions and practices of superiority, of racist ideologies. It is tempting and deceiving on the part of such abusers of power to invoke structural causes and external factors in order to camouflage violations of human rights which they are consistently committing, thus adding immensely to the suffering which is already prevalent as a result of the contextual circumstances.

8. We would submit that a structural and global approach is definitely called for, if we want to build up a human order, in which political freedom and social justice prevail, if we want to build up a just and participatory society. But the call for a structural and global approach cannot serve as an excuse for not devising as a matter of urgency and immediacy "Ways and means of improving the capacity of the United Nations to put a stop to violations of human rights wherever they may occur."[9] The necessity of combining the structural and global approach with immediate means and methods was aptly pointed out in a recent UNESCO publication which put it in the following terms: ". . . while the full achievement of human rights presupposes patient efforts in the furtherance of development, the dissemination of knowledge and the equalization of opportunities for acquiring it, the humanizing of the environment and the background of life, the enhancement of cultures and communication between them and the promotion of a genuine mutual communication system among people, this does not mean that active measures for the protection, achievement and extension of human rights can be put off until tomorrow except at the cost of an intolerable abdication. It is one thing to take into account, as we must, the fact that circumstances are difficult, the need for patient improvement of conditions determining the life of every society and the extent and level of what it can achieve, the limited amount and precarious nature of the resources that can be mobilized for this purpose, and the need for a determined and prolonged effort to build a better and a juster world. It would be quite another to disregard the obligation, admitting of no compromise, to tackle without further ado all the clear denials of human rights which are already such a scandal."[10]

---

[8] See Stephen Marks, "Development and Human Rights; Some reflections on the study of development, human rights and peace", in *Bulletin of Peace Proposals,* 1977, pages 236-246, at pages 238-239.

[9] General Assembly resolution 2144 A(XXI) of 26 October 1966.

[10] Thinking Ahead; UNESCO and the Challenges of Today and Tomorrow, (1977) page 28.

9. It is against this background that we should pay attention to the main elements and proposals which were prominent in the debate in autumn 1977 at the thirty-second session of the United Nations General Assembly on the item "Alternative approaches and ways and means within the United Nations system for improving the effective enjoyment of human rights and fundamental freedoms". The thrust of this debate centered around two proposals. The first called for an over-all analysis of existing problems in the field of human rights and for increased efforts in finding appropriate solutions for the effective promotion and protection of human rights and fundamental freedoms taking into account the experiences and contributions of both developed and developing countries.[11] This proposal, which became General Assembly resolution 32/130 of 16 December 1977, contained a number of important concepts which should be taken into account in the approach to the future work within the United Nations system with respect to human rights questions. We will revert later to this proposal and to some of the concepts defined therein, largely reflecting the structural and global approach. The other proposal called for the establishment, under the authority of the Secretary-General, of a United Nations High Commissioner for Human Rights, possessing the degree of personal independence, prestige and integrity required for the discreet and impartial performance of his functions.[12] Without going into the details of the latter proposal – which was a revised version of similar proposals which were put forward in earlier years but never commended themselves to the majority of the United Nations membership – the essence of it was to establish an independent authority that could, in an expeditious and tangible manner, deal with immediate human rights concerns without being subject to political decision making. It is my view that a United Nations High Commissioner for Human Rights could be one of the "ways and means of improving the capacity of the United Nations to put a stop to violations of human rights wherever they may occur" and could be considered as a complementary device to the structural and global approach of the other proposal. However, the main proponents of the latter proposal deemed otherwise by achieving that the vote on the draft resolution relating to the High Commissioner for Human Rights was deferred.

10. Turning to the concepts contained in General Assembly resolution 32/130, they reaffirm the indivisibility and interdependence of all human rights, civil and political as well as economic, social and cultural; they ask for a global examination of human rights in the over-all context of the

---

[11] A/C.3/32/L.17/Rev. 1.
[12] A/C.3/32/L.25/Rev. 1.

various societies; they call for the realization of the new international economic order as an essential element and a priority basis for the effective
promotion of human rights; they wish the international community to
accord priority to the search for solutions to the mass and flagrant violations of human rights of peoples and persons. It should be noted that the
preoccupation with mass and flagrant violations of human rights is further
qualified inasmuch as they are "resulting from *apartheid,* from all forms
of racial discrimination, from colonialism, from foreign domination and
occupation, from aggression and threats against national sovereignty,
national unity and territorial integrity, as well as from the refusal to recognize the fundamental rights of peoples to self-determination and of every
nation to the exercise of full sovereignty over its wealth and natural resources" (para. 2 (e)).

11. Earlier, we tried to identify the validity and the deficiency of the
structural and global approach. This approach is valid since it relates
human rights to the purposes of the United Nations, in particular the
achievement of international cooperation in solving international
problems of an economic, social, cultural or humanitarian character as
well as the maintenance of international peace and security and the
development of friendly relations among nations based on respect for the
principles of equal rights and self-determination of peoples. It rightly
emphasizes that the establishment of new international structures, devoid
of the exploitation of poor nations by rich nations and of the abuse of economic, political and military power to the detriment of large masses, is essential for the fate and well-being of large parts of the world population. In fact,
it rightly enjoins the rich and powerful nations, communities of nations and
transnational entities to make the human rights component a predominant
factor in their international dealings. However, resolution 32/130 falls
short where it does not connect the international order to the domestic
orders, where it calls for tackling mass and flagrant violations of human
rights mainly resulting from external factors and neglects the human rights
responsibilities at national and local levels and the gross violations which
occur as a result of the flouting of these responsibilities. Finally, it tends to
generalize (or "globalize") human rights responsibilities so that one fails to
discover the human person who should be the ultimate concern of all
endeavours.

12. The difficulties of making resolution 32/130 operational surfaced at
the thirty-fourth session of the Commission on Human Rights, which was
requested by the General Assembly to undertake, as a matter of priority,
an over-all analysis of the alternative approaches and ways and means

within the United Nations system for improving the effective enjoyment of human rights and fundamental freedoms in the light of the concepts outlined in resolution 32/130. In carrying out this mandate at its thirty-fourth session, the Commission rather concentrated on more practical institutional proposals, aiming at establishing national and local institutions in the field of human rights[13] and regional arrangements for the promotion and protection of human rights[14] and at making the working methods of the Commission and other human rights organs more effective, than on the question of analyzing and elaborating the concepts contained in General Assembly resolution 32/130.[15] Apparently many members of the Commission were more inclined to work on practical and immediate means in order to enhance the United Nations capacity to deal with human rights problems, in particular consistent patterns of gross violations, than to enter into a further reflection on conceptual guidelines. This does not mean that such further reflection in the light of present-day facts, needs and requirements is not called for. The Commission on Human Rights will have in fact a good opportunity to broaden and deepen its conceptual outlook and its framework of action when it will consider at its thirty-fifth session the study of the Secretary-General on the subject "The international dimensions of the right to development as a human right in relation with other human rights based on international cooperation, including the right to peace, taking into account the requirements of the New International Economic Order and the fundamental human needs."[16]

13. Thirty years have passed since the adoption of the Universal Declaration of Human Rights. In those years fundamental changes have been taking place in terms of decolonization, increase in population, mass destruction capabilities, energy consumption, environmental conditions and many other factors having a fundamental impact on humanity as a whole or at least on the masses at large. General Assembly resolution 32/130 considered that the thirtieth anniversary of the Universal Declaration of Human Rights should be marked by an over-all analysis of existing problems in the field of human rights and by increased efforts in finding appropriate solutions for the effective promotion and protection of human rights and fundamental freedoms, taking into account the experiences and contributions of both developed and developing countries. A pertinent question is whether the Universal Declaration is still a valid and pertinent

---

[13] Commission on Human Rights resolution 23 (XXXIV).
[14] Commission on Human Rights resolution 24 (XXXIV).
[15] See report of the thirty-fourth session of the Commission on Human Rights, doc. E/1978/34, chapter IX.
[16] Commission on Human Rights resolution 4 (XXXIII).

international instrument, particularly in the light of the concepts of General Assembly resolution 32/130.

14. It is no doubt true that the Universal Declaration is a product of its time – which applies to all major documents – and that its scope and content were largely determined by the limited membership of the United Nations at the time of its drafting and adoption. This explains why the Universal Declaration focusses nearly exclusively on the rights of the individual person and hardly elaborates on the rights of the community and the duties of the individual.[17] It is also true that the drafters of the declaration were somewhat pretentious in their contentions that the declaration had universal dimensions and validity by calling it *Universal* Declaration of Human Rights, while a large part of the world was still under colonial rule and therefore unable to participate in the framing of the document. It should, however, not be overlooked that the United Nations in later years, with the participation of representatives of large sectors of the Third World, have in many ways reaffirmed the validity of the Universal Declaration and *ipso facto* recognized and endorsed this document as a valid and authoritative statement of human rights. In the struggle against colonialism and racism the United Nations stated in the Declaration on the Granting of Independence to Colonial Countries and Peoples (adopted by General Assembly resolution 1514 (XV) in 1960) and in the Declaration on the Elimination of All Forms of Racial Discrimination (adopted by General Assembly resolution 1904 (XVIII) in 1963) that all States shall faithfully and strictly observe the Universal Declaration of Human Rights. In adopting the International Covenants on Human Rights in 1966 (General Assembly resolution 2200A (XXI)), and thereby completing the International Bill of Human Rights, the United Nations agreed upon a juridical elaboration of the Universal Declaration. In the Proclamation of Teheran, adopted by the International Conference on Human Rights in 1968 and containing a list of human rights imperatives in relation to major world-wide problems and concerns, it was solemnly proclaimed that "the Universal Declaration of Human Rights states a common understanding of the peoples of the world concerning the inalienable and inviolable rights of all members of the human family and *constitutes an obligation for the members of the international community*" (my italics). It is the Universal Declaration which serves as the human rights yardstick in the important procedure, based on Economic and Social Council resolution 1503

[17] See René Cassin, "De la place faite aux devoirs de l'individu dans la Déclaration universelle des droits de l'homme", in: *Mélanges offerts à Polys Modinos* (Editions A. Pédone, Paris, 1968) pp. 479-488.

(XLVIII) which is aimed at identifying situations appearing to reveal a consistent pattern of gross and reliably attested violations of human rights and fundamental freedoms. Many more examples can be adduced in order to show that the Universal Declaration is constantly invoked at various levels and in numerous fora, legal and political, thus reaffirming its value as an authoritative statement of human rights.[18]

15. It is hard to see that approaches and pronouncements adopted in the period after the adoption of the Universal Declaration would invalidate the declaration. Such instruments as the Proclamation of Teheran and General Assembly resolution 32/130 relate human rights to urgent concerns of a global nature, affecting life, liberty and well-being of millions, and underscore that peace and justice are indispensable to the full realization of human rights and fundamental freedoms. These instruments may constitute a challenge to the peoples and nations that were the original framers of the Universal Declaration and they may reflect goals and aspirations of many new nations and their peoples. We would submit that the Universal Declaration is not superseded but supplemented by new concepts, new approaches and new instruments.[19] The Universal Declaration will no doubt continue to serve within and outside the United Nations, as "a common standard of achievement for all peoples and all nations" and as "a common understanding of the peoples of the world concerning the inalienable and inviolable rights of all members of the human family." But the message is clear: unless fundamental changes are brought about in the political, economic and social relations and conditions *among* States and *within* States, "the advent of the world in which human beings shall enjoy freedom of speech and belief and freedom from fear and want" will remain an utopia on our globe.

May, 1978

---

[18] See United Nations Action in the Field of Human Rights (doc. ST/HR/2); Part One, Chapter II, The International Bill of Rights: the Universal Declaration of Human Rights.

[19] See also Report on the thirty-fourth session of the Commission on Human Rights, doc. E/1978/34, para. 162.

CHAPTER V

STANDARD-SETTING: FUTURE PERSPECTIVES

DR. B.G. RAMCHARAN*

A. STANDARD-SETTING: THE PRESENT STATE

Upon the establishment of the United Nations in 1945, events indicated the directions of standard-setting in the field of human rights. The atrocities committed during the Second World War led to strong demands for the inclusion of human rights provisions in the Charter of the United Nations. At the San Francisco Conference, however, there was not enough time to draft an International Bill of Human Rights and it was therefore decided that this should be a priority task of the new organization – a task which was entrusted to the Commission on Human Rights envisaged.in Article 68 of the Charter. The Commission on Human Rights set to work on an International Bill of Human Rights which has now been realized with the adoption of the Universal Declaration of Human Rights, the International Covenant on Economic, Social and Cultural Rights, the International Covenant on Civil and Political Rights and the Optional Protocol thereto. While work was under way on the International Bill of Human Rights, standard-setting was also undertaken in areas such as self-determination and racial discrimination, upon which much emphasis was placed in the United Nations. Work was also undertaken in other areas as problems requiring international action were identified, or as governments or interest groups pressed for action on them.[1] Related activities were likewise undertaken in the specialized agencies and in regional intergovernmental organizations.

All of these efforts have resulted in a considerable body of human rights law and standards supplementing the International Bill of Human Rights

---

* All views expressed in this paper are those of the author in his purely personal capacity.

[1] See generally, Human Rights: A compilation of International Instruments, UN Publication, Sales No. E.73.XIV.2; United Nations Action in the Field of Human Rights, U.N. Publication, Sales No. E.74.XIV.2; ILO, the International Labour Code (1966); L. Sohn and T. Buergenthal, The International Protection of Human Rights (1973); ILO, the Impact of Conventions and Recommendations; U.N. doc. A/CN.4/1/Rev. 1: Survey of international law in relation to the work of the ILC; A/CN.4/245; A/32/143; A/C.6/32/SR.46-50.

in areas dealing with diverse aspects such as the right to self-determination, the prevention of discrimination, war crimes and crimes against humanity, slavery, servitude, forced labour and similar institutions and practices; nationality, statelessness, asylum; rights of refugees; freedom of information; freedom of association; employment policy; political rights of women; marriage and the familiy; childhood and youth; social welfare; progress and development; the right to enjoy culture; and international cultural development and co-operation. Most of these instruments are contained in the United Nations Publication, "Human Rights: A compilation of International Instruments of the United Nations".[2] Notable instruments adopted after 1973, the date of the current edition of this publication are: The International Convention on the Suppression and Punishment of the Crime of Apartheid, the Declaration on the Prohibition of Torture and the Declaration on the Rights of Handicapped Persons.

The methods employed by the United Nations for setting and urging the application of standards in human rights thus far have included the making of recommendations, the adoption of declarations or bodies of principles and the preparation and adoption of international treaties (designated as conventions, agreements, covenants, protocols, etc.). Methods utilized in more recent times have included: standards suggested in studies prepared by rapporteurs; standards suggested by the Secretariat; standards suggested by working groups of human rights organs; drafts submitted by NGOs and standards proposed by Governments. There has been an increasing tendency in the last few years to send drafts to Governments for comments before they are finalized. This was done recently in relation to the draft body of principles on the rights of persons born out of wedlock, the draft code of conduct for law-enforcement officers, the draft declaration on the rights of non-citizens, the draft convention on the rights of the child; the draft declaration on the rights of minorities, and the draft convention against torture.

The practice as to the use of the terms "Declaration" and "Recommendation" was described in the following terms in a memorandum prepared in 1962 by the Office of Legal Affairs and submitted to the Commission on Human Rights at its Eighteenth session in 1962:

3. In United Nations practice, a "declaration" is a formal and solemn instrument, suitable for rare occasions when principles of great and lasting importance are being enunciated, such as the Declaration of Human Rights. A recommendation is less formal.

---

[2] *Op. cit.* in note 1 above. (UN Publication Sales no. E.73.XIV.2).

4. Apart from the distinction just indicated, there is probably no difference between a "recommendation" and a "declaration" in United Nations practice as far as strict legal principle is concerned. A "declaration" or "recommendation" is adopted by resolution of a United Nations organ. As such it cannot be made binding upon Member States, in the sense that a treaty or convention is binding upon the parties to it, purely by the device of terming it a "declaration" rather than a "recommendation". However, in view of the greater solemnity and significance of a "declaration", it may be considered to impart, on behalf of the organ adopting it, a strong expectation that Members of the international community will abide by it. Consequently, in so far as the expectation is gradually justified by State practice, a declaration may by custom become recognized as laying down rules binding upon States.

5. In conclusion, it may be said that in United Nations practice, a "declaration" is a solemn instrument resorted to only in very rare cases relating to matters of major and lasting importance where maximum compliance is expected.[3]

B. STANDARD-SETTING IN THE FUTURE

What lessons can we learn from the experience over the last thirty years? How are the existing standards facing up to the passage of time? In what areas are standards particularly lacking? What new areas require the development of standards? Are there any particular areas which should be accorded priority treatment? What methods should be adopted in the future for the updating and supplementation of existing standards and for the development of new standards? Can measures be taken to increase the bindingness of standards presently contained in recommendations, declarations or bodies of principles? Are there any areas in need of consolidation?[4] What measures should be taken to teach and disseminate standards in the field of human rights?

1. Basic policy considerations

In its resolution 32/130 of 16 December 1977, the General Assembly recommended that the approach to future work within the United Nations system with respect to human rights should take into account certain concepts or guidelines, including the following:

---

[3] See United Nations Action in the Field of Human Rights, *op. cit.* in note 1 above, p. 163.

In a draft resolution submitted to the International Conference on Human Rights (1968),
[4] (A/CONF.42/C.2/L.20), Nigeria suggested the codification of international instruments in the field of human rights adopted by the United Nations into a single international code of human rights.

(g) It is of paramount importance for the promotion and protection of human rights and fundamental freedoms that Member States undertake specific obligations through accession to or ratification of international instruments in this field; consequently, the standard-setting work within the United Nations system in the field of human rights and the universal acceptance and implementation of the relevant international instruments should be encouraged.

While encouraging further standard-setting it will be necessary to maintain a balance between this and the implementation of existing standards. It is the widely acknowledged policy of the United Nations nowadays that after the first era of activity in the United Nations wherein primacy was attached to standard-setting, emphasis should be placed henceforth on the implementation of those standards. A balance therefore needs to be struck between implementation and standard-setting. It should be borne in mind, however, that the standard-setting process is an inherent and important part of the process of implementing human rights. If, for example, it is revealed that certain human rights are being violated, an important part of the response of the international community is to call for standards to guide conduct in these areas. Sometimes the United Nations addresses violations of human rights by elaborating standards thereon. Often, this is the only type of response that can be agreed upon.

A report prepared by the Secretary-General of the United Nations which summarized proposals and suggestions made by Governments, specialized agencies and NGOs over several years, on the programme and methods of work of the Commission on Human Rights, bears out the preceding points. Thus, it was suggested that since a number of important international instruments in the field of human rights had been adopted, the Commission on Human Rights should now pay more attention to the implementation of the standards contained in them.[5] However, it was pointed out that, "although the standard-setting achievements of the United Nations had been impressive, its work was by no means complete."[6] It was suggested that the United Nations should continue to formulate rules of conduct regarding human rights in the form not only of draft declarations and conventions but also of practical guidelines for their application.[7] In the Commission on Human rights in 1978 also, it was suggested that existing gaps in international law relating to human rights should be filled by promulgating additional standards through international treaties, codes, model

---

[5] E/CN.4/1273, para. 19.
[6] A/32/178, para. 52.
[7] *Ibid.,* para. 67.

rules, bodies of principles and other similar instruments.[8]

2. A global perspective

The report of the Club of Rome on Reshaping the International Order advanced the idea that the aims, means, and institutions of the new international order should eventually be laid down in legal rules and standards governing the behaviour of States, international organizations, transnational enterprises and other subjects of law. The law should also provide legal remedies and effective sanctions in case of transgressions of these rules and standards. It suggested the adoption of a framework treaty which clearly lays down the ground rules for international co-operation and the guiding principles to be adopted by nation-States in building the new order.[9] The fundamental aim of the world community was defined as being "to achieve a life of dignity and well-being for all world citizens."[10] This fundamental aim was said to have its roots in the conviction that all human beings have an equal right to a life of dignity and to satisfaction in their threefold capacities as citizens, producers and consumers. Six guiding elements to shape development efforts were identified as likely to prove of decisive importance: Equity, freedom; (as recognized in the Universal Declaration of Human Rights) democracy and participation; solidarity; cultural diversity; and environmental integrity. New development strategies must, it was asserted, be shaped by five main components: the satisfaction of needs; the eradication of poverty; self-reliant and participatory development; the exercise of public power and balanced eco-development.

Such a global perspective should be kept in mind in future standard-setting activities. The existing human rights instruments already provide a basic stock of norms which are at the heart of the legal structure of the international order. However, they need to be emphasized more in strategies for development. This should be one of the results of the study currently being prepared for the Commission on Human Rights by the Secretary-General of the United Nations on the human right to development. Human rights organs should seek to make human rights inputs in the legal structure of the new international order. They should seek to consolidate two central components of the new international order: a new human order and a new social order.

[8] Report of the Commission, 1978, doc. E/1978/34, Chapter IX.
[9] J. Tinbergen (Co-ordinator), *Reshaping the International Order. A Report to the Club of Rome* (1976), pp. 114-117.
[10] *Ibid.*, p. 61.

3. A planned approach to standard-setting?

It is probably the case that the clarity of direction of standard-setting activities which was felt at the beginning of the United Nations is now becoming somewhat blurred. The following trends may be detected in standard-setting at the present time:

(a) Topics under consideration

(1) There are some outstanding topics still on the agenda, on which: (i) political agreement has been difficult to attain, for example, freedom of information, religious intolerance and the right of persons to be free from arbitrary arrest or detention; or (ii) on which work has been protracted, for example, the rights of minorities.

(2) Some governments or non-governmental organizations interested in certain questions call for international action on them, including the adoption of new standards. The Polish proposal at the thirty-fourth session of the Commission on Human Rights for a convention on the rights of the child is a case in point.

(3) Some existing or emerging human rights problems of great importance, or problems endowed with new dimensions are being studied with a view to determining the nature of international action. Such studies often reveal gaps in present international standards or the need for their updating. Questions currently under study in United Nations human rights organs include: the right to self-determination; the adverse consequences for the enjoyment of human rights of political, military, economic and other forms of assistance given to régimes violating human rights; slavery and related practices; genocide; the right to development; the rights of minorities; the rights of indigenous populations; the rights of migrant workers; the rights of non-citizens; humans rights and scientific and technological developments; the right to be free from torture; the human rights of persons subjected to any form of detention or imprisonment; human rights in emergency situations, duties of individuals to the community and limitations imposed on human rights and fundamental freedoms; freedom of information; and religious intolerance.

(4) The following is a list of topics on which standards are either being drafted at the present time, or are likely to be drafted in the future or which have been suggested for the adoption of standards:
-The right of everyone to live in conditions of international peace and
  security

- The right to self-determination
- Standards against *apartheid* in sports
- Terrorism
- The adverse consequences for the enjoyment of human rights of aid given to Governments violating human rights
- The negative consequences of the activities of transnational corporations on the enjoyment of human rights
- The need for legal guarantees aimed at ensuring the enjoyment of economic, social and cultural rights
- The right to development
- The rights of the child, including the rights of children born out of wedlock
- The rights of minorities
- The rights of indigenous populations
- The rights of migrant workers
- The rights of non-citizens
- Human rights and scientific and technological developments
- The right to be free from torture, inhuman, cruel or degrading treatment or punishment
- The human rights of persons subjected to any form of detention or imprisonment
- Human rights in emergency situations
- The duties of individuals to the community and limitations which can be imposed on human rights and fundamental freedoms
- Freedom of information
- Religious intolerance
- Discrimination against women
- The rights of consumers
- Freedom of cultural expression and exchange
- The rights of youth
- Strengthening the rights and freedoms of trade union organizations
- Draft code of offences for law enforcement officials
- Judicial settlement of grievances pertaining to violations of human rights and fundamental freedoms
- Code of procedure for collecting, sifting, presenting and weighing evidence before international fact-finding bodies.

(5) The foregoing list reveals that standards have been proposed for four main areas;

(i) Standards in novel areas, e.g. human rights and scientific and technological development.

(ii) Standards elaborating rights contained in existing instruments e.g. freedom from torture.

(iii) Procedural standards, e.g. code of procedure for collecting, sifting, presenting and weighing evidence.

(iv) Standards in areas dealing with violations of human rights, e.g. the consequences of aid given to régimes violating human rights.

Suggestions are also being made for the codification of certain areas, e.g. the right to self-determination.

(b) Organs engaged in standard-setting

(6) Universal standards are being elaborated in five main groups of United Nations organs:

(i) The Commission on Human Rights and the Sub-Commission on Prevention of Discrimination and Protection of Minorities.

(ii) The Commission on the Status of Women.

(iii) The Committee on Crime Prevention and Control and the United Nations Congress on the Prevention of Crime and the Treatment of Offenders.

(iv) The Special Committee against *Apartheid.*

(v) The Economic and Social Council and the General Assembly, either independently or in conjunction with the preceding bodies.

(c) The standard-setting process

(7) The following standard-setting processes may be detected:

(i) Study by a rapporteur and/or the Secretariat, recommendations in study, debate in Sub-Commission and/or Commission on Human Rights, consideration in ECOSOC and/or General Assembly and pronouncement by ECOSOC or General Assembly, either of resolution, recommendation, declaration or convention.

(ii) Study and recommendations, sometimes including draft body of principles, approved by Sub-Commission and noted and/or approved by Commission or ECOSOC.

(iii) Draft convention or declaration proposed by Governments in Sub-Commission, Commission on Human Rights, ECOSOC or General Assembly.

(iv) Draft instrument circulated and promoted by non-governmental organizations.

(v) Standards contained in resolutions adopted by organs when considering particular questions or particular situations of violations of human rights.

(vi) Standards implicit in positions taken by organs when examining complaints of violations of human rights.

(d) Consultation of Governments

(8) There is a growing tendency to consult Governments in the standard-setting process. Governments are either asked for their views when studies are being undertaken or when a draft is in the process of elaboration it is sent to them for their comments.

The question may be raised whether the most urgent topics are currently being considered, or whether the method of including topics for standard-setting is the most efficient. There seems to be too high a dependence upon the initiative of particular Governments in proposing topics. This same dependence also influences the mode of standard-setting employed.

The ILO has recently carried out an in-depth survey of its standard-setting activities which is highly pertinent to our subject-matter. A study prepared by the International Labour Office for this review raised the question whether a planned approach to standard-setting should be adopted. It was suggested that if it were felt desirable to adopt a more systematic approach, the ILO long-term plans could be used as a basis for establishing a programme of standard-setting during the period to which the plans relate. The draft plan could include a section indicating the various questions which appeared ripe for action and suggesting priorities which might be related to areas of emphasis of the plan. An outline programme of items to be placed on the agenda for standard-setting during the plan period could be drawn up. This programme would not constitute final decisions on the agenda in the years in question, but would provide guidelines for future work. The existence of such a programme, it was felt, would facilitate the necessary technical preparation and research.[11]

There is a case of more planning and more careful consideration of priorities in standard-setting activities in the field of human rights. The present system operates on too *ad hoc* a basis and, often, not enough objective groundwork is done before the standard-setting exercise is begun. The need for standards, the selection of topics and the mode of treatment for each topic is in need of more expert scrutiny.

The Sub-Commission on Prevention of Discrimination and Protection of Minorities is an expert body of general competence which has been studying issues and drafting standards for many years. The Sub-Commis-

[11] G.B.194/PFA/12/5: In-depth review of international labour standards; GB.198/PFA/11/22: Analysis of the questionnaire on international labour standards; GB.201/14/32: Report of the Committee on Standing Orders and the application of conventions and recommendations.

sion has an item on its agenda each year entitled "Review of further developments in fields with which the Sub-Commission has been concerned."
Under this item the Sub-Commission conducts a general debate on recent
developments in its field of work. It is suggested that the Sub-Commission
should extend its review to "Developments in the Field of Human Rights"
and that one of the matters which it should specifically review is the position with respect to standards. The Sub-Commission could, for example, at
the beginning of each (three-year) term of its members, entrust one of its
members with the task of preparing, with the assistance of the Secretariat,
a short annual report on developments in the field of standards. This report
would aim at pointing out any noteworthy experience in the application of
existing standards and any areas in which new, modified or additional
standards appear to be called for. For the preparation of this report the
Secretariat could annually invite the views of Governments, non-governmental organizations, specialized agencies, members of United Nations
human rights organs and relevant international and regional intergovernmental bodies.

This report could be examined by a regular committee of the Sub-Commission on standard-setting with a view to making recommendations to the
Sub-Commission, including its views as to whether a topic is ripe for
standard-setting; if so what priority should be given to it, and what mode is
most likely to yield the best results.

The recommendations of this standing committee, together with the
views of the plenary Sub-Commission thereon, could be transmitted to the
Commission on Human Rights which will then be in a position to take
decisions or to make recommendations to the Economic and Social
Council, as appropriate.

The suitability of the Sub-Commission to be entrusted with the task we
are suggesting is borne out by its record of concern for "strengthening the
legal bases of human rights in order to make respect for them increasingly
effective at the national and international levels." In its resolution 6
(XXIX) adopted on 31 August 1976, the Sub-Commission, considering
that in the implementation of resolutions and declarations adopted by the
main organs of the United Nations in the field of human rights, doubts and
difficulties often arise concerning their legal nature which may restrict
United Nations action in this sphere, and considering that, to be able to
make progress and maintain the pace of international standard-setting and
codification in this matter, it is important to define the legal nature, impact
and scope of declarations and resolutions of the main organs of the United
Nations in the field of human rights, recommended that the Commission

on Human Rights should suggest to the Economic and Social Council that it request an advisory opinion of the International Court of Justice on the following legal question: "What is the legal nature, scope and impact of declarations and resolutions of the main organs of the United Nations, in particular the General Assembly, in the field of human rights?". Unfortunately, the Commission on Human Rights has not yet acted on this recommendation. In the Commission in 1978, it was suggested that standard-setting should be handled in the future mainly by the Sub-Commission.[12]

One particular practice of the ILO which may merit further consideration in the United Nations is that of dealing, item by item, with distinct aspects of social policy. In this way a comprehensive body of instruments has been built up in the ILO. Many of these instruments serve to spell out in detail the contents of rights recognized in the Universal Declaration of Human Rights and the International Covenants on Human Rights. Some studies carried out within the United Nations, for example in regard to the administration of justice, suggest that more detailed standards of this kind could perform a most useful function.

Greater use could also be made in the future of more flexible modes of standard-setting than the drawing up of conventions. Recommendations, bodies of principles, model codes and declarations could be utilized to greater advantage.

C. CO-ORDINATION IN THE FIELD OF STANDARD-SETTING

In a communication dated 15 March 1977, addressed by the Director-General of the ILO to the Secretary-General of the United Nations the problem was raised of conflicts which could arise in the standard-setting process. At its sixty-second session, the Economic and Social Council had before it the draft of a Convention on the Elimination of Discrimination against Women prepared by the Commission on the Status of Women. The ILO felt that one provision of this draft, concerning the relations between the proposed convention and other conventions adopted under the auspices of the United Nations or its specialized agencies involved legal difficulties which could adversely affect the standard-setting activities of the United Nations and the specialized agencies.

Article 16, paragraph 2 of the draft read as follows: " . . . Nothing in

[12] Report of the Commission, 1978, E/1978/34, para. 172.

this convention should affect existing conventions adopted under the auspices of the United Nations or its specialized agencies and having as their object the regulation of various aspects of the status of women if they provide for more extensive rights for women." The intent of the paragraph, the ILO pointed out, was not altogether clear. It appeared to imply that the new convention will supersede existing conventions adopted under the auspices of the United Nations or its specialized agencies unless these provide for more extensive rights for women. Is it possible, the ILO asked, to deal in this manner with the inter-relationship between conventions adopted in different constitutional frameworks and creating obligations for Governments? Subsidiarily the ILO also raised the question of the meaning to be given to the term "more extensive" – does it mean more detailed, or more favourable, and by reference to what standard would this be determined?

International conventions, the ILO went on, are designed to create legal obligations for Governments, "Such obligations are not immutable; they are likely to be open to modification by some appropriate and orderly system of amendment or revision. They are also normally open to unilateral denunciation; however, in many conventions such unilateral withdrawal is possible only at specified, relatively infrequent intervals. In all these circumstances, it is important to ensure that the competent organs of different organizations do not give States conflicting directives and obligations."[13]

In 1972, a number of organizations of the United Nations system recommended that the United Nations' Administrative Committee on Co-ordination (ACC) should develop a common approach, at the inter-secretariat level, to the legal and practical difficulties that may arise as a result of overlaps in the standard-setting activities of the system. Difficulties mentioned related to potential or actual divergencies regarding the nature and scope of the obligations laid down in overlapping instruments, the interpretation to be given to similar provisions of such instruments,[14] and the supervision of their application.

The ACC considered the matter and remitted it to an *ad hoc* meeting of legal experts in the United Nations system which met at Geneva from 16-17 July 1973, under the chairmanship of the Legal Counsel of the United Nations. The main recommendation formulated by the meeting – which

---

[13] E/5938.
[14] The study of this problem was called for in a draft resolution sponsored by Austria at the thirty-fourth session of the Commission on Human Rights (E/CN/4/L.1387). The question will be considered at future sessions of the Commission.

was fully endorsed by the ACC – was that it would be preferable, as a matter of general policy, to avoid duplication in the legislative work of the different organizations and that, where this is not possible, conflict and erosion of standards should be avoided by appropriate drafting techniques.[15] The ACC also concurred in the conclusion of the meeting that the fundamental concerns in the co-ordination of the legislative work of international organizations, within and outside the United Nations system, given the overriding purpose of developing an integrated system of international treaty law, are threefold:

(a) To prevent unnecessary duplication;

(b) To prevent conflict between the obligations undertaken by the States under different instruments, as well as in the interpretation and supervision of the implementation of instruments adopted by various organizations; and

(c) To ensure that statutory provisions on complex technical subjects are established and supervised by those most competent to do so.

In endorsing the conclusions of the meeting as to the co-ordination methods that should be applied to meet these concerns, the ACC stressed the ultimate responsibility of the competent legislative organs and noted that it was up to them to decide in each case, the extent to which such concerns should be taken into account. On the other hand, the ACC felt that if a full knowledge and understanding of the needs, the precedents and possible solutions could be provided by the secretariats whenever the possibility of duplication arose, it should go a long way towars meeting the objectives and concerns mentioned above. The ACC also recognized that while it was necessary to explore a wider range of methods of co-ordination and to systematize some which so far have been applied only on an *ad hoc* basis, there was already extensive and largely effective co-operation between organizations in this field.

The ACC shared the sense of importance attached to information-sharing and co-operation both within each organization and between them, and endorsed the recommendation that the legal offices of the various organizations should serve as information centres endeavouring to obtain and disseminate, at regular intervals, perhaps annually, the details of all projected legislative activity within the organization concerned as well as of

---

[15] The term "legislative work", as defined by the *ad hoc* meeting, included "all international and regional norms and standards designed to be applied by the Member States of the various organizations, whether they were in the form of conventions, declarations, recommendations, resolutions and regulations such as the International Health Regulations or Codex Alimentarius Standards or model codes and other guides to national legislative activity".

the projected programmes of other organizations.

The ACC considered it important that any arrangements that might be developed to strengthen co-ordination should not be such as to impede the development of international legislative activities, since it was felt that there is at present considerable room for expansion of international norms and standards. At the same time, the ACC felt that it is normally preferable to bring such norms and standards up-to-date in the technical and organizational framework in which they were originally adopted. Thus, as a consequence of the process of information-sharing and consultation, which should be as wide as possible, it may be found necessary to introduce in a new instrument being drafted either cross-references to existing instruments or saving clauses, or to resort to such means as "mutual reference" or "desistment" from legislative action.

The ACC also shared the view of the meeting of legal experts, that, in view of the importance of achieving uniform interpretation of standards, analysis of compliance with standards should as far as possible be carried out by those with the greatest competence in the field. Where more than one organization has a concern in an instrument, it would be desirable for provision for co-operation to be made in the terms of the instrument itself and for such co-operation to bear both on mutual representation and on full exchange of information and observations as appropriate.[16]

One question which may deserve attention in the future is the need for the various bodies engaged in the development of international law to take account of developments in the law occurring in other areas. A study which analysed the international law making process in 1972, predicted that the broad division of functions between bodies concerned with human rights and those occupied with other areas of international law may be expected to continue. It added, however, that as the law in one or other sphere develops there may be an increasing need to reflect the progress made elsewhere – for the law relating to human rights to take account of developments in other areas of international law, and, *vice versa,* for efforts undertaken with respect to the codification and development of other branches of international law to take cognizance of the degree of recognition now given to human rights.[17] While human rights organs generally take into account developments in other branches of international law, the reverse sometimes does not happen in organs working in other parts of international law.

[16] E/5488, paras. 200-209.
[17] A/CN.4/245, para. 395.

D. CONCLUSIONS

The conclusions reached in this paper may be summarized as follows:

1. The General Assembly has determined that the standard-setting work in the United Nations system in the field of human rights and the universal acceptance and implementation of the relevant international instruments should be encouraged.

2. A balance needs to be struck between the implementation of existing standards and the elaboration of new standards. The emphasis should be on the former, always mindful, though, that standard-setting is an inherent part of the process of implementing human rights.

3. Human rights standards should be aimed at the establishment of a new human order and a new social order alongside the new international economic order. Human rights standards should also be brought to bear upon efforts to establish a new international economic order so as to ensure that the human factor is never lost sight of.

4. There is need for better planning and more careful consideration of priorities in standard-setting activities. The present system operates on too *ad hoc* a basis and sometimes not enough detached groundwork is done before the standard-setting exercise is begun. Responsibility for planning could be entrusted to the Sub-Commission on Prevention of Discrimination and Protection of Minorities.

5. Greater use should be made of more flexible forms of standard-setting, for example recommendations, bodies of principles, model codes and declarations, especially when standards are being elaborated to spell out rights contained in existing instruments.

6. There is need for the ongoing collection, analysis, systematisation and dissemination of procedural standards being developed in the application of implementation procedures as well as those contained in resolutions of human rights organs.

CHAPTER VI

IMPLEMENTING HUMAN RIGHTS: PRESENT STATUS AND FUTURE PROSPECTS

MR. MOSES MOSKOWITZ*

Of the present state of international implementation of human rights it may be said that it provides neither comfort nor remedy; the term has become a slogan wrapped in language that had long ago surrendered much of its ability to describe reality. As defined in the dictionary, implementation means putting into effect, fulfilling or carrying through, be they ideas, statutes, laws or promises; it presupposes the existence of certain conditions, principally an implementing authority and agreement on the connotative value of words. But those conditions are absent from international implementation of human rights. Different connotative values placed on the same words aid and abet different meanings of the text, while the implementing organs and agencies have yet to command the authority and stature to affect events. The United Nations, which carries over-all responsibility in the field of human rights, has too often become hostage to the mean-minded and prejudiced to summon the moral power and prestige to compel compliance with international rules of conduct and conscience. When texts are wrenched out of their orbits in order to fill ellipses shaped by governments and different criteria enter into the making of moral judgements, we cannot yield to the notion of implementation without taking deep thought.

Strictly speaking, the term implementation applies to the principles, procedures and modes of enforcement of the international Covenants on Human Rights and similar multilateral treaties providing for enforcement measures. States Parties to such treaties undertake not only to respect and observe the covenanted rights and freedoms, but also to place them under international protection. The essence of international protection of human rights is the accountability of the States Parties for their international obligations. Article 16 of the Covenant on Economic, Social and Cultural Rights provides that

---

*Secretary-General, Consultative Council of Jewish Organizations. Author, Human Rights and World Order; The Politics and Dynamics of Human Rights; International Concern with Human Rights.

The States Parties to the present covenant undertake to submit in conformity with this part of the Covenant reports on the measures which they have adopted and the progress made in achieving the observance of the rights recognized herein.

According to Article 40 of the Covenant on Civil and Political rights,

The States Parties to the present Covenant undertake to submit reports on the measures they have adopted which give effect to the rights recognized herein and on the progress made in the enjoyment of those rights: (a) within one year of the entry into force of the present Covenant for the States Parties concerned and (b) thereafter whenever the Committee so requests.

In addition, as provided for in Article 41,

A State Party to the present Covenant may at any time declare under this article that it recognizes the competence of the Committee to receive and consider communications to the effect that a State Party claims that another State Party is not fulfulling its obligations under the present Covenant.

Carrying one step further, Article 1 of the Optional Protocol to the International Covenant on Civil and Political Rights provides that

A State Party to the Covenant that becomes a party to the present Protocol recognizes the competence of the Committee to receive and consider communications from individuals, subject to its jurisdiction, claiming to be victims of a violation by that State Party of any of the rights set forth in the Covenant.

From the very beginning, however, the term implementation has come to apply also to procedures evolved by the United Nations for dealing with breaches of human rights independently of the Covenants and similar treaties, and to statements critical of general or specific situations and actions and programs of a promotional nature in support of human rights. Surely the difference between the procedures laid down in the Covenants and those improvised by the General Assembly and other organs of the United Nations is fundamental; but what they share in common is perhaps more decisive than what separates them. Both sets of procedures are shackled to the burdens of history and traditions, ideas and perceptions, which lie astride all efforts at international protection of human rights.

Neither the Universal Declaration of Human Rights, nor the International Covenants nor the myriad recommendations for positive action to promote human rights adopted by United Nations bodies over the years truly reflect international reality; they are but part of the conscious and unconscious universal effort to change that reality and to reconstruct international relations on new foundations. While the United Nations may lay plans, schemes tending to preempt the course of its work are hatched somewhere else. We cannot ignore the ideological division of the world, anymore than we can disdain the diversity of perception which stems from differences in culture and history; they lie at the heart and core of international implementation and provide the keys to an understanding of the human rights situation anywhere, anytime. It is striking, for example, that whereas as of the end of 1977 16 of the 44 States which had ratified the Covenant on Civil and Political Rights had also subscribed to the Optional Protocol, only six had chosen to be bound by Article 41 concerning State-to-State complaints. The reason is simply the fear of inviting intervention in the domestic affairs of States under the pretext of concern for human rights.

As we shall see, the vision of a world in which human rights are universally respected and internationally safeguarded is not a static one in which the right principles prevail and govern: it is a dynamic world of untidy accommodations between competing principles and doctrines and of tensions that cannot be wished away. The debate in the Third Committee of the thirty-second session of the General Assembly in the fall of 1977 on alternative approaches and ways and means within the United Nations system for improving the effective enjoyment of human rights and fundamental freedoms, is a warning that our passion for resolution of problems must not overwhelm our sense of life as a process, choice or struggle, nor lure us into a teleology that will one day resolve all intellectual and moral contradictions. To disappear into the clouds of a universality that leaves the larger world stranded far below, is a disservice to the cause.

A spirit of revisionism is abroad at the United Nations which questions many of the fundamental premises on which the International Bill of Human Rights was erected and which underlie much of the human rights program of the world body. There exists great pressure for recognition of the notion that different regimes move towards the goal of humane government from different circumstances wrought in the crucible of national experience. As originally conceived, the purpose of the Declaration was to define the human rights and fundamental freedoms asserted in the United Nations Charter and to place them before the world as a standard of achievement for all peoples and all nations. The purpose of the International Covenants was to translate the moral commitment of the Declaration into legally binding international obligations. The measures of implementation, as already suggested, were designed to place those obligations under international supervision and to provide a remedy, however feeble, for breaches of the covenanted freedoms. A distinction was drawn between political and civil rights, which were regarded as enforceable by a

State Party to the Covenants without any prior conditions, and economic, social and cultural rights, whose enjoyment was predicated on the existence of certain material conditions which time and effort would create. The presumption throughout has been that whatever philosophical and ideological differences existed among the nations which determined their perceptions, those differences in no way affected their common understanding of the practical meaning of human rights and fundamental freedoms and of their moral and legal obligations.

All that has now been put in question. After we have examined the debate in the Third Committee of the thirty-second session of the General Assembly, we are no longer sure of the authenticity of the rights and liberties spelled out in the various international instruments, of their relation to each other and to the international community, their order of importance, and their absoluteness or dependency.

Opening the debate in the Third Committee on 10 November 1977,[1] the representative of Cuba declared that the fundamental principles which had originally governed the activities of the United Nations in the field of human rights were based on the experience of a group of nations that were economically highly developed and wielded a predominant influence in the world body. Although the admission to membership in the United Nations of the many newly independent States gave to the consideration of human rights problems a new impetus, a new orientation and a new dimension, certain tendencies of old persisted in the international organization which had a subtle but very real influence on its human rights program. He referred especially to the question of interdependence of the two categories of human rights which, in his view, made the exercise of civil and political rights impossible without the effective enjoyment of economic, social and cultural rights. It was therefore essential, the Cuban representative concluded, to ensure economic development in order that all citizens might exercise not only their economic, social and cultural rights but also, simultaneously, their civil and political rights. The failure of the United Nations, he added, to give due attention to such problems as the right to work in developed countries and the impact on human rights in developing countries of the persistence of an unjust international economic order, was a direct consequence of the refusal to give full recognition to the truth of the interdependence of the two sets of rights. He urged that in any reappraisal of the United Nations human rights program care should be taken not to

---

[1] For the summary records of the debate, see A/C.3/32/SR.42-44, 49-55, 62, 64, 65 and 67-69.

distort the general concept of human rights and not to give undue attention to any specific category of fundamental rights, and to take into account the development of society as a whole.

Continuing in that vein, the representative of the Soviet Union said that the promotion of human rights must be viewed within the general context of Chapter IX of the United Nations Charter, which referred to the promotion of higher standards of living, full employment, and conditions of economic and social progress and development, as well as the solution of international economic, social and related problems. The effectiveness of the United Nations in the field of human rights, he noted, was directly linked to the general world situation. Only world peace could ensure economic and social development and the enjoyment of human rights, and especially the inalienable right to life. The first task of the United Nations, therefore, was to work for détente, for curtailment of the arms race and for the promotion of peace. The more consistently the United Nations fought against aggression, colonialism and racism and the more actively it supported national liberation struggles and the vital interests of the workers, the more favorable would be the conditions for enhancing its effectiveness in securing the inalienable rights of peoples and human freedoms.

Earlier in his statement Ambassador Troyanovsky referred to the recently adopted Soviet Constitution as an example at the national level of how Member States could implement the goals of the Charter in their foreign and domestic policy. Nodding in approval, Hungary's representative declared that the socialist system itself was a guarantee of the effective enjoyment of human rights because it safeguarded the rights of everyone rather than those of favoured groups only, and because it recognized that economic rights, such as the right to work, were the prerequisites for all the others.

The representative of the Ukrainian SSR agreed that the question of enhancing the effectiveness of the United Nations in the field of human rights could not be considered separately from the maintenance of international peace and security and that cooperation among States in the furtherance of human rights could be successfully carried on only within the framework of détente. He went on to suggest that human rights and fundamental freedoms were violated primarily in those regions of the world which were subjected to aggression, colonialism and neo-colonialism, racism, suppression of national liberation movements and exploitation of man by man. The remedy, he implied, depended largely on the effectiveness of the United Nations in strengthening international peace and security and deepening détente, eliminating hotbeds of aggression, racism and colonialism and supporting the national liberation movements and the workers' struggle for their rights and social progress.

What the representative of the Ukraine suggested has been a basic tenet of Soviet policy dating back to the early years of the United Nations, when the propriety of the world organization's intervention in the racial situation in southern Africa was still in question. It enabled the socialist States to support United Nations intervention in certain human rights situations while invoking the principle of non-intervention in the domestic affairs of States in others. Thus the representative of Bulgaria chastised those Western States that were seeking to transform the United Nations into a global supervisor of individual human rights, particularly where a mere handful of cases were concerned, while adamantly resisting the efforts of Member States to apply the relevant Charter provisions to cases of flagrant violations of human rights and basic freedoms where entire nations lived in conditions of colonial and imperialist slavery and occupation." All that, he said, only confirmed the need for the United Nations to continue and intensify its struggle against aggression, colonialism and racism and to defend the national liberation movements of colonial peoples and the vital interests of the working people.

Similar sentiments were voiced by other representatives of socialist countries. The representative of the German Democratic Republic declared that responsibility for safeguarding human rights fell within the jurisdiction of individual Member States and that was in full accord with reality; the rights of the individual could not be separated or isolated from the society in which he lived and that any outside attempts to "misuse" the human rights issue to isolate the individual from society and to bring him into conflict with the State, were essentially directed at undermining the sovereignty of States. Likewise, he added, any attempt to extend the competence of the United Nations against the will of the State offended the principles of the United Nations system and, rather than promoting human rights, put in peril the implementation of individual rights and freedoms insofar as they depended on the maintenance of international peace and friendly relations among States.

The Non-aligned world, in general, shared the views of the socialist States regarding the interdependence and indivisibility of human rights, the relative importance of individual and collective rights, and the different path taken by developed and developing countries in pursuit of humane objectives. While the Western countries stressed the rights of the individual, said Princess Ashraf Pahlavi of Iran, the developing Countries were thinking of the rights of entire peoples; while the former spoke of the immediate implementation of civil and political rights, the latter strove to establish economic rights. She regretted the narrow interpretation of concepts that were differently understood in different parts of the world and cautioned against treating human rights in isolation from all other human problems, in particular economic problems. Warning that there could be no real cooperation in the implementation of individual rights if no such cooperation was forthcoming for the implementation of the rights of peoples, Princess Ashraf declared that the will of the developed countries to put an end to the difficulties experienced by the developing countries would govern the development of individual rights. This did not mean that the world had to wait for utopia before taking action against certain impermissible acts and practices, such as torture and other cruel and inhuman treatment. But the question of human rights was exceedingly complex when other aspects of individual rights were raised, and they had to be dealt with from an over-all perspective which imposed a specially arduous task upon the developing world. She pleaded with the West to remember that what was asked of the developing world took the developed countries centuries to accomplish.

The representative of Mali thought that the universal values underlying the ideals of the Charter were often in conflict with the concerns of States, because a universally accepted definition had not yet been found for the rights enunciated in the Charter, the Universal Declaration and the International Covenants. Restrictive definitions, she said, could lay no claim to universal truth and suggested the need for a universally acceptable policy based on the different values of various societies. A society, she went on to say, which ignored the basic rights of the individual became dictatorial, but recognition of individual rights alone led to anarchy. Human rights must be viewed as part of a network of indivisible and interdependent socio-political relationships and could not be limited to one set of rights. By the same token, the Mali representative concluded, if human rights were to be upheld and realized to the fullest extent, the requirements of society must take precedence over the guarantee of individual rights. That involved a philosophical and political choice which determined the form of administration chosen by peoples to guarantee their survival as a group.

In the view of the Philippines, the context in which the principles of the Universal Declaration could be given meaning was undergoing changes. All countries, the representative of the Philippines said, have contributed to the evolution of the United Nations human rights program. For example, the emphasis on civil and political rights in the Charter and in the Universal Declaration had been inherited from Western political thought, while the importance which the international community attached to economic, social and cultural rights had been the unique contribution of the socialist States. Developing countries tried at their own pace and in their own way to deal with the various human rights and their experience provided a new insight into the role of human rights in the development process which might expand the traditional concepts of human rights. These countries were concerned with balancing the claims of the individual and the needs of the community and no one group of countries had a monopoly of the best methods of implementing human rights. Some countries had been able to accord civil and political rights to their citizens, while others were more advanced in implementing economic, social and cultural rights. Still others placed more emphasis on the role of government in promoting human rights and liberties which, in the opinion of the Philippine representative, attested to a close partnership between the citizen and his government in the attainment of national goals and could not be construed as subordination of the individual to the State. All that called for a new system of measuring the implementation of human rights which heretofore was confined to reporting and fact-finding systems.

India's representative suggested that if basic philosophical concepts regarding human rights and fundamental freedoms could be defined, it would be much easier to evaluate the comparative merits of alternative approaches to the question. She hailed the growing recognition by countries belonging to different political and economic systems of the interdependence of all human rights and urged giving increasing attention to the realization of economic, social and cultural rights, the denial of which was causing grave problems especially in developing countries, and thought that the establishment of a new economic order would be a definite step forward towards the advancement of human rights. She pleaded that the implementation of human rights and freedoms required an over-all view and an appreciation of the special problems of each region.

The representative of Pakistan alluded to the breakdown of the consensus that was thought to have prevailed regarding the meaning of rights, and questioned many of the assumptions which guided the United Nations human rights activities. He spoke of the inability of governments in developing countries with democratic structure to promote economic and social welfare, which complicated their ability to adhere to acknowledged standards of civil and political rights, and regretted that insufficient account had been taken of those complexities. He warned that overemphasis on the need for practical compliance with uniform human rights standards might erode even the existing consensus with regard to the general scope and content of particular human rights and thought that the practical enforcement of such rights depended on the underlying values of each society; to some, for example, the right to freedom of expression was more important than the right to work, while to other societies it was the reverse. The Pakistan representative opposed any and all doctrinaire approaches and saw the best hope in an approach that provided a harmonious blend between different principles and preconceptions.

The representative of Nigeria accused the technically advanced countries of having ignored the social and economic rights of the poorer countries, thus making it difficult for them to establish the infrastructure essential for the creation of a truly egalitarian society. Arguing that repression and intolerance were almost directly proportionate to economic backwardness, governments presiding over countries with low standards of economic development are often tempted to resort to unacceptable methods in order to maintain order and ensure national security when faced with socio-economic insecurity. Economic problems he added, often led to dictatorship or totalitarianism and neither regard for the personal value of the individual nor family stability, nor the structure of community life could resist the corrosive force of unemployment.

Emphasis on economic, social and cultural rights, Jamaica's representative noted, had evolved from the historical development of the countries of the southern hemisphere, warning against any underestimation of the impact of the experience of the developing countries on the intellectual and moral principles which governed United Nations activities – an experience which had led the international community to an increasing acceptance of the indivisibility and interdependence of all human rights. Economic and social justice, the Jamaican representative continued, was a fundamental aspect of the economic system and a full guarantee of the enjoyment of all human rights; the struggle against global economic inequity and poverty, through the establishment of a new international economic order, was becoming integral to any strategy for the implementation of human rights.

The Latin American nations were generally sympathetic to the problems faced by the developing countries in their efforts to comply with the international standards of human rights, while they maintained intact their traditional position of human rights as inherent in the individual and independent of social, economic, cultural or legal circumstances. As was noted by the representative of Bolivia, all political philosophies were valid provided that they were not imposed by force; the only difference lay in the methods employed by each system. Those which subordinated individual freedom to economic development were giving primacy to the system itself as a means of social development, thus placing individual aspirations on a secondary plane and subjecting them to an abstract concept of collective welfare. The cruel paradox, he said, was that human rights were respected only insofar as they were not in opposition to the system, and the available guarantees were valid only for those who obeyed supreme decrees without doubt or consent. To downgrade the protection of the individual in favor of other considerations, he warned, would be to distort the very purpose of the Universal Declaration of Human Rights and all efforts to find alternative approaches and ways and means within the United Nations system for improving the effective enjoyment of human rights and fundamental freedoms. He saw only conflict in the field of human rights in the proposal to examine human rights questions globally, taking into account the overall context of the various realities in which they presented themselves, and to give priority to the implementation of the new international economic order.

Differences of opinion among Western nations as to the limits of their reservations to the proposals and suggestions put forward by the non-aligned world divided Australia, Denmark, Finland, New Zealand, Norway and Sweden from the nine Members of the European Community. Australia, for example, welcomed the initiative of the developing countries in forcing the United Nations to address issues on which it thought the international community must focus in the years ahead. New Zealand went so far as to urge upon all Member States to make a determined effort to produce approaches based on an understanding of different traditions, values, stages of development and cultural and social systems, and to forge a new consensus on human rights with a view to implementing them. Canada agreed on the importance of establishing priorities in the field of human rights in the future. Their main concern was to maintain a balance between individual and collective rights. The Members of the European Community rejected the notion that the enjoyment of economic, social and cultural rights should precede the realization of civil and political rights; they also rejected the allegation made in the course of the debate that the exercise of civil and political rights was peculiar to affluent countries; they insisted on the reciprocity of the indivisibility of civil and political rights and economic, social and cultural rights and on a clear distinction between individual and collective rights. While acknowledging the importance of collective rights and their interaction with individual rights, they refused to consider the enjoyment of collective rights as indispensable to the enjoyment of human rights as defined in the Universal Declaration. When those desiderata were not satisfied and all attempts to amend the draft resolution which emerged from the debate came to naught, the Members of the European Community decided to abstain in the voting, both in Committee and in plenary.

The draft resolution, sponsored by Angola, Argentina, Bangladesh, Benin, Bulgaria, Burundi, Comoros, Cuba, Egypt, Ethiopia, Finland, Hungary, India, Iraq, Jordan, Kenya, Libyan Arab Jamahiriya, Madagascar, Mali, New Zealand, Pakistan, Papua New Guinea, Peru, Philippines, Sweden, Syrian Arab Republic, United Republic of Tanzania, Vietnam, Yemen, Yugoslavia and Zambia, was adopted on December 16, 1977, by a vote of 123 to none, with 15 abstentions. The abstentions included, in addition to the nine Members of the European Community, Chad, Israel, Ivory Coast, Paraguay, Spain and the United States of America. The text follows:

ALTERNATIVE APPROACHES AND WAYS AND MEANS WITHIN THE UNITED NATIONS SYSTEM FOR IMPROVING THE EFFECTIVE ENJOYMENT OF HUMAN RIGHTS AND FUNDAMENTAL FREEDOMS

The General Assembly,

Convinced that the obligation of all States to observe the purposes and principles of the United Nations Charter is fundamental for the promotion and respect of human rights and fundamental freedoms and for the realization of the full dignity and worth of the human person,

Conscious that is the duty of the United Nations and of all Member States to achieve international co-operation in solving international problems of an economic, social, cultural or humanitarian character and in promoting and encouraging respect for human rights and for fundamental freedoms for all, without distinction as to race, sex, language or religion.

Convinced that such co-operation should be based on a profound understanding of the variety of problems existing in different societies and on the full respect for their economic, social and cultural realities,

Bearing in mind the Universal Declaration of Human Rights,

Acknowledging the progress achieved by the international community in the promotion and protection of human rights and fundamental freedoms, particularly, with respect to the standard-setting work within the United Nations system,

Noting with satisfaction the entry into force of the international Covenants on Human Rights and of a large number of other important international instruments in the field of human rights,

Considering that the acceptance by Member States of the obligations contained in the said instruments is an important element for the universal realization and respect of human rights and fundamental freedoms,

Recognizing that, in accordance with the Universal Declaration of Human Rights, the ideal of free human beings enjoying freedom from fear and want can only be achieved if conditions are created whereby everyone may enjoy his economic, social and cultural rights, as well as his civil and political rights,

Profoundly convinced that all human rights and fundamental freedoms are interrelated and indivisible,

Recognizing that *apartheid,* all forms of racial discrimination, colonialism, foreign domination and occupation, aggression and threats against national sovereignty, national unity and territorial integrity, as well as the refusal to recognize the fundamental rights of all peoples to self-determination, and of every nation to exercise full sovereignty over its natural wealth and resources constitute situations which in themselves are and generate mass and flagrant violations of all human rights and fundamental freedoms of peoples as well as of individuals,

Deeply concerned at the continuing existence of an unjust international economic order which constitutes a major obstacle to the realization of the economic, social and cultural rights in developing countries,

Considering that the approach to the future work within the United Nations system in the field of human rights should take into due account the experiences and the general situation of, as well as the efforts made by, the developing countries to implement human rights and fundamental freedoms,

Considering that the thirtieth anniversary of the Universal Declaration of Human Rights should be marked by an over-all analysis of existing problems in the field of human rights and by increased efforts in finding appropriate solutions for the effective promotion and protection of human rights and fundamental freedoms taking into account the experiences and contributions of both developed and developing countries.

Having considered the reports by the Secretary-General on this item,

1. *Decides* that the approach to the future work within the United Nations system with respect to human rights questions should take into account the following concepts:

(a) All human rights and fundamental freedoms are indivisible and interdependent; equal attention and urgent consideration should be given to the implementation, promotion and protection of both civil and political, and economic, social and cultural rights;

(b) ". . . the full realization of civil and political rights without the enjoyment of economic, social and cultural rights is impossible. The achievement of lasting progress in the implementation of human rights is dependent upon sound and effective national and international policies of economic and social development" as recognized by the Proclamation of Teheran (1968);

(c) All human rights and fundamental freedoms of the human person and of peoples are inalienable;

(d) Consequently, human rights questions should be examined globally, taking into account both the over-all context of the various societies in which they present themselves, as well as the need for the promotion of the full dignity of the human person and the development and well-being of the society;

(e) In approaching human rights questions within the United Nations system, the international community should accord or continue to accord priority to the search for solution to the mass and flagrant violations of human rights of peoples and persons affected by situations such as those resulting from *apartheid,* all forms of racial discrimination, colonialism, foreign domination and occupation, aggression and threats against national sovereignty, national unity and territorial integrity as well as of the refusal to recognize the fundamental rights of peoples to self-determination, and of every nation to exercise full sovereignty over its wealth and natural resources;

(f) The realization of the New International Economic Order is an essential element for the effective promotion of human rights and fundamental freedoms and should also be accorded priority;

(g) It is of paramount importance for the promotion of human rights and fundamental freedoms that Member States undertake specific obligations through accession or ratification of international instruments in this field. Consequently, the standard-setting work within the United Nations system in the field of human rights and the universal acceptance and implementation of the relevant international instruments should be encouraged;

(h) The experience and contribution of both developed and developing countries should be taken into account by all organs of the United Nations system in their work related to human rights and fundamental freedoms;

2. *Requests* the Commission on Human Rights:

(a) To undertake, as a matter of priority at its thirty-fourth session an over-all analysis of the alternative approaches and ways and means within the United Nations system for improving the effective enjoyment of human rights and fundamental freedoms, in the light of the above concepts;

(b) To comply with the mandate established in Economic and Social Council resolution 1992 (LX) and its decision 4 (XXXIII), also in the light of this resolution;

(c) To submit to the General Assembly, at its thirty-fourth session, a report with its conclusions and recommendations of the work done with respect to (a) and (b) above, and to present a progress report to the General Assembly, at its thirty-third session;

3. *Requests* the Secretary-General to transmit this resolution to all United Nations organs and specialized agencies concerned;

4. *Decides* to include in the provisional agenda of its thirty-third session the item "Alternative approaches and ways and means within the United Nations system for improving the effective enjoyment of human rights and fundamental freedoms."

Resolution 32/130 confirms what has become a truism that, were it not for the avoidance of a conceptual confrontation between the historical traditions and ideological commitments represented in the United Nations, it is doubtful whether agreement could have been reached on the Universal Declaration of Human Rights in 1948, on the International Covenants on Human Rights, and on many human rights activities which the United Nations has been carrying on for more than thirty years. The late Professor Jacques Maritain gave succinct expression to that truism even while the Universal Declaration was being drafted, when he said:

Where it is a question of rational interpretation and justification of speculation or theory, the problem of human rights involves the whole structure of moral and metaphysical (or anti-metaphysical) convictions held by each of us. So long as minds are not united in faith or philosophy, there will be mutual conflicts between interpretations and justifications.

In the field of practical conclusions, on the other hand, agreement on a joint declaration is possible, given an approach pragmatic rather than theoretical, and cooperation in the comparison, recasting and fixing of formulae, to make them acceptable to both parties as points of convergence in practice, however opposed the theoretical viewpoints.

. . . It is not reasonably possible to hope for more than the convergence in practice in the enumeration of articles jointly agreed. The reconciling of theories and a philosophic synthesis in the true sense are only conceivable after an immense amount of investigation and elucidation of fundamentals, requiring a high degree of insight, a new systematization and authoritative correction of a number of errors and confusions of thought . . .[2]

A careful reading of the resolution leaves little doubt that the moment of truth is at hand. The debate in the Third Committee revealed a deep-seated desire for revision of all traditional thinking of the United Nations in the area of human rights, and for new approaches to the subject based on an understanding of different traditions, values, stages of development and social and economic systems. To be sure, among the large majority which supported the resolution a sizeable number was motivated by patently ideological and political considerations; others may have seen in it a way out of onerous obligations they found increasingly difficult to live with. For the most part, however, the resolution corresponded to the needs and realities of the majority of the peoples of the world. Human rights were bound to lose in depth what they gained in range, and they could not be reduced to routine and formulae and maintain their inspirational quality. Obviously, the hope for an international human rights program based on the superficial similarities of cultures without comprehending their differences fell far short of the mark; human rights has not become a movement which could be caught in one beautiful, all embracing act. While it is too early to tell whether or not the quest for change in United Nations perception of human rights is likely to result in a reconciliation of theories and bring about a philosophic synthesis by redressing the imbalances and errors of the past, the fact is that the United Nations has been put on notice that henceforth it must pay close attention to the new trends in the human rights field and cut the strings that tie it to traditional concepts. Too many countries have gone on record as resentful of the tendency to minimize the impact of their experiences on the intellectual and moral prin-

[2] Human Rights; comments and interpretations (a Symposium edited by UNESCO with an introduction by Jacques Maritain, pp. 11-12).

ciples which govern United Nations activities to be ignored.

That the adoption of a resolution challenging the very validity of the Universal Declaration of Human Rights and seeking to set a new course of human rights in the future coincided with increasing emphasis on international implementation of human rights, with the intense search for new procedures and new institutions for their enforcement, and with the emergence in 1977 of human rights as a central theme of American foreign policy, was no accident. The collision of contrary emphases by the several groupings of the States Members of the United Nations had been edging up over the years and was unavoidable. And it was precisely the confluence of factors seemingly favoring the development of international human rights that triggered the realization of how preposterous it was to deal with an issue so pregnant with consequences through a contest for votes in the General Assembly and other United Nations bodies. This awareness was perhaps greatest among those States Members which had successfully manipulated the human rights issue to promote political or ideological issues, but the underlying problems affected all alike.

To begin with, the precise role and limits of United Nations concern with human rights and the point at which such concern merges into interference in the domestic affairs of States, are questions which theoretically might better remain moot but practically raise issues of great consequence to nations. While the Soviet Union and its allies have made no secret of their views that human rights could fall within the jurisdiction of the United Nations only in cases where mass violations of human rights occurred on a scale which constituted a threat to international peace and security, or where they accompanied aggression, occupation or foreign domination, many other States Members were never far behind in holding to a similar point of view. This is the intent and purpose of operative paragraph 1 (e) of the resolution, as follows:

In approaching human rights questions within the United Nations, the international community should accord or continue to accord, priority to the search for solutions to the mass and flagrant violations of human rights of peoples and persons affected by situations such as those resulting from *apartheid,* from all forms of racial discrimination, from colonialism, from foreign domination and occupation, from aggression and threats against national sovereignty, national unity and territorial integrity, as well as from the refusal to recognize the fundamental rights of people to self-determination and of every nation to the exercise of full sovereignty over its wealth and natural resources.

There is in this paragraph all that is needed to justify past, present and future acts of omission or commission in respect to violations of human rights: it provides standard reasons for United Nations intervention in some situations and inaction in others and, above all, it establishes criteria which ultimately have little to do with human rights but with effects of violations of human rights on external situations determined by political instances on the basis of judgements and considerations not even remotely related to the original issue. United Nations intervention in defense of human rights in Chile following the overthrow of the Allende regime in September 1973, for example, was made possible because powerful political and ideological forces at play found shelter behind the assertion that the coup d'etat was aided and abetted by foreign powers which sought economic domination over Chile and denied the Chilean people full sovereignty over their wealth and natural resources. On the other hand, nations whose gross violation of human rights was hardly in dispute escaped international censure because none of the conditions stipulated in paragraph 1 (e) of resolution 32/130 readily applied.

Similarly, the issue of the relationship between economic, social and cultural rights and civil and political rights, their dependence upon each other or their interdependence, and their relative status in the hierarchy of human rights, gives aid and comfort to Governments which seek refuge in excuses for policies and actions that are violative of human rights. The authoritarianism introduced by former Prime Minister Indira Gandhi to ensure economic development of India and subsequently repudiated in the national elections of 1977, is a case in point; the desires of the human will do not necessarily coincide with objective necessity.

Thus, operative paragraph 1 (B) of the resolution providing that

The full realization of civil and political rights without the enjoyment of economic, social and cultural rights is impossible; the achievement of lasting progress in the implementation of human rights is dependent upon sound and effective national and international policies of economic and social development, as recognized by the Proclamation of Teheran,

is hardly a redeeming proposition for the conduct of international affairs; it establishes causal relationships of undetermined validity and places responsibility on all and none. Surely Paragraph 1 (b) does not move from evidence through reasoning to conclusion to serve as a practical guide to action. Ultimately the relationship between economic, social and cultural rights and civil and political rights is not far different from the relationship, for example, between constitutional guarantees of a free press and the guarantees of privacy and a fair trial, which are often in conflict with each other; the resolution of this conflict lies not in the suppression or subordination of one right or the other, but in a harmonious, all-embracing set of relationships. Unless problems are treated comprehensively in such a way that a solution in one area does not lead to catastrophe in another, there is always danger of succumbing to the treacheries of mere conjecture. Reliance upon factors which elude, to all intents and purposes, human control is to wait for a curtain that never goes up. There is no conceivable authority in the offing that can define, prescribe and enforce universally applicable sound policies of economic and social development at the national level, as there is no international policy which can bridge the disparities among nations to produce a common standard of economic and social development.

Similarly, the provision in Paragraph 1 (d) that

> human rights questions should be examined globally, taking into account both the overall context of the various societies in which they present themselves, as well as the need for the promotion of the full dignity of the human person and the development and well-being of the society;

belong to the category of philosophical views which can hardly be translated into tangible propositions; we are hard put to distinguish factual statements from cant and compulsory clichés in which the resolution abounds. The fact is that the resolution has created awkward nettles which will have to be grasped in the future. The resolution is certainly no model of an integrated approach to international human rights; it lacks an interlocking series of rigorously disciplined facts, attitudes, judgements and movements that are related to clearly-defined objectives.

The deep divisions among nations in their perception of human rights, as well as in objectives, brought into such sharp relief by the debate in the Third Committee, cast grave doubt on the viability of the very notion of international implementation. As long as one part of the world regards human rights as inherent in the human person and therefore universal and timeless; as long as another part recognizes the supremacy of the collectivity over the individual, and still another part looks upon human rights as the satisfaction of vital, active and concrete human needs, international implemenation of human rights will remain a snare and delusion. While this does not necessarily imply the eventual dissolution of existing institutions and procedures of implementation such as, for example, the Committee on Human Rights established by the International Covenant on Civil and Political Rights, their relevance to the human rights situation in the world in the concrete is bound to diminish in time. The insistence, for example, that the full flowering of civil and political rights must await the enjoyment of economic, social and cultural rights, or the resolution of the issue of peace and war, is more likely to prevail than the libertarian philosophy of the Western world.

But even the area of implementation associated with the human rights activities of the General Assembly, the Economic and Social Council, the Commission on Human Rights and the Sub-Commission on Prevention of Discrimination and Protection of Minorities cannot long escape the impact of resolution 32/130. One of the major preoccupations of those organs of the United Nations has been their adversary proceedings of different kinds against States Members accused of gross violations of human rights. These proceedings have often been hailed as milestones on the road to international protection of human rights and witnesses to the development of United Nations concern with human rights. In reality, however, they proved to be but convenient ploys for engaging the United Nations in national, regional, territorial and ideological disputes for the promotion of patently partisan objectives. For example, it was not abstract justice that sustained and nourished the thirty-year long campaign against *apartheid,* but the emergence of the African continent into independence and the quest of the newly emancipated nations for equality and dignity; similarly, it was not the merits of the Middle East dispute that pitted the great majority of States Members against Israel, but the power of the Arab-Afro-Asian Alliance supported by the so-called socialist States. And, finally, it was not the rare cruelty of the Chilean junta that brought down the wrath of so many States Members upon that Latin American country, but the ability of the Soviet Union to mobilize support for an ideological vendetta in the guise of concern for human rights. But once the focus on political and civil rights dissolves in the concern for peoples' economic needs and social aspirations, the opportunities for exploiting human rights for partisan purposes will lessen, and with it much of the reason and motivation behind the implementation of such rights by the General Assembly and the other organs concerned in the form of adversary proceedings against Governments will have disappeared.

Obviously, if human rights are perceived in the spirit of General Assembly resolution 32/130, the stress in the United Nations will be increasingly on forms of implementation designed to further economic development and social progress. Unlike civil and political rights which involve setting limits to a Government's freedom of action and, by definition, creates an adversary relationship between the organized international community and Governments, economic and social development invites their participation and cooperation rather than conflict. And since the promotion of economic and social development calls for greater intervention of Government in the lives of people, responsibility for any infringements on civil and political rights that may result from such intervention will be shared by all and, therefore, by none. Thus, whatever fate may be in store for civil and political rights, their international implementation is bound to be affected by the spirit and letter of the resolution of December 16, 1977.

That in this the thirtieth year of the Universal Declaration of Human Rights that great historic document should have reached what some may call a shattering denouement could have been anticipated. It is not that the world has turned its back on the ideas and concepts that gave birth to it; it just could not keep up with the demands made upon it by the Declaration, it was nothing short of bias towards self-deception to believe that the Declaration could bridge in such a relatively short time the Western, Communist and Third worlds and be counsel to each. Perhaps the West was too quick to chart the road of political and moral responsibilities to the rest of the world, and too slow to purge the language of words that confuse law and order with democracy and hammer out the twisted logic that professes to rationalize the murder of innocents as a response to social injustice. It was as preposterous to believe that outward conformity supports commitment, as to suggest that human rights issues, so pregnant with consequences, could be dealt with through a contest of votes in United Nations bodies whose membership remains divided by history and tradition, national interests and ideological differences, and to place uncritical trust in the historical efficacy of verbal constructs.

Perhaps too great a burden was placed on the Third World, which was expected to negotiate painlessly the uneven and fateful transaction between tradition and modernity, between communal and individual expression, and between its own survival and its peoples' acculturation. Perhaps, too, too much confidence was staked on the act of judgement by reference to the Western standards without further analysis and without seeking new directions. As was recently suggested by Jahangir Amuzegar, Iran's representative to the International Monetary Fund and the World Bank,

. . . if a sharper focus on basic human rights is to result in the betterment of the human condition in the world . . .

Care should be taken not to paper over certain harsh economic realities in the developing countries with a mere magnificent facade – that is, not to crucify their basic human needs on the altar of abstract "human rights" . . .

As fas as the third world is concerned, they are largely one-sided, passive and abstract. They reflect political rights for the redress of grievances, personal immunity from unlawful and unnecessary search and seizure, *habeas corpus* privileges, due process of law for incarceration or imposition of fines, the absence of cruel and inhuman punishment, and a host of other individual freedoms of action.

But they are silent about the society's obligation toward the individual; they say precious little about the right to economic opportunities, the right to employment, the right to obtain a meaningful education, the right to enjoy a minimum of life's amenities. These "active" and "positive" sides (that is, society's obligations) are either ignored or considered as secondary in the roster of Western "human rights" . . .

In the third world countries suffering from poverty, widespread illiteracy and a yawning gap in domestic distribution of incomes and wealth, a constitutionally guaranteed freedom of opposition and dissent may not be as significant as freedom from despair, disease and deprivation. The masses might indeed be much happier if they could put more into their mouths than empty words; if they could have a health-care center instead of Hyde Park corner; if they were ensured gainful employment instead of the right to march on the Capitol. The trade-offs may be disheartening and objectionable to a Western purist, but they may be necessary or unavoidable for a majority of nation . . . States . . .

To champion the cause of "human rights" is an admirable pursuit. But let us not forget that empty heads and empty stomachs may find the "due process" also frightfully empty.[3]

But we need not give up our goals, only our illusions. Human rights can never become merely a model of other people's expectations and maintain a continuity of conviction. By the same token, international concern with human rights is bound to die of its own pretensions unless it is rooted in the reciprocal acceptance of the cultural and ethical values of the different societies which make up the community of nations. The future of international human rights depends upon our ability to reach for the connection between the evidence and the pressing question about the human condition; what is called for is an integrated approach that takes into account all relevant factors which bear upon the subject and seeks to resolve the internal and external contradictions which block the road to the achievement of the great objectives. It is not specific blueprints that come to mind, but courage to look through the darkest negations and work through to the light. What is needed is a leap of faith, not a reckless optimism of the reformer; intellectual discipline to rescue the United Nations from its own excesses, not caution to the point of nullity; and a clear distinction between fashionable fads and critical causes, not belligerence of righteous indignation and turgid griefs. Only in an atmosphere cleansed of cant can we hope for persuasion and rational compromise.

It is not a question of creating new institutions or of refining old procedures, but one of perception and understanding; what is called for is

---

[3] New York Times, opp. ed. page. January 29, 1978.

an integrated approach that takes into account all important factors which bear upon the subject and seeks to resolve the internal and external contradictions blocking the evolution of international human rights.

But first we must rid ourselves of certain notions which encumber the United Nations human rights programme and contribute to its general disorientation. For example, in our eagerness to pass from standard-setting to implementation, or from word to deed, we have tended to overlook the broad area of promotion and its vast opportunities and possibilities for constructive achievement, in favour of a role for the United Nations in redressing violations of human rights outside the framework of the International Covenants on Human Rights. Whatever the immediate reasons which prompted some or all of us to force the world body into a role for which it was ill-equipped constitutionally, politically, as well as morally, it has become abundantly clear that international protection of human rights will not be achieved by reproach or condemnation, whether by majority vote or consensus. As Dr. van Boven, Director of the Human Rights Division of the United Nations, pointed out in his maiden speech at the opening of the thirty-fourth session of the Commission on Human Rights on 6 February 1978, the misconception that the Commission should deal with violations of human rights by either condemning a Government or by instituting an investigation may be one source of the Commission's difficulties in handling allegations of violations of human rights. The same applies to the General Assembly and other United Nations organs concerned. A careful examination of United Nations intervention in the racial situation in southern Africa, in the Middle East dispute and, more recently, also in Chile, shows that the world body has little to offer to the resolution of problems short of complete submission or capitulation. Moreover, these three cases of United Nations experience with situations involving allegations of gross violations of human rights, have been patently acts of political assertion and can hardly serve as models for the conciliation of disputes and the redressing of wrongs. Rather, they would indicate that the authority of the United Nations might be invoked to better advantage by the general acceptance of the undisputed and uninhibited right of every State Member to inveigh in every major organ of the Organization against what it regards as grave injustices and to raise issues of gross violations of human rights without the encumbrance of formal procedures and without formal conclusions and recommendations.

Let us leave the Covenants on Human Rights to work out their own historical dialectics and to contribute their just share to the growth of an international human rights jurisprudence as a reliable and predictable guardian of the liberties of man. For the rest, the most constructive work in which the United Nations might engage with great profit in the immediate future, is to turn its attention to a systematic examination of the conceptual political and practical problems which impede the realization, in whole or in part, of the Universal Declaration of Human Rights, with a view to removing such impediments. Surely, if the United Nations had been engaged in an examination of that kind, resolution A/32/130 could never have proved by assertion what it could not assert by fact. The resolution is only symptomatic of the intellectual chaos which pervades the international human rights field; there are no valid reasons why in this the thirtieth year of the Universal Declaration that document, which was conceived of the ages should have been shaken to its foundations. The great task before the United Nations is to restore intellectual discipline to its work in human rights, to draw clear distinctions between fashionable fads and critical causes, and to cleanse the human rights programme of all cant and pretense. Only then can we hope for a rational approach that will permit the consolidation of the achievements of the past and ensure progress in the future.

CHAPTER VII

SOME REFLECTIONS ON IMPLEMENTING HUMAN RIGHTS

DR. KAMLESHWAR DAS*

There is need to be concerned with implementing human rights in the thirtieth anniversary year of the proclamation of the Universal Declaration of Human Rights. Are there, however, "experts on human rights" who can write about it with breadth of vision, a multi-disciplinary approach, a world-wide knowledge and understanding, and a dispassionate objectivity? The author has spent a lifetime studying and learning about human rights but he lays no claim to being more than someone who is deeply committed to their realization. If he has learnt any lesson, it is to ponder on the scarcity, on the one hand, of material concerning implementing human rights within different countries, and the abundance, on the other hand, of documentation of international origin. Writing on implementing human rights is like facing what Jalal-unDin Rumi wrote in the thirteenth century about the "Unseen Elephant":[1]

The Elephant was in a dark house: some Hindus had brought it for exhibition.
As seeing it with the eye was impossible, everyone felt it in the dark with the palm of his hand.
The hand of one fell on his trunk: he said, 'This creature is like a water-pipe'.
Another touched its ear: to him it appeared like a fan.
Another handled its leg: he said, 'I found the Elephant's shape to be like a pillar'.
Another laid his hand on its back: he said, 'Truly this Elephant resembles a throne'.
Had there been a candle in each one's hand, the difference would have gone out of their words.

Lacking that candle, these brief reflections will relate to human rights of all, without special reference to women, youth, children, etc., and draw attention to a certain want of focus. This arises out of conflicts in the objectives of the Charter of the United Nations, their interdependency, and

*M.A., Ph.D. (Cantab); of the Inner Temple, Barrister-at-Law; former Deputy Director of the Division of Human Rights of the United Nations Secretariat.
[1] *Tales of Mystic Meaning, being selections from the Mathnawi* (translated by R.A. Nicholson, 1931), p. 111.

a co-ordinated approach to them. It arises out of absence of knowledge about, and the possibilities of, national action and co-operation. It also arises out of failure to discuss flexible international measures.

The peoples of the United Nations have set out their aims in the preamble to the Charter. It was not the peoples, however, but their respective Governments who agreed to the Charter. Those Governments and others have interpreted the Charter provisions in different ways. For instance, what is the meaning to be attributed to the provisions of Articles 55 and 56 in relation to Article 2 (7)? Dot the purposes and the means set out to accomplish them take precedence over the principles, or do the latter frustrate the accomplishment of the purposes? Do the proceedings at San Francisco limit possibilities of action? What value is to be attached to the practice of United Nations organs? There is no need to catalogue all the issues. The effectiveness of any effort or decision by the United Nations may suffer to the extent a Member State does not agree with it, but is that not a fundamental characteristic of the Organization whether or not Article 2 (7) is invoked?

Mahatma Gandhi, in replying to a questionnaire from UNESCO, may have given a clue to a better understanding when he responded that he learnt from "his illiterate but wise mother that all rights to be deserved come from duty well done. Thus the very right to live accrues to us only when we do the duty of citizenship of the world."[2] Without life there would be no human beings and without them there would be no State. Needless to say we would not be concerned then with human rights. This "duty of citizenship of the world", may, accordingly, be said to apply equally to the peoples who have set out their goals in the Charter and to Member States whose obligations are inscribed in it. Can peoples or States prosper or achieve anything lasting without each other? It is also delusory to conceive in the world of today either one, particularly any State, being able to force upon others a course of conduct which may result in implementing human rights everywhere. What is required is co-operation in the common quest in ordered complexity and harmonized multiplicity.[3]

[2] *Human Rights: comments and interpretations* (a symposium edited by UNESCO, 1949), p. 18.

[3] Speaking in 1946 the representative of the United Kingdom, Mr. Philip Noel-Baker, a past awardee of the Nobel Peace Prize, observed: "We have to develop the means by which international law can be most wisely and most rapidly developed, the means by which it can be effectively applied, the means by which day to day practical co-operation between Governments can be obtained. We shall often find ourselves, I hope, led to discard the old ideas and the old practices of national sovereignty . . . From the broadest point of view, our task may be stated thus. In 1939, after twenty years of so-called peace and so-called social progress, there were in the richest countries of the world anything up to half of the population who had not

It is necessary to acknowledge the inter-connectedness of the Charter provisions, since proposals to include provisions to protect human rights or to incorporate a bill of rights in the Charter were considered too ambitious at San Francisco. As the late Secretary-General U Thant put it in 1963:[4]

What is surprising is not that provisions on human rights were included in the Charter, but it took humanity so long to acknowledge the inter-connexion between human rights and its other aspirations. For what purpose is international peace and security to be maintained, if not to preserve the right to life, liberty and the pursuit of happiness? What is the use of economic development if it does not, in the words of the Charter "promote better standards of life in larger freedom".

This inter-dependency was ignored for a long time and is still not fully comprehended. The multi-dimensional problem posed by it demanded both co-operative and co-ordinated action. Such action might have been spurred if the Universal Declaration had been followed quickly by the completion of the other parts of the "grand design" of the International Bill of Human Rights containing norms and fundamental aims of a world society. Instead, to take Article 55 as an example, policies, programmes and institutions were adopted with insufficient regard for the provisions of the article as a whole. The Commission on Human Rights itself has never undertaken to scrutinize the relationship of human rights to the other objectives of the Charter. If the Commission continues to ignore a concerted approach, its inability to adopt a realistic work programme to implement human rights will broaden.

Co-ordination was emphasized in 1945 by the Preparatory Commission of the United Nations and since then various efforts to achieve it have been made.[5] In the last fifteen years human rights have found a place in most

---

enough to eat, there were slums unfit for human habitation, there were ignorance and preventable disease. In 1946 we can produce the wealth, we have the organizing power, we have the material and spiritual contact between all the continents which are needed to enable us to abolish these monstrous evils that have afflicted us too long . . . In the Atlantic Charter our government promised that that would be done. In our Charter the promise was renewed that all the men in all the lands shall be free from want. Whatever other agencies may be set up, it is on the Council that the prime responsibility for that great task must lie. I believe we shall succeed in the measure in which we remember the solidarity of the interests of the nations and in the measure in which we can create international loyalty on the part of the people of the United Nations". *Official Records of the Economic and Social Council, First Session,* 1st Meeting, p. 18.

   [4] United Nations, OPI/146, p. 4.

   [5] The Preparatory Commission recommended to the Economic and Social Council the advisability of setting up a Co-ordination Commission "entrusted with duties of organizing the machinery for co-ordinating the activities of various organs of the Council and the specialized agencies". This co-ordinating task, while being a function of the Council itself, the Preparatory Commission pointed out, "is also necessary at the Commission level, and the work of the Council will be greatly facilitated if the reports and recommendations coming forward from any one commission take full account of the point of view of others". To

United Nations programmes and activities, but blueprints for a new international order often fall short of providing an adequate link to implementing human rights.[6] Will resolution 32/447 of 1977 of the General Assembly
on restructuring of the economic and social sectors of the United Nations
system inaugurate a more desirable objective to meet the multi-dimensional
problem to which attention has been drawn?

There is insufficient knowledge and appreciation of implementing
human rights nationally. Exactly what part do the State and its organs play
in achieving recognition of, and safeguarding enjoyment of, human rights
and fundamental freedoms? How do national action and efforts become
embedded in the life and practice of a country?[7] Why do Governments
invoke reasons of State? What causes them to bristle at outside criticism?
What is their experience with internal conflicts, and why do they arise?
How do they deal with problems arising out of the past or the present? Can
anything lasting be accomplished without the will of governments and
peoples to understand each other and pursue common goals in mutual
co-operation? How do these take into account the just demands of the
individual, the community, the Government, and, if you will, the international order?

In 1958, Mrs. Eleanor Roosevelt asked where, after all, do universal
human rights begin, and answered:[8]

In small places, close to home – so close and so small that they cannot be seen on
any map of the world. Yet they are the world of the individual person; the neigh-
bourhood he lives in; the school or college he attends; the factory, farm or office
where he works. Such are the places where every man, woman and child seeks
justice, equal opportunity, equal dignity without discrimination. Unless these rights
have a meaning there they have little meaning anywhere. Without concerted citizen
action to uphold them close to home, we shall look in vain for progress in the larger
world.

How much is known about the implications of Mrs. Roosevelt's answer,
and particularly about what goes on in the non-public sphere.[9] What is
known about the role in different countries of efforts at self-regulation and

---

"facilitate collaboration between commissions working in allied fields, suitable arrangements
for reciprocal representation should be made". Document PC/20, pp. 36 and 39.

[6] See, for instance, a report to the Club of Rome by Jan Tinbergen and others in *Reshaping
the International Order* (1976).

[7] See an innovating attempt in R.P. Clause (editor), *Comparative Human Rights* (1976).

[8] *Teaching Human Rights,* United Nations Publication, Sales No. 63.I.34, p. 1.

[9] See, for example, D.W. Ewing, *Freedom Inside the Organization: bringing of civil
liberties to the work place* (1977).

self-discipline, codes of honour and ethics, and similar methods used in various walks of life and professions in countries to assert many rights and freedoms and to protect them against practices and abuses which impinge upon their enjoyment, whether or not they involve the State?[10] How far are such methods encouraged, used or permitted, and what has been the outcome of their practice? Does initiative for them come from the community or the Government? Are they subject to sanctions and, if so, what kinds of sanctions are invoked? Is there any sign of human rights becoming a common feature of concern almost on a street to street level?[11]

There are many documents on most facets of United Nations activities but few of them supply a coherent picture of implementing human rights and fundamental freedoms nationally. Direct means to obtain such information have rarely met with total success. There has never been published a guide on national legal institutions and procedures for the protection or promotion of human rights called for in 1962. There is not enough practical information available from the Yearbooks on Human Rights, the periodic reports or the studies on specific subjects. Declarations and conventions have been prepared and adopted without prior collection and analysis of national experience and practices relating to their subject-matters. Guidance for the future may come from the General Assembly which is now considering the question of the multi-lateral treaty making process. Requests to governments for observations, suggestions and answers to questionnaires on conventions and other matters have not led to eliciting the required data, and the majority of States have not responded. Similar requests extended to non-governmental organizations have not been more successful. Sometimes valuable information is furnished in papers contributed to seminars, but they are available to participants only and brought out in the language of submission.

There have been promising developments relating the procedures connected with reports asked from States Parties to certain conventions by extending invitations to them to attend meetings to encourage a dialogue between them and the bodies receiving the reports. The author made a number of suggestions concerning direct contact with such States in relation to the International Convention on the Elimination of All Forms of

---

[10] See the opening address of U Thant in the *Final Report of the International Non-Governmental Organizations' Conference,* held in Paris in September 1968, p. 12.

[11] See the author's remarks in the *Proceedings of the Second Annual Conference of the Canadian Council of International Law* (1973), p. 181.

Racial Discrimination.[12] Subsequently, following a General Assembly recommendation the Committee on Elimination of Racial Discrimination
extended invitations to States Parties to participate at meetings when their
reports are considered. Lately, another suggestion was taken up by the
Committee when it invited seven States Parties which had failed to submit
more than one report to send representatives to discuss their difficulties at
private meetings at the Committee's summer session in 1978. The example
of inviting States Parties to meetings was followed by the Committee on
Human Rights for reports under the International Covenant on Civil and
Political Rights. Recently it was also espoused by the Working Group of
the Commission on Human Rights set up under the Convention on the
Suppression and Punishment of the Crime of Apartheid. It may be expected that a similar course will be followed by the working group established
by the Economic and Social Council to examine reports from States Parties
to the International Covenant on Economic, Social and Cultural Rights.
Direct contacts between States Parties offering opportunity for dialogue
and other forms of co-operation and assistance, as the author wrote in his
article mentioned above, and the various bodies provide better means for
gauging national actions and for achieving the objectives of conventions.

There is room for direct contact and involvement of governments in the
sensitive area of violations of human rights. While it is impossible here to
go into all the questions and problems concerned with such violations outside of conventions, some observations may be in order.

Economic and Social Council resolution 1503 (XLVIII) lays down procedures whereby the Sub-Commission on Prevention of Discrimination
and Protection of Minorities, under rules of receivability prescribed by it,
is to examine communications, mainly originating from non-governmental
sources, alleging violations of human rights, together with any replies
received from the Governments concerned. The Sub-Commission may, as
a result of such examination, draw the attention of the Commission on
Human Rights to particular situations which appear to reveal a consistent
pattern of gross and reliably attested violation of human rights. The Commission may decide to make a study of any such situation or initiate an
investigation after obtaining the consent of the Government concerned and

---

[12] See the author's article, "Measures of implementation of the International Convention
on the Elimination of All Forms of Racial Discrimination with special reference to the provisions concerning reports from States Parties to the Convention", *Human Rights Journal*
(1971), Vol. IV, pp. 253-258.

in constant consultation with it. The Commission has, for the first time, in 1978, listed countries on which it held private meetings, as envisaged in the Council resolution, and took confidential measures; the countries named were announced as Bolivia, Equatorial Guinea, Malawi, Republic of Korea, Uganda, Ethiopia, Indonesia, Paraguay and Uruguay. The Commission also agreed to invite States concerned to attend its meetings when it considers any situations regarding them brought to its attention by the Sub-Commission. Further, acting outside that Council resolution the Commission asked the Government of Democratic Kampuchea to submit comments on the proceedings of the Commission in which references were made to reported violations of human rights there.[13]

Thus, the Commission has started to apply a more direct approach to governments. But whether it be a situation brought to its attention by the Sub-Commission or otherwise, why should the Commission not look at, for example, the experience of the ILO procedure concerning allegation of trade union rights? To act in cases of such allegation coming from governments or employers or employees organizations the ILO established a Fact Finding and Conciliation Commission. It is not this body, which has been used rarely, but a Committee of Three established by the Governing Body of the ILO to carry out preliminary explorations that has played a central role and acted on allegations with direct approach to governments concerned.[14] The Commission could without undue publicity and without prejudice to a Government's position or to those alleging violations, hold informal consultations with Governments by, say, involving one or more Governments of the same region as the State concerned. Regional machinery, where available, might be used both formally and informally. Preliminary consultations might be entrusted to persons of eminence, such as former Presidents of the General Assembly, former Justices of the International Court of Justice, or existing or former chief justices of the highest courts of States. Thought might be given also to assigning, in agreement with a Government concerned, a particular situation or issue to national bodies. Moreover, it is time to hold national, regional and other discussion on the model rules of procedure for United Nations bodies dealing with violations of human rights. A request for such rules originated from the International

---

[13] As the proceedings and the report of the Commission were not available the actions of the Commission mentioned were taken from United Nations Press Release HR 1624 of 13 March 1978.

[14] See C.W. Jenks, "The International Protection of Trade Union Rights", in: E. Luard (editor), *The International Protection of Human Rights* (1967), chapter 9, as well as *Official Bulletin of the International Labour Office* for various years.

Conference on Human rights in 1968. Draft rules were prepared by the Secretariat and considered by two working groups of the Commission. The results were taken note of by the Council in 1974 and brought to the attention of all organs and bodies of the United Nations dealing with questions of human rights and fundamental freedoms. If there can be substantial agreement on such rules by Member States it would go a long way in creating confidence and strengthening efforts to implement human rights and freedoms.

Governments can request assistance in the form of experts, seminars, training courses, fellowships and documentary material under the programme of advisory services in the field of human rights and other programmes within the United Nations system, which offer possibilities for implementing human rights and freedoms nationally, regionally and internationally. They may be used to advantage in preparing declarations, conventions, model rules and in discussing principles and other conclusions of studies.

Equally promising for fostering national action and co-operation is the new impetus given by the Commission on Human Rights in 1978 to establishing national institutions and their functions, which are to be discussed also in July 1978 by a seminar; earlier initiatives in this regard going back to 1946 led nowhere. Side by side with national institutions revival by the General Assembly and the Commission to encourage regional arrangements may be found useful, as they have been by the Council of Europe, the League of Arab States, the Organization of African Unity and the Organization of American States. Such arrangements may not be favoured by all countries in all regions, just as they may not show enthusiasm for national institutions. There is also no reason why sub-regional or other groupings of interested States should not find a place. Discussions and other functions performed by institutions and groups can only enhance national co-operation, lead to exchange of experience, and conduce a community interest arising out of commonly shared values. They may also help to solve problems peculiar to any country or group of them.

Time may be ripe for a comprehensive review with governments and non-governmental organizations concerning the arrangements for consultations prescribed by the Economic and Social Council pursuant to Article 71 of the Charter. Provision for such consultation was welcomed and much praised in the early days of the United Nations when it was even suggested that the organizations should enjoy privileges commensurate with their importance and competence as they were, in a sense, the only link directly provided in the Charter with the peoples of the United Nations. Over the years the organizations have by and large played a constructive part in co-operating with the United Nations to achieve its goals. Many of them met in 1955 and 1959 in conferences convened by the Council to discuss the eradication of prejudice and discrimination. But over the same years consultative privileges have been curtailed, and in recent years there has been criticism of some of the organizations and their activities connected with violations of human rights.[15] Surely, here is an opportunity to convene meetings nationally, regionally and internationally to clear up misunderstandings, to formulate a sounder arrangement for consultation, and to agree upon better means of co-operating in implementing human rights. Be it remembered, consultative status is not confined to international organizations but may be granted to national organizations; one national organization in consultative status, for example, considers itself the largest women's organization in the world.

The remainder of this contribution is devoted to exploring some means to implement human rights and fundamental freedoms which link national and international concerns. What is being suggested for discussion is a protocol of a general nature for eventual adoption by the General Assembly consisting of a scheme whereby States may accept certain minimum undertakings and optionally adhere to greater commitments. Its object is far from engendering conflict and division but, on the contrary, to invite constructive co-operation and dialogue. It recognizes, on the one hand, what appears to be generally agreed amongst Member States to accept the conventional method. It also takes into account, on the other hand, what the representative of Ghana said during the preparation of the International Convention on the Elimination of All Forms of Racial Discrimination, namely, that any State progressive enough to declare that its citizens should enjoy a certain right ought not to have to await the agreement of other States before granting that right. He made his remark as a sponsor to a proposal on individual communication in article 14 of that convention in opposing a Swedish proposal to require prior acceptance by ten States Parties before article 14 could come into effect, which was based on article 25 of the European Convention on the Protection of Human Rights and Fundamental Freedoms.[16] Sweden appears to have accepted the Ghanian

[15] See Economic and Social Council resolutions 2/3, 288 B (X), 454 (XIV), 1296 (XLIV), 1391 (XLVI), 1919 (LVIII), and the latest report of the Council Committee on Non-Governmental Organizations in document E/1978/13.

[16] See *Official Records of the General Assembly. Twentieth Session, Third Committee,* 1362nd meeting, paras. 13 and 14; and 1363rd meeting, para. 9.

position in article 20, relating to individual communication, of its proposed draft International Convention against Torture and Other Cruel, Inhuman or Degrading Treatment or Punishment submitted to the 1978 session of the Commission on Human Rights.

It would be left to the General Assembly to decide to apply the protocol to existing or future conventions, whether or not they include measures for their implementation, because it would allow States Parties to various conventions to weigh and decide for themselves whether they wish to go beyond those measures and subscribe to more far-reaching obligations. This does not exclude discussion, decision or inclusion in conventions of appropriate provisions for their implementation, as recommended by the Economic and Social Council in its resolution 1101 (XL) of 2 March 1966, or to ignore the Council's urging for full utilization of the organizational and procedural arrangements for the implementation of existing conventions.

Besides conventions, the General Assembly may open the protocol to implementing certain Declarations or parts of them which it would designate, since there may well be subjects on which a declaration need not be followed by a convention. This would not be a novel or an entirely new departure when it is recalled, for example, that the General Assembly set up by its resolution 1654 (XVI) of 27 November 1961 a Special Committee to examine the application of the Declaration on the Granting of Independence to Colonial Countries and Peoples, to make suggestions and recommendations on the progress and extent of the implementation of the Declaration, and directed the Committee to carry out its task by "employment of all means which it will have at its disposal within the framework of the procedures and modalities which it shall adopt for the proper discharge of its functions".

The proposed protocol might also be utilized with regard to specific Recommendations, which may be designated by the General Assembly relating to special subjects for which neither a convention nor a declaration may be most suitable, or when some particular objective of a limited scope is contemplated. Special procedures apply in specialized agencies, particularly in the ILO and in UNESCO, to mention only two of them, for implementing designated Recommendations, but the United Nations has not developed any comparable general procedures. One example is the Recommendation on Consent to Marriage, Minimum Age for Marriage and Registration of Marriages adopted by the General Assembly in 1965.

To emphasize the importance to be attached to certain conventions, declarations and recommendations to which the protocol may apply it may be required that their designation be made by a two thirds vote of the General Assembly. To recognize the inter-connectedness of human rights and fundamental freedoms with the other purposes and goals of the Charter, the designation may not be influenced decisively by the organ or body which originated the convention, declaration or recommendation. The criterion would be whether any of them set out norms on fundamental aims which are deemed to be essential and needed for the achievement of human rights and fundamental freedoms. The protocol might be applied, for example, for implementing the Standard Minimum Rules for the Treatment of Prisoners, adopted more than twenty years ago by the First Congress held by the United Nations on the Prevention of Crime and the Treatment of Offenders and approved by the Economic and Social Council in its resolution 1663 C (XXIV) of 31 July 1957. The effective implementation of the Rules has been discussed for some time without any conclusions.[17]

It is intended that the protocol will be open to voluntary acceptance by States and to allow them complete freedom on how far they wish to assume far-reaching obligations. Therefore, there appears to be no barrier to include in it alternative provisions, including those for an International Court of Human Rights. This is desirable also because it is difficult to envisage easy passage of suitable alterations to the Statute of the International Court of Justice. The International Law Commission, it will be recalled, came to the conclusion that an international criminal court was both possible and desirable but it recommended a separate institution rather than a criminal chamber of the Court.[18] Thereafter, the General Assembly appointed Committees which considered the draft statutes for a separate court. However, the Assembly considered that the problems raised were closely related to defining aggression and to the draft code of offences against the peace and security of mankind and deferred discussion until those two questions were taken up. Since then, the Assembly in 1974 adopted a text defining aggression and it has agreed to place the draft code of offences against the peace and security of mankind on the agenda of its 1978 session. Not only the Convention on Prevention and Punishment of the Crime of Genocide but the Convention on the Suppression and Punishment of the Crime of Apartheid also provide for trial of persons charged with either crime by an international tribunal if there is one. There has been

[17] See *Fifth United Nations Congress on the Prevention of Crime and Treatment of Offenders.* United Nations Publication, Sales No. 76.IV.2 , chapter II.
[18] See *Official Records of the General Assembly, Fifth Session Supplement No. 12,* part IV.

discussion about international criminal jurisdiction in connexion with other subjects, including the Convention on the Non-Applicability of Statutory Limitations to War Crimes and Crimes against Humanity.

It was as long ago as 1946 that a proposal for an International Court of Human Rights was first advanced by Australia at the Paris Peace Conference, and later submitted to the Commission on Human Rights. It was never discussed extensively. In 1950 the Commission rejected reference of proposals regarding implementation of human rights by international jurisdiction to the International Law Commission.[19] In 1961, the representative of Colombia proposed in the Sixth Committee of the General Assembly that the question of the establishment of an international tribunal for the protection of human rights should be placed on the agenda of the 1962 session of the Assembly, but it was agreed to include in the Committee's report an expression of hope that the Secretary-General would convey to the Commission on Human Rights the proposal and the observations made in the Committee.[20] The Commission took no action. In 1968, the question of an international court of human rights was raised in a paper submitted to the International Conference on Human Rights by a present judge of the International Court of Justice, Mr. T.O. Elias of Nigeria.[21]

During the twenty-fifth anniversary year of the United Nations, President Kaunda of Zambia, speaking before the General Assembly on 19 October 1970, also in his capacity as Chairman of the Organization of African Unity and Chairman of the Third Summit of Non-Aligned Countries, directed attention to the "dire need for reform" if the United Nations "is to cope with the new and complex international community," and the second of these needs, he said, was that "the United Nations should, during the rest of the century, devote its attention to the improvement of the machinery for the implementation of human rights which has become a very urgent and desperate problem in many parts of the world". He continued, "human rights laws, which the United Nations has adopted in the form of conventions and human rights covenants, are dishonoured with impunity. Therefore what is needed now is not more law but an effective system of implementing all the conventions which have been

---

[19] *Official Records of the Economic and Social Council, Eleventh Session, Supplement No. 5,* document E/1681, paragraph 46. For a comprehensive proposal by Australia see *Official Records of the Economic and Social Council, Ninth Session. Supplement No. 10,* document E/1371, annex III.

[20] *Official Records of the General Assembly, Sixteenth Session, Annexes,* agenda item 70, document A/5036, para. 38.

[21] A/CONF.32/L.3.

adopted. There is need to give the United Nations agencies enforcement powers. To this end the establishment of an international crime register must be decided as a matter of priority so that those who commit crimes against humanity do not get away with it. In addition, the creation of an international tribunal to deal with complaints against violations of human rights must be given serious consideration''.[22] It is hardly necessary to refer to the existence of judicial machinery in the European Convention, which has been functioning for some years, or in the 1969 American Convention on Human Rights, both provide for optional judicial recourse.

It is impossible to set out a complete and full text of a draft protocol which is being suggested for consideration, if only because of limited space. What can be done is to furnish a rough scheme touching upon the main points but deficient in drafting, in details, and in explanations. It may be called a General Protocol for Promotion and Protection of Human Rights and Fundamental Freedoms. It might consist of a number of parts. Parts I and II might contain certain general provisions. Part III might deal with national reporting systems, and part IV with international reporting. All these parts with parts IX and X on reservations and declarations and final clauses, respectively, might be the minimum to which a State Party to the protocol would commit itself. The other parts would all be optional subject to individual declarations under various conditions. These parts might include: part V, good offices and conciliation: part VI, communications from individuals, groups of individuals and non-governmental organizations; part VII, mediation; and part VIII, international court of human rights. While parts V to VIII would be tied to each other to some extent, flexibility lies in the ability to subscribe to all or any of them or to none of them. All of these parts would be open to separate declarations. A State Party may be willing, for example to subscribe to good offices and conciliation but to go no further. Another State Party may feel mediation to be the proper method. Still another State may be willing to allow the court to have a limited or wide jurisdiction, which could be either in con-junction·with all or any parts or independently of them.

A simple method of accession may be sufficient. It may also be thought that the number of acceding States could be as low as possible in order not to deny equality of opportunity to States in their desire to undertake obligations. Perhaps accession by two States might suffice to bring the protocol into effect. Financial considerations often dominate United

---

[22] *Official Records of the General Assembly, Twenty-Fifth Session, Plenary Meetings,* 1872nd meeting.

Nations deliberations and they would have to be carefully weighed by the General Assembly against the advantages to be derived from the existence of the protocol and the seriousness with which implementing human rights is to form part of co-operation between States and the United Nations.

As the protocol will be applicable to conventions, declarations and specified recommendations designated by the General Assembly it may be considered as proper to refer to them by the term "instrument", being fully aware that the term is often used in a wider sense as well as in a more strict sense as applying only to treaties and conventions. It is for the Assembly to determine what it believes to be the best term to use.

PART I. GENERAL PROVISIONS

Article I[23]

1. This protocol shall apply to any conventions, declarations, or specific recommendations (hereinafter referred to as "instrument"), designated by two thirds majority vote of the General Assembly of the United Nations.

2. The General Assembly may indicate any parts of this protocol which shall or shall not apply to any conventions designated in accordance with paragraph 1.

3. All actions contemplated by this protocol shall be consonant with the object and purpose of the instruments, particularly those arising out of the provisions of parts IV to VIII of this protocol.

4. The General Assembly shall determine the emoluments and other financial expenditures to be incurred in the operation of this protocol and the sources to be utilized in meeting them.

5. The Secretary-General of the United Nations shall be responsible for providing the Secretariat for all bodies other than national bodies contemplated in this protocol unless provided otherwise in the protocol.

6. Nothing in this protocol shall be interpreted as impairing the provisions of the Charter of the United Nations and of the constitutions of the specialized agencies. The General Assembly may provide other conditions concerning comparable provisions established by the United Nations or under its auspices, or by specialized agencies, or by inter-governmental organizations in particular regions.

---

[23] As stated earlier these suggestions are incomplete, deficient in all details which may be required and in drafting, as well as omitting many connected provisions which will be required, but the aim is to set forth what is hoped are the main topics on which the scheme is built and are indispensable in discussing it. Accordingly, numbering of articles is simply for purposes of easy reference.

Article 2

1. Each State Party to this protocol undertakes to take all necessary measures to bring the text of the instruments other than a convention to which it is a State Party before the competent constitutional authorities for appropriate action.

2. Each State Party shall inform the Secretary-General not later than two years after it has submitted the instrument to the authorities as provided in the preceding paragraph and furnish details of the measures, if any, taken by them.

3. Each State Party shall inform the Secretary-General as and when it has taken measures to comply with the provisions of the instrument, indicating whether such measures extend to the whole instrument or to parts of it, and in the latter case furnish any observations on difficulties which prevent compliance with the whole instrument.

4. The Secretary-General shall report to the General Assembly on the information received under the preceding two paragraphs and on any information which the General Assembly may decide upon in furtherance of the objectives of the aforementioned paragraphs.

Article 3

1. Member States of the United Nations and such other States as the General Assembly may determine shall inform the General Assembly through the Secretary-General, within one year of the adoption of this protocol by the General Assembly, whether they have brought the protocol to the attention of the competent constitutional authorities empowered to accede to this protocol and of the action taken or contemplated by them, including observations concerning any obstacles to accession to this protocol.

2. After the period specified in the preceding paragraph if a State referred to therein has not acceded to this protocol it shall submit at intervals determined by the General Assembly the information asked for under the provisions of paragraph 1.

PART II. NATIONAL REPORTING SYSTEM

Article 4

1. Each State Party undertakes to establish or designate a National Body, independent from its legislature, executive and the administration, to carry out the functions provided in this protocol.

2. States Parties undertake to submit to their National Bodies within one year of the entry into force of this protocol for the States Parties concerned reports on the measures they have taken to give effect to the provisions of the instrument or to such parts as they have accepted with such particulars as the National Bodies may request.

3. The National Bodies shall examine the aforementioned reports with the representatives of the States Parties and submit to their respective States Parties general appraisal on the reports, including such comments, conclusions, suggestions and recommendations as the National Bodies have agreed upon.

4. If any disagreement between States Parties and National Bodies arises which is not settled by any means available within the States Parties, the National Bodies concerned may by a two thirds majority vote of all their members refer any unresolved question to the Human Rights Board established under part III of this protocol.

5. The States Parties may at any time avail themselves of any advice or assistance from their National Bodies in preparing their reports for submission to the Human Rights Board as provided in part III of this protocol.

PART III. INTERNATIONAL REPORTING SYSTEM

Article 5

1. The General Assembly of the United Nations shall set up a Human Rights Board (hereafter referred to as the Board) consisting of twenty-one members elected by the General Assembly from candidates of high moral character and recognized competence in the field of human rights and fundamental freedoms nominated by Member States of the United Nations with functions and powers as set forth in this protocol.

2. The members of the Board shall be elected for a term of six years. At the initial election the President of the General Assembly shall choose by lot the names of one third of the members elected whose term of office shall terminate at the end of three years.

3. Outgoing members of the Board shall be eligible for re-election if re-nominated but the General Assembly shall take into account the need over a period of time for the Board to include nationals from every Member State.

4. Not more than one national of a Member State shall be elected or be a member of the Board at any time.

5. Consideration shall be given in the election to equitable geographical distribution of membership bearing in mind the size of the population whose human rights and fundamental freedoms are involved, and to the representation of different forms of civilization, of economic and social systems, of cultures, and of the principal legal systems, as well as to adequate representation of women and youth.

6. Every member of the Board shall serve in his personal capacity and, before taking up his duties, make a solemn declaration that he will perform his functions impartially and conscientiously.

Article 6

1. The Board shall elect its officers for a term of three years.

2. The Board shall establish its own rules of procedure, but they shall provide for a quorum of at least half the members, and decisions of the Board shall be made by majority vote of the members present unless provided otherwise in this protocol.

3. The Board shall normally meet at the Headquarters of the United Nations or at any of the headquarters of the regional commissions of the Economic and Social Council as determined by the General Assembly from time to time.

4. The Board shall report annually, through the Secretary-General, to the General Assembly on its activities under this protocol and those of the mediation committee that may be set up under part VII of this protocol.

PART IV.

Article 7

1. States Parties undertake to submit to the Board, through the Secretary-General, every three years after the entry into force of this protocol for the States Parties concerned reports relating to the instrument or part of it which they have accepted dealing with all measures taken and difficulties encountered in ensuring the application in practice of the provisions thereof, which shall include any unresolved questions between States Parties and their National Bodies as provided in part II, article 4, paragraph 4 of this protocol.

2. The Board shall study the reports and such further information as it may request or the States Parties may have supplied and transmit its observations on them to the States Parties.

3. States Parties shall be entitled to be present at meetings of the Board when their reports or further information furnished by them or at the

request of the Board are considered, and to make statements, offer explanations, and give assurances, as well as to submit their own observations on the observations of the Board made in accordance with the previous paragraph within such time limits as the Board may decide upon.

4. The General Assembly shall make arrangements for attendance and the mode of participation at meetings of the Board of representatives of specialized agencies and other United Nations bodies concerned, and for information to be supplied by them to the Board, as well as methods for co-operation between them and the Board to attain the objectives of any instrument.

PART V. GOOD OFFICES AND CONCILIATION (OPTIONAL)

Article 8

1. Each State Party may make a declaration either at the time of its accession or at any time thereafter by notification to the Secretary-General accepting this part of the protocol as regards any instrument or part of it, unconditionally or for a specified period, which shall be renewable, and on the condition of reciprocity, if any, if the instrument is a convention.

2. Each State Party agrees to forward to its National Body any communication from another State Party that it is not giving effect to any of the provisions of the instrument binding on itself if the matter is not settled between the States Parties within three months after the receipt by the receiving State of the initial communication.

3. Thereafter, if the National Body is unable within three months to settle the matter and certifies that all local remedies have been exhausted, either State may refer the matter to the Board.

4. If the Board, after obtaining all required information from the States is unable to resolve the matter, it may by a two thirds majority vote of its members submit its suggestions on the matter to the States.

5. Either State may notify the Board, through the Secretary-General, within six months, whether it accepts the suggestions of the Board and if not the reasons therefor, or that the matter has been settled by the States concerned in the meanwhile.

6. If the matter still remains unsettled it may be referred by the Board or by either State to a Mediation Committee under part VII of this protocol or to the International Court of Human Rights, provided the States concerned have made prior declarations or a declaration *ad hoc* accepting any such referral. Otherwise the Board shall submit its suggestions with all documentation to the General Assembly.

PART VI. COMMUNICATIONS FROM INDIVIDUALS, GROUPS OF
INDIVIDUALS OR NON-GOVERNMENTAL ORGANIZATIONS (OPTIONAL)

Article 9

1. Each State Party may make a declaration either at the time of its accession to this protocol or at any time thereafter by notification to the Secretary-General accepting this part of the protocol as regards any instrument or part of it, unconditionally or for a specified period, which shall be renewable.

2. Individuals, groups of individuals or non-governmental organizations claiming that any of the rights or freedoms enumerated in an instrument or part of it to which a State Party to this protocol has given acceptance has been violated by that State, provided all available local remedies have been exhausted, unless the application of the remedies is unreasonably prolonged or it is contended that no remedies exist, may submit a written communication to the National Body of the State concerned.

3. If the National Body considers a communication non-receivable, or an abuse of the right to submit such a communication, or if the communication is submitted indirectly on behalf of an individual, groups of individuals or a non-governmental organization concerned, the National Body may request the sender of the communication and the State Party involved to furnish all necessary information required by the National Body to decide upon any questions or problems arising therefrom.

4. The National Body when satisfied that the various conditions have been met shall deal with a communication in the following manner:

(a) if the communication emanates from an individual, group of individuals or a non-governmental organization within the territory and jurisdiction of the State concerned whose National Body has received the communication, the National Body shall make its suggestions to the State which shall inform the author of the communication of its views and if the matter is not settled the National Body shall forward its suggestions with all the documentation to the Board;

(b) if the communication emanates from an individual or groups of individuals or a non-governmental organization outside the territory or jurisdiction of the State concerned at the time when its National Body receives the communication, the National Body shall make its suggestions to the State and inform the author of the communication of the State's view, and if the matter is not settled, the National Body shall forward its suggestions with all the documentation to the Board.

Article 10

1. If the Board decides by a majority vote of two thirds of its members that a claim in any of the communications referred to it is well founded it may call upon the State concerned and the author of the communication to furnish the Board with such further information as it considers necessary and proceed to examine the communication with all the material in closed meetings, and, thereafter, forward its suggestions on the communication to the State concerned and to the individual, groups of individuals or the non-governmental organization concerned.

2. In the event that the State concerned does not accept the suggestions of the Board, the latter may refer the matter with all the documentation to a Mediation Committee or to the International Court of Human Rights, as may be agreed by the State concerned and the author of the communication, provided the State concerned has made a declaration beforehand or on an *ad hoc* basis accepting such referral, such a declaration also dispenses with the requirement of agreement between the State concerned and the author of a communication as aforementioned. Otherwise the Board shall submit a brief report on the matter to the General Assembly.

3. In the event of a referral to a mediation committee the State concerned and the author of the communication concerned shall be entitled to submit to either body further information as they may deem necessary.

PART VII. MEDIATION (OPTIONAL)

Article 11

Each State Party may make a declaration either at the time of its accession to this protocol or at any time thereafter by notification to the Secretary-General accepting this part of the protocol as regards any instrument or part of it, unconditionally or for a specified period, which shall be renewable, and on the condition of reciprocity if the instrument is a convention, as regards another State Party. Such declarations may also relate to the acceptance of this part of the protocol in relation to the provisions contained in parts V and VI of this protocol concerning referral of matters under those parts to mediation. Alternatively, such declaration may insofar as disputes between States Parties are concerned be made applicable without prior recourse to the provisions of part V on the condition of reciprocity.

Article 12

1. A panel of mediators shall be established under this protocol con-

sisting of persons whose names have been submitted to the Secretary-General by Member States and whose qualifications are not less than those required for members of the Board. The panel may consist of a national of each Member State.

2. The members of the panel may be designated to serve for such periods as the Member States may specify. After the specified period the same member or another member may be appointed to the panel by the Member State concerned.

3. The Secretary-General shall be responsible for keeping Member States and States Parties to this protocol informed of the membership of the panel initially and whenever any changes occur.

Article 13

1. Any matter submitted to mediation shall be determined by a Mediation Committee consisting of five members from the panel.

2. In a matter submitted to mediation under part V of this protocol or otherwise involving States Parties to this protocol, each State Party shall be entitled to nominate two members from the panel, the fifth member shall be chosen by the four members so nominated and he shall serve as President of the Mediation Committee. If several States Parties should have the same interest in the matter, they shall be considered as a single party for purposes of nominating the members of the Committee.

3. In a matter submitted to mediation under part VI of this protocol or otherwise involving a State Party and an individual, group of individuals or a non-governmental organization, each party to the matter shall be entitled to nominate two members from the panel, the fifth member shall be chosen by the four members so nominated and he shall serve as President of the Mediation Committee. If several individuals, group of individuals or non-governmental organizations should have the same interest in the matter they shall be considered as a single party for purposes of nominating the members of the Committee.

4. Each member of the Mediation Committee shall serve in the Committee in his personal capacity and, before taking up his duties, make a solemn declaration that he will perform his functions impartially and conscientiously.

Article 14

1. The Mediation Committee shall provide for its own rules of procedure, but any decision taken by it shall require the affirmative vote of at least two thirds of the members of the Committee. The rules shall provide

also for the contents of any report to be sent by the Committee to the Board for inclusion in the Board's annual reports to the General Assembly pursuant to the provisions of part III, article 6, paragraph 3 of this protocol.

2. The proceedings of the Committee may be held in closed meetings at the request of either party to a matter submitted to the Committee.

3. The Committee shall afford all opportunities to all parties concerned in the matter to present their points of view.

4. If efforts at mediation fail the Committee may submit the matter to the International Court of Human Rights, provided the State Parties concerned have made prior declarations accepting such a procedure, unconditionally or for a specified period, which shall be renewable. Otherwise the Mediation Committee shall include in its report to the Board under paragraph 1 of this article a summary of its proceedings.

PART VIII. INTERNATIONAL COURT OF HUMAN RIGHTS

Article 15

1. An International Court of Human Rights shall be established consisting of fifteen judges elected in their individual capacity from among persons of high moral character who possess the qualification required in their respective States for appointment to the highest judicial offices, nominated by Member States and States Parties to this protocol.

2. Each Member State or State Party to this protocol shall be entitled to nominate for election one candidate who may be a national of that State or any other Member State or State Party to this protocol.

3. The General Assembly shall elect the judges from the nominations made by an absolute majority vote of the Assembly.

4. No two judges may be nationals of the same State.

5. The judges of the court shall be elected for a period of seven years. They shall be eligible if renominated to be re-elected for one more term of seven years.

6. Each judge shall, before taking up his duties, make a solemn declaration in open court that he or she will perform his or her function impartially and conscientiously.

7. Each judge of the court and the Registrar of the court appointed by it in accordance with the provisions of this part of the protocol shall receive an annual salary and such allowances as may be determined by the General Assembly, which shall not be decreased during the term of office.

Article 16

1. The jurisdiction of the court shall comprise:

(a) all cases concerning the interpretation, observance, and application of an instrument;

(b) all matters referred to it under parts V, VI or VII of this protocol subject to the conditions provided therein;

(c) all other matters on which jurisdiction has been conferred on the court by any State Party.

2. Prior declarations by a State Party to this protocol accepting the Jurisdiction of the court relating to paragraph 1 (a) and 1 (c) may be made at the time of the State Party's accession to this protocol or at any time thereafter by notification to the Secretary-General or on an *ad hoc* basis. Under paragraph 1 (c) a State Party in its declaration may agree to recourse to the Court by individuals, groups of individuals or non-governmental organizations within the jurisdiction of that State Party claiming to be a victim of violation by that State Party of the provisions of an instrument or part of it which that State Party has accepted. Any such declarations may extend to all the instruments, to some parts of them or to any particular part of them.

3. As regards acceptance of jurisdiction set forth in paragraph 1 (b) the conditions for declarations prescribed in parts V, VI or VII of this protocol shall apply.

4. A State Party to this protocol making a declaration subject to condition of reciprocity may waive the condition by notification to the Secretary-General in any particular case or matter or on an *ad hoc* basis, or the condition may be set aside by the court if the court considers the condition to be opposed to the object and purpose of an instrument concerned only if it so decides by a vote of at least ten judges of the court.

Article 17

1. Nine judges shall constitute a quorum for the transaction of any business of the court.

2. All decisions and judgements of the court shall be by a majority vote of the judges present, unless provided otherwise in this part of the protocol.

3. The court shall decide upon any question relating to its jurisdiction.

4. The judgement or decision of the court shall be final. It shall state the reasons on which it was based, and include any separate opinion of any judge agreeing or dissenting from such judgement or decision.

5. If the Court finds that there has been a violation of a right or freedom which is in conflict with the obligations accepted by a State, the court shall

afford just satisfaction to the injured party by ensuring the enjoyment of the right or freedom violated or decide on the suitable remedy, including fair compensation.

6. Any disagreement as to the meaning or scope of a judgement or decision of the court shall be decided by the court at the request of any party concerned within such time limits as the court may lay down for the submission of such a request.

Article 18

1. The court shall draw up its own rules of procedure for the purposes of carrying out its functions.

2. The rules of procedure shall include rules relating to:

(a) election of President and Vice-Presidents of the court;

(b) the participation on an *ad hoc* basis of a judge national of a State party to a case or matter before the court in the absence of such a national judge sitting in the court;

(c) the method of presentation of cases or other matters to the court;

(d) the procedure to be followed in the conduct of the court's proceedings and in obtaining information relating thereto;

(e) occupation of judges which may interfere with their judicial functions as judges of the court;

(f) participation of judges of the court in proceedings relating to any case or matter in which they have previously taken part in any capacity whatsoever;

(g) the manner of appointment, and the appointment, of the court's Registrar and his functions;

(h) the preparation and contents of an annual report on the activities of the court to the General Assembly.

Article 19

1. The court may give an advisory opinion on the interpretation, observance or application of any instrument or on the operation of any parts of this protocol at the request of:

(a) the General Assembly of the United Nations;

(b) any other organ or body designated by the General Assembly;

(c) the Human Rights Board or the Mediation Committee provided for in parts III and VII of this protocol;

(d) a State Party to this protocol which has made a prior declaration at any time by notification to the Secretary-General accepting such recourse to the court, unconditionally or for a specified period, which shall be renewable, or on an *ad hoc* basis;

(e) individuals, groups of individuals or non-governmental organizations within the jurisdiction of a State Party to this protocol.

2. Questions upon which an advisory opinion of the court is requested shall be submitted to the court by a written request containing an exact statement of the question upon which an opinion is required, accompanied by all documents likely to throw light upon the question.

Article 20

1. A quorum of at least twelve judges of the court shall be required for proceedings relating to an advisory opinion.

2. An advisory opinion shall be given by a majority of not less than ten judges of the court.

3. The court shall adopt rules of procedure for the purposes of carrying out its functions with respect to advisory opinions taking into account the other provisions in this part of the protocol, including the rules of procedures adopted under them, to the extent to which the court recognizes any of them to be applicable.

PART IX. RESERVATIONS AND DECLARATIONS[24]

Article 21

1. A State at the time of acceding to this protocol shall declare in regard to each instrument designated by the General Assembly in accordance with article 1 of part I of this protocol whether it accepts the whole instrument or parts of it, indicating in the latter case the exact parts or part which it accepts. If the declaration relates to part only of an instrument the State may at any subsequent time by notification to the Secretary-General accept other parts or the whole instrument.

2. As regards reservations to conventions designated by the General Assembly in part I of this protocol the provisions on reservations contained in the conventions shall apply, otherwise in the absence of any such provi-

---

[24] This part is set out in a very preliminary manner and it may eventually be the part where all provisions concerning its subject matter have to be included. In the draft there are provisions for declarations inserted where they were thought to be most relevant for purposes of getting an over-all view of the provisions and for making discussion of them easier.

sions the relevant articles of the Vienna Convention on the Law of Treaties may be made applicable if so determined by the General Assembly.

3. While no reservation shall be permitted to parts I, II, III, IV of this protocol, States Parties bound by reporting procedures or other provisions in conventions may make reservations concerning subject matters on which they have already assumed obligations by being parties to those conventions. In this and other regards as it relates to conventions the application of the provisions of this protocol is subject to decisions of the General Assembly under part I, article 1, paragraph 2 of this protocol.

4. Any reservations or declarations made to this protocol shall not affect any matters already under consideration or already initiated under parts III, IV, V, VI, VII or VIII of this protocol if the State Party is bound by any such parts by a prior declaration.

PART X. FINAL CLAUSES

Article 22

1. This protocol is open to accession by all Member States of the United Nations and by any other State as invited by the General Assembly of the United Nations.

2. Accession shall be effected by a deposit of an instrument of accession with the Secretary-General of the United Nations.

Article 23

This protocol shall enter into force on the thirtieth day after the date of the deposit with the Secretary-General of the second instrument of accession, and for States acceding thereafter within the same time limit.

Article 24

1. A request for the revision of this protocol may be made at any time by one third of the Member States of the United Nations by means of notification in writing addressed to the Secretary-General.

2. The General Assembly shall decide upon the steps, if any, to be taken in respect to such request.

3. The General Assembly shall every five years after this protocol is in effect carry out a review of its operation and request for this purpose such documents and other material it may determine are required.

Article 25

1. This protocol, of which the Arabic, Chinese, English, French, Russian and Spanish texts are equally authentic, shall be deposited in the archives of the United Nations.

2. The Secretary-General of the United Nations shall transmit certified copies of this protocol to all States who are eligible to accede to it.

CHAPTER VIII

IMPLEMENTING THE INTERNATIONAL COVENANTS ON HUMAN RIGHTS

DR. B.G. RAMCHARAN*

> ... Our task now is to see to it that these new Covenants are
> strictly observed everywhere.

> Statement by Mr. Nasinovsky (USSR), in
> the General Assembly, after the adoption
> of the Covenants on 16 December 1966.**

Upon the adoption of the International Covenants on Human Rights in the General Assembly on 16 December 1966, Mr. Abdul Rahman Pazhwak of Afghanistan, the President of the General Assembly, stated: "I think that those who realize the importance of this achievement would feel able to entitle me to congratulate the United Nations . . . Universal respect for human rights is inseparable from world peace . . . At the root of all strife and tyranny, in the present as in the past, lies a violation of human rights in one form or another".[1] Secretary-General, U Thant declared: "It is my sincere belief that our decision today will bring us nearer to the kind of world our organization is committed to build. I earnestly hope that, by early action, which Member States alone can take, the International Covenants on Human Rights will soon become a living reality".[2]

The International Covenant on Economic, Social and Cultural Rights[3] finally became a living reality when it entered into force on 3 January 1976. The International Covenant on Civil and Political Rights and the Optional Protocol thereto entered into force on 23 March 1976.[4] These instruments are of historic significance inasmuch as they constitute the first universally promulgated code of human rights binding upon States which have accep-

---

*All views expressed in this paper are those of the author in his purely personal capacity.
**A/PV.1496, para. 145.
[1] *Ibid.*, para. 64.
[2] *Ibid.*, para. 75.
[3] As at 1 June 1978, 51 States had ratified or acceded to this instrument.
[4] As at 1 June 1978, 49 States had ratified or acceded to the Covenant and 19 States to the Protocol.

ted them. Their entry into force represents a major achievement in the work begun since the inception of the United Nations to establish an effective International Bill of Rights.

This paper will look at the implementation provisions of the Covenants and the Optional Protocol, particularly at action taken to bring them into operation. In so doing we shall bear in mind how the drafters of the Covenants envisaged that their procedures of implementation should be applied. We shall also look at certain practical issues which could usefully be borne in mind at the commencement of their work by the Human Rights Committee established under the Covenant on Civil and Political Rights and the Working Group decided upon by the Economic and Social Council for the examination of reports submitted under the Covenant on Economic, Social and Cultural Rights.[5]

A. THE INTERNATIONAL COVENANT ON ECONOMIC, SOCIAL AND CULTURAL RIGHTS

Under the International Covenant on Economic, Social and Cultural Rights each State Party undertakes to take steps, individually and through international assistance and co-operation, especially economic and technical, to the maximum of its available resources, with a view to achieving progressively the full realization of the rights recognized in the Covenant by all appropriate means, including the adoption of legislative measures (Article 2, paragraph 1). Among the rights recognized in the Covenant are the right of peoples to self-determination and to dispose freely of their natural wealth and resources; the equal right of men and women to the enjoyment of economic, social and cultural rights; the right to work; the right to just and favourable conditions of work; trade union rights; the right to social security; the right to protection and assistance of the family; the right to an adequate standard of living; the right to the

---

[5] See generally, F. Capotorti, "The International Measures of Implementation included in the Covenants on Human Rights", *(Nobel Symposium* 7, Oslo, September 25-27, 1967), Stockholm, 1968, pp. 132-148. E. Schwelb, "Notes on the Early Legislative History of the Measures of Implementation of the Human Rights Covenants", *Mélanges Modinos,* Paris, 1968, pp. 270-289. "The Nature of the Obligations of the States Parties to the International Covenant on Civil and Political Rights", *René Cassin Amicorum Discipulorumque Liber I,* Paris, 1969, pp. 270-289. "Civil and Political Rights. The International Measures of Implementation", *A.J., I.L.* Vol. 62, pp. 827-868 (1968). "Some Aspects of the Measures of Implementation of the International Covenant on Economic, Social and Cultural Rights", *Revue des droits de l'homme,* Vol. 1 no. 3, pp. 363-377 (1969). "Some aspects of the International Covenants on Human Rights of December, 1966". *Nobel Symposium* 7, pp. 103-129.

enjoyment of the highest attainable standard of physical and mental health; the right to education; the right to take part in cultural life; and the right to enjoy the benefits of scientific progress. /

Under Article 2, paragraph 2, the States Parties to the Covenant undertake to guarantee that the rights enunciated in the Covenant will be exercised without discrimination of any kind as to race, colour, sex, language, religion, political or other opinion, national or social origin, property, birth or other status.

1. Implementation provisions

Under Article 16, the States Parties to the Covenant undertake to submit to the Economic and Social Council reports on the measures which they have adopted and the progress made in achieving the observance of the rights recognized therein. Article 18 also provides that the Economic and Social Council may make arrangements with the specialized agencies in respect of their reporting to it on the progress made in achieving the observance of the provisions of the Covenant falling within the scope of their activities. Under Article 17, the reports are to be furnished in stages in accordance with a programme to be established by the Economic and Social Council within one year of the entry into force of the Covenant after consultation with the States Parties and the specialized agencies concerned.

2. Inter-Agency Consultations

In preparation for the entry into force of the Covenant, the Division of Human Rights held consultations with the specialized agencies within the framework of the activities of the United Nations Administrative Committee on Co-ordination concerning various matters pertaining to the implementation of the Covenants. Meetings were held on 9-10 September 1974 and from 14-16 January 1976 at which questions relating to the implementation of the Covenants were examined as they affected the United Nations and the specialized agencies concerned. These meetings agreed, *inter alia,* on suggestions for the reporting programme to be established under Article 17 of the Covenant on Economic, Social and Cultural Rights, on suggestions for the submission of reports by specialized agencies, and on the modalities for the transmission to the specialized agencies, as appropriate, of copies of the reports submitted by States Parties under the Covenants. As regards the reporting programme under the International Covenant on Economic, Social and Cultural Rights, it was suggested that the Economic and Social Council might wish to adopt provisional arrangements whereby within a six-year period States Parties would report under Article 16 of the Covenant and the specialized agencies concerned under Article 18, in the following stages: First year: rights covered by articles 6-7, second year: rights covered by article 11, third year: rights covered by articles 13-14, fourth year: rights covered by article 12, fifth year: rights covered by articles 9-10, sixth year: rights covered by articles 8 and 15.

3. Action by the Economic and Social Council for the implementation of the Covenant

Following the entry into force of the Covenant on 3 January 1976 the Economic and Social Council at its organizational session in January 1976 requested the Secretary-General to carry out on its behalf consultations with the States Parties and the specialized agencies, under Article 17 (1) of the Covenant, regarding the establishment by the Council of a programme for the submission of reports by the States Parties and the specialized agencies on the observance of the rights set forth in the Covenant, and to prepare a note with recommendations on procedures for the implementation of the Covenant, taking into account the provisions of that instrument and the relevant decisions on the rationalization of the work of the Council. A note prepared by the Secretary-General in accordance with the above-mentioned decisions of the Council was submitted to the sixtieth session of the Council.[6]

In paragraph 26 of this note the Secretary-General made recommendations to the Council concerning, *inter alia,* the programme for reports from the States Parties and the specialized agencies; the submission of the first set of reports; an outline of headings to be proposed to Governments for their assistance and guidance in the submission of reports; and the study of the various reports and comments. On the basis of this note the Economic and Social Council discussed the question at its sixtieth session[7] held in 1976 and on 11 May 1976 adopted resolution 1988 (LX) in which it established the following programme under which the States Parties to the Covenant will furnish their reports in biennial stages: First stage: rights covered by articles 6-9; second stage; rights covered by articles 10-12; third stage: rights covered by articles 13-15. The Council invited States Parties to the Covenant to submit to the Secretary-General in accordance with the foregoing programme, reports on the measures that they have adopted and

[6] E/5764.
[7] See E/CN.4/SR.1987, 1988 and 1999.

the progress made in achieving the observance of the rights recognized in the Covenant, and to indicate, when necessary, factors and difficulties affecting the degree of fulfilment of their obligations under the Covenant. The reports on the rights included in the first stage of the programme were scheduled for transmission by 1 September 1977, and the reports on the subsequent stages at biennial intervals thereafter.

The Council also called upon the specialized agencies to submit to the Economic and Social Council, in accordance with the same programme, and bearing in mind the provisions of article 16, paragraph 2, of the Covenant, reports on the progress made in achieving the observance of the provisions of the Covenant falling within the scope of their activities. The reports on the rights included in the first stage of the programme were scheduled for transmission by 1 December 1977, and the reports on the subsequent stages at biennial intervals thereafter.

The Council also decided that: (a) A sessional working group of the Economic and Social Council, with appropriate representation of States Parties to the Covenant, and with due regard to equitable geographical distribution, shall be established by the Council whenever reports are due for consideration by the Council, for the purpose of assisting it in the consideration of such reports; (b) Representatives of specialized agencies concerned may take part in the proceedings of the working group when matters falling within their respective fields of competence are considered. An appeal was made to States to include, if possible, in their delegations to the relevant sessions of the Economic and Social Council, members competent in the subject-matters under consideration.

During the discussion in the Council the representative of Italy thought that the resolution adopted by the Council provided for a speedy and smooth procedure which had various positive aspects: it avoided placing upon States a heavy reporting burden under the Covenant; if fully respected the provisions of article 16 of the Covenant as far as the main and direct responsibility of the Council was concerned, without excluding the contribution of the Commission on Human Rights as outlined in article 19; it ensured[8] the participation of experts in the examination of the reports of the States parties without creating *ad hoc* bodies or establishing special sessions of the existing ones; finally, it settled the aspects connected with the competence and reporting obligations of the specialized agencies.[9] The representative of Canada, on the other hand, regretted that the Council

---

[8] "Foresees" is perhaps more accurate than "ensures".
[9] E/SR.1999, p. 5.

had not placed adequate stress on the need for expert assistance in the consideration of the reports which States were asked to submit under the Covenant.[10] She feared that the machinery provided for in operative paragraph 9 of resolution 1988 (LX) would not ensure thorough consideration of those reports by persons possessing expertise in the various fields covered. Her delegation also regretted that nowhere in the draft resolution was there any provision for enlisting the services of the Commission on Human Rights, which at its thirty-second session had expressed its desire to play a role in the implementation of the Covenant. She emphasized her delegation's understanding that the task entrusted to the Council's Working Group under paragraph 9 (a) of Council resolution 1988 (LX) would allow of its recommending to the Economic and Social Council that reports, or parts of reports, should be transmitted to the Commission on Human Rights for study, as provided in article 19 of the Covenant.[11] The representative of Austria trusted that the Council would avail itself of the possibility provided in article 19 of the Covenant of transmitting reports to the Commission on Human Rights, particularly as the Commission had expressed its readiness to assume the responsibilities involved. The representative of Yugoslavia also thought that the resolution should have envisaged the active participation of the Commission on Human Rights.[12]

4.   The Working Group of the Council

As regards the composition of the sessional Working Group of the Council, certain guidelines were contained in resolution 1988 (LX), viz. that there should be appropriate representation of States parties to the Covenant, that there should be equitable geographical distribution and that Governments should include in their delegations members competent in the subject-matter under consideration by the Working Group. However, when the establishment of the Working Group arose in the Council in 1978, the resolution gave rise to conflicting interpretations. In paragraph 9 (a) of the resolution, the Council had decided that "A sessional working group of the Economic and Social Council, with appropriate representation of States parties to the Covenant, and with due regard to equitable geographical distribution, shall be established by the Council whenever reports are due for consideration by the Council, for the purpose of assis-

[10] Cf. the proposal made in the Third Committee of the General Assembly in 1966 for a committee of experts on economic, social and cultural rights – A/6546, pp. 10-13.
[11] E/SR.1999, pp. 4-5.
[12] Ibid., p. 5.

ting it in the consideration of such reports". In paragraph 3 (d) of its decision 1978/1, the Council decided "to request Mr. V.N. Martynenko, Vice-President of the Council, to undertake consultations on the composition of the sessional working group . . . ; to invite members of the Council to notify the Secretary-General as early as possible of their interest in participating in that working group, without prejudice to the final decision of the Council on the composition thereof to be adopted at the outset of the first regular session, 1978; and to request the Secretariat to make an interim report on the notifications received by 15 March 1978". Pursuant to this decision, the Secretariat received notifications of interest from fifteen members of the Council including five States that were not Parties to the Covenant (see E/1978/L.19).

When the resolution and decision referred to above were approved by the Council, there was no record of the discussions which could have clarified the purport of the above-quoted texts. Consequently, interpretation of paragraph 9 (a) of ECOSOC resolution 1988 (LX) had to be based on its wording in the context of the entire resolution, taking into consideration the relevant provisions of the Covenant.

It was argued on one side that the words "with appropriate representation of States parties to the Covenant" in paragraph 9 (a) meant that only States parties to the Covenant which are members of the council could participate in the working group. This argument was supported "on the basis of generally accepted principles of international law";[13] more specifically that "in ratifying the Covenant States assumed responsibilities and also acquired particular rights so that it would be illogical for States parties and States not parties to the Covenant, as members of the sessional working group, to have the same rights in considering reports from States parties to the Covenant".[14] It was further argued that "if States not parties to the Covenant were allowed to join the sessional working group, States parties to the Covenant would be placed in an unequal situation as the non-party States would have no obligations but would have the right to discuss the reports of other States, while the States parties in addition to that right would have their obligations under the Covenant. That situation would be in contradiction with one of the basic principles of contemporary international law or, in other words, of *jus cogens,* namely, the sovereign equality of States. Under contemporary international treaty law, international instruments created rights and obligations for the parties only,

---

[13] Mr. Martynenko (USSR), E/1978/SR.9, p. 3.
[14] *Ibid.*

and any bodies that might be established to consider reports submitted under a convention were composed of representatives or experts from States parties".[15]

On the other side, it was argued that the sessional working group was established by the Council for the purpose of assisting it in the consideration of reports submitted by States Parties to the Covenant. In establishing the working group, the Council attached two conditions, namely, that it should have "appropriate representation of States Parties to the Covenant" and that due regard should be given to "equitable geographical representation". In this context, unless records clearly indicated otherwise, "appropriate" representation cannot be taken to mean "exclusive" representation.[16] Moreover, in paragraph 10 of the same resolution (i.e. resolution 1988 (LX)), the Council appealed to States "to include, if possible, in their delegations to the relevant sessions of the Economic and Social Council, members competent in the subject matter under consideration". This was to ensure that all members of the Council including those that are not parties to the Covenant should have representatives competent to discuss the subject matters of the reports submitted by Parties to the Covenant.

It was further argued that in its decision 1978/1, the Council had invited *members* of the Council to notify the Secretary-General of their interest in participating in the working group. Although this was done without prejudice to the final decision of the Council on the composition of the working group, the fact remained that the invitation was addressed to all members of the Council including States that were not Parties to the Covenant.[17]

It was pointed out also, that article 16 of the Covenant provided that reports from States parties to the Covenant shall be submitted to the Secretary-General who shall transmit copies "to the Economic and Social Council for consideration in accordance with the provisions of the present Covenant". While it was clear that reports were submitted only by Parties to the Covenant, nowhere in the Covenant was it indicated or implied that consideration by the Economic and Social Council should in the first instance be made only by those members that are Parties to the Covenant.[18]

[15] Mr. Kudryavtsev (Byelorussian SSR), E/1978/SR.9, p. 7. See similarly Mr. Zachmann, (German Democratic Republic), *ibid.*, p. 11.

[16] Mr. Fauris (France), E/1978/SR.9, p. 13.

[17] Mr. Fauris (France), E/1978/SR.9, pp. 4-5.

[18] See Mr. Merkel (Federal Republic of Germany), E/1978/SR.9, p. 5: "the proposal that the working group should consist only of States parties to the Covenant had been discussed and rejected at the time of the adoption of the Covenant by the General Assembly". See similarly Mrs. Wells (USA), *ibid.*, p. 6.

On the basis of these points, it was argued that the phrase "with appropriate representation of States parties to the Covenant" meant that States parties to the Covenant should be represented by an appropriate number on the sessional working group. It did not require from a legal point of view that the sessional working group should be composed exclusively of those members of the Council that are Parties to the Covenant. The representative of the United States stated at the 12th meeting of the Council that his delegation and others had obtained an opinion from the United Nations Legal Counsel confirming this interpretation of resolution 1988 (LX).[19] Some delegations requested that the Legal Counsel be formally asked to advise the Council on the interpretation of resolution 1988 but the view prevailed that "the problem was political and not legal" and therefore the request for a legal opinion was not acceded to by the majority of the Council.[20] However, the Council did decide to allow members wishing to do so to bring legal officers into the informal consultations.[21]

In the end a compromise was adopted by the Council by which it decided: (a) to establish, for the purpose of assisting the Council in the consideration of reports, a sessional working group composed of 15 members of the Council which are also States parties to the Covenant, 3 members from the Group of African States, 3 members from the Group of Asian States, 3 members from the Group of Eastern European States, 3 members from the Group of Latin American States and 3 members from the group of Western European and other states; (b) to invite the President of the Council, after due consultations with the regional groups to appoint the members of the working group in accordance with paragraph (a) above; (c) to invite to participate in the proceedings of the working group as observers: (i) other members of the Council; (ii) States parties to the Covenant which are not members of the Council; (iii) Member States which express interest in the deliberations of the working group; (iv) the representatives of the specialized agencies concerned, when matters falling within their respective fields of competence are considered; (d) to request the working group to prepare for the consideration of the Council recommendations on its methods of work for the consideration of the reports of States parties to the Covenant; and (e) to review this decision at its first regular session in 1981, taking into account the principle of equitable geographical distribution and the increase in the number of States parties to

---

[19] E/1978/SR.12, p. 7.
[20] Mr. Abdallah (Tunisia), E/1978/SR.9, p. 16.
[21] E/1978/SR.9, p. 17.

the International Covenant on Economic, Social and Cultural Rights. Because the decision on the composition of the Working group was taken practically at the end of the Council's session, it was not possible for the working group to meet during this session. The working group will now meet in 1979 at the Spring session of the Council.

A number of issues still remain to be ironed out. The working group has been asked to submit to the Council, recommendations on its methods of work for the consideration of reports. Some of the issues which will engage its attention were touched upon in the Council during the debate on the composition of the working group. Regarding the role of the working group, Council resolution 1988 had stated that its purpose would be to assist the Council in the consideration of reports. What is meant by "assistance" is not yet clear. Thus, in the Council in 1978 it was envisaged "either that the group would make an expert evaluation of reports before they were considered by the Council or that the group would make a more substantive examination of them and submit a general report to the Council, so as to reduce the work to be done in plenary meetings". The first view was preferred by the speaker in question.[22] A related view was that the group "should simply help to prepare for the Council's general discussion of reports from States parties".[23] Another view was that "the role of the working group would be to prepare working papers for consideration by the Council".[24]

Will the working group follow the methods of bodies such as the Committee on the Elimination of Racial Discrimination or the Human Rights Committee, which consider the reports of States parties country by country, in the presence of a representative of the Government concerned, or will it consider reports collectively on an article-by-article basis? The preference in the Council seems to have been for article-by-article examination. Thus the representative of Finland suggested that the working group should review reports "on a global basis, article-by-article rather than country-by-country".[25] Similarly, the representative of the USSR stated that "the Group would not consider the report of each country in detail but would submit general views on the implementation of groups of articles of the Covenant by States parties as a whole and on any difficulties encountered by States in implementing particular articles".[26] The represen-

[22] Mr. Marshall (UK), E/1978/SR.9, p. 9.
[23] Mr. Tornudd (Finland), E/1978/SR.9, p. 9.
[24] Mr. Abdallah (Tunisia), E/1978/SR.12, p. 10.
[25] E/1978/SR.9, p. 9.
[26] *Ibid.,* p. 12.

tative of the Federal Republic of Germany also felt that it would be "best for the reports to be considered on an article-by-article, rather than on a country-by country-basis".[27] In line with this view it was suggested, and the Council agreed, that the Secretariat should "prepare analytical reports (of the reports of States Parties) in order to facilitate the work of the sessional working group".[28]

It was also the clear understanding of delegations which voted in favour of the resolution adopted by the Council that "the intention was that the working group should not vote" and that decisions of the working group should be taken by consensus.[29] The representative of Finland expressly stated that "his delegation had finally sponsored the draft resolution on the express understanding that the working group would take its decisions by consensus".[30]

Regarding the role of the Council itself, it was pointed out that "the role of the Council would remain, as it would consider the reports of the working group established to assist it".[31] It was also underlined that "the working group was intended to be an ephemeral body, not a permanent subsidiary body of the Council, and it could therefore not replace the Council in the consideration of reports".[32] Neither, it was said, could it delegate its tasks under Article 16 of the Covenant completely to a limited sessional organ.[33]

A pertinent assessment of the arrangements decided upon by the Council in 1978 was offered by the representative of the United Kingdom. His delegation, he said, was concerned at a number of significant omissions from the Council's decision: for instance, there was no indication of when the Working group was to be established, or of how long it would take to formulate recommendations on its methods of evaluating reports from States parties. Moreover, there was no way of ensuring that, should members of the Group fail to agree on a given issue they would not resort to a vote. The decision also failed, he said, to indicate when the Council would consider the reports submitted by the working group.[34]

In addition to the above observations it might be asked whether it is a

---

[27] *Ibid.,* p. 14.
[28] E/1978/SR.12, p. 14.
[29] E/1978/SR.12, p. 11. See also Mr. Smirnov (USSR), E/1978/SR.9, p. 12 "there should be no need for the working group to take any votes".
[30] E/1978/SR.12, p. 8. See also Mr. Abdallah (Tunisia), *ibid.,* p. 10.
[31] Mr. Smirnov (USSR), E/1978/SR.9, p. 11.
[32] Mr. Fauris (France), E/1978/SR.12, p. 5.
[33] *Idem,* E/1978/SR.9, p. 4.
[34] E/1978/SR.12, pp. 8-9.

satisfactory state of affairs that such a temporary arrangement has been adopted. The existence and composition of the working group will be subject to review in 1981. If some methods of work are decided upon in 1979, will they be open to changes soon after, in 1981? If the working group is not re-established in 1981 will new arrangements have to be introduced then for the examination of reports? This atmosphere of uncertainty is not the healthiest environment in which to commence the functioning of the Covenant.

Three emerging patterns can be discerned at the 1978 session of the Council. In the first place, there was a partial tendency to follow the pattern of the Committee on the Elimination of Racial Discrimination and the Human Rights Committee inasmuch as these bodies are composed of persons elected from nominees of States parties. However, in the case of the Council's working group, there was no election, and the members will not necessarily sit in their individual capacities. Secondly, there were attempts to assimilate the role of the sessional working group to that of the Human Rights Committee inasmuch as it was suggested that the reports of States parties should first be examined by the sessional working group and that the reports of this working group, in turn, should be considered by the Council, in like manner as the Council considers the annual report of the Human Rights Committee. On the other hand, there appears to be a departure from the practice of the Committee on the Elimination of Racial Discrimination and the Human Rights Committee which examine reports on a country-by country basis. Thirdly, an incipient movement can be detected back to an idea advanced, but not adopted, in the General Assembly in 1966. It may be recalled that it had been proposed then that a Committee similar to the Human Rights Committee should be established to consider reports received under the International Covenant on Economic, Social and Cultural Rights. However, this idea was defeated in favour of consideration of reports by the Council. Now, in the Council itself, the majority view prevailed that reports should be examined initially by a working group composed principally of States parties to the Covenants. One difference between the 1966 idea and the 1978 decision of the Council is that as pointed out above, the working group is to be composed of representatives of States instead of persons sitting in their individual capacities.

5. The Future?

The Working Group and the Council will need to be mindful of two basic criteria which lie at the heart of the implementation system of the Covenant: that "the reports submitted in pursuance of the Covenant should receive adequate treatment and study, and the study of the reports should lead to meaningful recommendations providing an incentive for international co-operation and national action".[35] They should also heed the words of caution expressed by the Irish delegate to the Third Committee in 1966: "If implementation was limited to a reporting system (as it is) it must be ensured that the reports submitted were given very careful and thorough scrutiny, otherwise there would be no advance over the existing system of periodic reports on human rights".[36]

The basic premise, (advanced by the Polish delegate in the Third Committee in 1966 speaking of the progressive nature of the obligations undertaken under the Covenant), was that ". . . the obligation by which a State was bound under the terms of the Covenant, although progressive, was nevertheless a real obligation from the outset, and while the extent of the obligation depended on the possibilities of each State it was always feasible in the light of these possibilities to see immediately whether its contents were being fulfilled".[37] The Covenant imposes on the States parties "An obligation to strive for general progress" in the field covered.[38] The words of caution expressed by the Bulgarian delegate should also be kept in mind: "legislative enactments could not by themselves ensure the implementation of rights . . . ".[39]

As regard the techniques which should be followed, Mr. Paolini (France) said in the Third Committee in 1966 that "the Council should act within the field of its general competence under the Charter and should extend positive assistance – perhaps even technical assistance – for the purpose of promoting practical progress in a country in the field of human rights. The reports should be considered not as means of attacking other countries but as a manifestation of international solidarity and an effort of international co-operation in the field of human rights".[40] Mr. MacDonald (Canada)

---

[35] Mr. Mommersteeg (Netherlands), A/C.3/SR.1400, para. 13.
[36] *Ibid.*, para. 2.
[37] A/C.3/SR.1396, para. 2.
[38] Lady Gaitskell (UK), A/C.3/SR.1396, para. 26.
[39] A/C.3/SR.1396, para. 10.
[40] A/C.3/SR.1399, para. 15.

felt that the Council should seek to provide guidelines for the implementation of the Covenant and for domestic programmes. Mr. Mommersteeg (Netherlands) suggested that the Council "might look for ways and means on the basis of the reports received of promoting the full realization of the rights recognized in the Covenant".[41] His delegation "considered that the implementation of economic and social rights was connected with the economic situation in countries and therefore to some extent with international co-operation in developing countries". "The Council was called upon to play an important role in those matters and it should accordingly take all possible action at the policy-making level."[42]

6. Report of the Economic and Social Council to the General Assembly

Under article 21 the Economic and Social Council may submit from time to time to the General Assembly reports with recommendations of a general nature and a summary of the information received from the States parties to the present Covenant and the specialized agencies on the measures taken and the progress made in achieving general observance of the rights recognized in the present Covenant.[43] This provision was carefully considered in the Third Committee in 1966. Mr. Saksena (India) thought that the reports of the Council "should form the basis for discussion in the Assembly".[44] Mr. Mohammed (Nigeria) "wanted the Economic and Social Council's reports to be the main source of guidance for the General Assembly".[45]

The words "from time to time" were adopted by a vote of 50-27-17. Mr. Carpio (Guatemala) had objected to them because they did not indicate any specific periodicity.[46] Mr. Saksena (India) and Mr. Mirza (Pakistan) said that the words had been deliberately used by their drafters to leave the question of periodicity to the Council and to give it maximum latitude.[47] Mr. Nasinovsky (USSR) felt that the Council's reports "could take several different forms. For example, the Council might submit a single report in three parts or three separate reports, possibly spread out over a three-year period".[48]

As to the words "general recommendations", the Nigerian representa-

---

[41] A/C.3/SR.1400, para. 14.
[42] *Ibid.*, para. 15.
[43] See also pp. 23-24 below.
[44] A/C.3/SR.1403, para. 4.
[45] *Ibid.*, para. 5.
[46] *Ibid.*, para. 12.
[47] *Ibid.*, paras. 15, 30. See similarly para. 57.
[48] *Ibid.*, para. 11.

tive stated that the sponsors of the text had intended the word "general" to give the Council the widest possible latitude in making recommendations referring to any part of the Covenant.[49] The United States representative referred to the competence of the Council under article 62 of the Charter which authorized the Council to make "recommendations" without any qualifying adjective.[50] Mr. Aboul Nasr (United Arab Republic) assured the United States representative that the sponsors never had in mind any restriction of the Council's competence as defined in the Charter.[51] Mr. Mohammed (Nigeria) felt that the phrase "recommendations of a general nature" was in keeping with the terms of article 62 of the Charter. However, he doubted whether any member of the Third Committee would wish the Council to be asked to make specific recommendations.[52]

Mr. Elmendorf (USA) referring to the clarifications given by two of the sponsors of the text and having regard to article 24 of the text of the Covenant expressed "the understanding that the Economic and Social Council would be able to make such recommendations under the Covenant as it could also make under the terms of article 62 of the Charter".[53]

As to the words "general observance" Mr. Mohammed (Nigeria) said that the word 'general' "was intended to give the Council the greatest possible latitude for formulating its recommendations, which themselves had to be general" (sic).[54]

Mr. Saksena (India) stated "the expression 'general observance' would allow the Council to make general observations on the general implementation of economic, social and cultural rights throughout the world".[55] Mr. Mirza (Pakistan) expressed his agreement with the views of the Indian and Nigerian representatives on the interpretation of the words 'general observance'.[56]

7. General Remarks

Perhaps the greatest advantage of the fact that reports on economic, social and cultural rights are to be considered by the Economic and Social Council is that the Council has a unique opportunity to integrate human

[49] *Ibid.*, para. 20.
[50] *Ibid.*, para. 21.
[51] *Ibid.*, para. 22.
[52] *Ibid.*, para. 23.
[53] *Ibid.*, para. 25.
[54] *Ibid.*, para. 26.
[55] *Ibid.*, para. 28.
[56] *Ibid.*, para. 31.

rights with economic, social and cultural questions in general.[57] One cannot help feeling at the present time that though human rights should be an essential part of the integrated approach to development this is often not recognized enough. It should be one of the objectives of the Council to get this idea across and to give effect to it. The Council could use its consideration of reports to link economic, social and cultural rights with action going on under other parts of its programme and in related bodies such as the Commission on Social Development, the United Nations University, the Regional Economic Commissions etc.

The Declaration on Social Progress and Development adopted by the General Assembly on 11 December 1969 (resolution 2542 (XXIV) emphasized in its eighth preambular paragraph "the interdependence of economic and social development in the wider process of growth and change, as well as the importance of a strategy of integrated development which takes full account at all stages of its essential aspects". Human rights are an integral part of this process. They have a role to play in the planning as well as in the execution of development policies. They also have an important mission of seeking to ensure that the benefits of development are passed on to those for whom they are intended – individual human beings. This should be an important perspective in the work of the Council in its implementation of the Covenant. The Council should seek to foster and to implement recognition of the fact that the International Covenant on Economic, Social and Cultural Rights represents in effect the human rights dimension of the New International Economic Order. In this connexion it may be noted that under article 42 of the American Convention on Human Rights the States parties are required to transmit to the Inter-American Commission on Human Rights a copy of each of the reports and studies that they submit annually to the executive committees of the Inter-American Economic and Social Council and the Inter-American Council for Education, Science and Culture, in their respective fields, so that the Commission may see to it that the rights implicit in the economic, social, educational, scientific and cultural standards set forth in the Charter of the Organization of American States as amended by the Protocol of Buenos Aires are being promoted.

---

[57] Professor Capotorti sees the function of the Council as follows: "The implementation machinery created by the Covenant on Economic, Social and Cultural Rights is closely linked with the general action of the United Nations and specialized agencies in the same field; it aims to promote and direct such action on the basis of the available information. This might be found to be more concrete and to give better results than the control on the fulfilment of the obligations undertaken by each State Party". – *Nobel Symposium, loc. cit.,* in note 5 above, p. 132.

B. THE INTERNATIONAL COVENANT ON CIVIL AND POLITICAL RIGHTS AND OPTIONAL PROTOCOL THERETO

Under the International Covenant on Civil and Political Rights each State Party undertakes to respect and to ensure to all individuals within its territory and subject to its jurisdiction the rights recognized in the Covenant without distinction of any kind such as race, colour, sex, language, religion, or other opinion, national or social origin, property, birth or status (Article 2, paragraph 1). Among the rights recognized in the Covenant are the right of peoples to self-determination and to dispose freely of their natural wealth and resources; the equal right of men and women to the enjoyment of civil and political rights; the right to life; protection from torture, cruel, inhuman or degrading treatment or punishment, protection from slavery, the right to liberty and security of person; the right, when deprived of liberty, to be treated with humanity and respect for the inherent dignity of the human person; the right to liberty of movement within the territory of a State; the right to leave any country; the right to equality before the courts and tribunals; the right to recognition everywhere as a person before the law; the right to privacy; the right to freedom of thought, conscience and religion; the right to hold opinions; the right of peaceful assembly; the right to freedom of association; the right to protection of the family and children; and rights for the protection of minorities.

1. Implementation provisions

Under article 40 of the Covenant, the States Parties undertake to submit reports on the measures they have adopted which give effect to the rights recognized in the Covenant, and on the progress made in the enjoyment of those rights, within one year of the entry into force of the Covenant for the States Parties concerned and thereafter whenever the Human Rights Committee so requests. Article 28 of the Covenant provides for the establishment of a Human Rights Committee consisting of 18 members, nationals of States Parties to the Covenant, who are persons of high moral character and recognized competence in the field of human rights. The Human Rights Committee is charged with the consideration of reports submitted by States Parties under article 40; the consideration of communications by a State Party to the Covenant under article 41 complaining that another State Party is not fulfilling its obligations under the Covenant; and

the consideration of communications submitted under the Optional
Protocol to the Covenant.

Under the Optional Protocol to the International Covenant on Civil and
Political Rights, a State Party to the International Covenant on Civil and
Political Rights that becomes a Party to the Protocol recognizes the competence of the Human Rights Committee to receive, under certain conditions, and consider, communications from individuals subject to its jurisdiction, who claim to be victims of a violation by that State Party of any of
the rights set forth in the Covenant.[58]

2. The Establishment of the Human Rights Committee

A meeting of States Parties to the Covenant for the purpose of the initial
election of members of the Human Rights Committee took place on 20
September 1976 at United Nations Headquarters in New York. The follow-
ing 18 persons were elected to the Human Rights Committee: Mr.
Mohamed Ben-Fadhel (Tunisia), Mr. Ole Mogens Espersen (Denmark),
Sir Vincent Evans (U.K.), Mr. Manouchehr Ganji (Iran), Mr. Bernhard
Graefrath (German Democratic Republic), Mr. Vladimir Hanga
(Romania), Mr. Haissam Kelani (Syrian Arab Republic), Mr. Luben G.
Koulishev (Bulgaria), Mr. Rajsoomer Lallah (Mauritius), Mr. Andreas V.
Mavrommatis (Cyprus), Mr. Fernando Mora Rojas (Costa Rica), Mr.
Anatoly Petrovich Movchan (USSR), Mr. Torkel Opsahl (Norway), Mr.
Julio Prado Vallejo (Ecuador), Mr. Fulgence Seminega (Rwanda), Mr.
Walter Surma Tarnopolsky (Canada), Mr. Christian Tomuschat (Federal
Republic of Germany), Mr. Diego Uribe Vargas (Colombia).

The Committee has so far held four sessions. At its first session the
committee elected the following officers for a term of two years: Chairman:
Mr. Andreas V. Mavrommatis, Vice Chairmen: Mr. Luben G. Koulishev,
Mr. Rajsoomer Lallah and Mr. Torkel Opsahl, Rapporteur: Mr. Diego
Uribe Vargas.

On the basis of a set of preliminary draft rules submitted by the Secretary-General (CCPR/C/L.2 and Add. 1-2), the Committee has adopted the
main part of its rules of procedure. Additional rules will be considered at
future sessions. Rules of procedure have to be drawn up, *inter alia,* in
respect of article 41 of the Covenant which is not yet in force.[59]

---

[58] See further, pp. 25-27 below.
[59] See on rules of procedure of human rights organs, R. Beddard, *Human Rights and
Europe* (1973), Chapter 5, Procedural Limitations to the Guarantee; Chapter 6, Further

The Committee has decided to hold sessions as may be required for the satisfactory performance of its functions in accordance with the Covenant. Normally two regular sessions will be held each year. The holding of special sessions is also provided for. Sessions of the Committee are normally to be held at the Headquarters of the United Nations or at the United Nations Office at Geneva. The meetings of the Committee and its subsidiary bodies will be held in public unless the Committee decides otherwise or it appears from the relevant provisions of the Covenant or Protocol that the meeting should be held in private.

Summary records of the public and private meetings of the Committee and its subsidiary bodies are to be prepared by the Secretariat. The summary records of public meetings of the Committee in their final form will be documents of general distribution, unless, in exceptional circumstances, the Committee decides otherwise. The summary records of private meetings will be distributed to the members of the Committee and to other participants in the meetings. They may be made available to others upon decision of the Committee at such time and under such conditions as the Committee may decide. Except as otherwise provided in the Covenant or elsewhere in the rules of procedures (CCPR/C/3.) decisions of the Committee are to be made by a majority of the members present. In connexion with this rule however, the members of the Committee have generally expressed the view that its method of work normally should allow for attempts to reach decisions by consensus before voting, provided that the Covenant and the rules of procedure are observed and that such attempts do not unduly delay the work of the Committee. Nevertheless, the Chairman may at any meeting, and at the request of any member shall, put a proposal to a vote.

3. Reports by States Parties

Under article 40 of the Covenant, as we have seen above, the States Parties

Impediments to the Guarantee; M.A. Eissen, *Le Nouveau Règlement intérieur de la Commission Européenne des droits de l'homme, Annuaire Français 1960,* pp. 774-790; J.E.S. Fawcett, *The Application of the European Convention on Human Rights* (1969), pp. 323-325; A.B. McNulty and M.A. Eissen, "The European Commission of Human Rights – Procedure and Jurisprudence", *Journal of the ICJ,* Vol. 1, No. 2, pp. 198-219; A.H. Robertson, *Human Rights in Europe* (1963), pp. 55-58; H. Rolin, "Le Rôle du Requérant dans la Procédure Prévue par la Commission européenne des droits de l'homme", *Revue hellénique de droit international,* 1956, pp. 3-14; A.P. Schreiber, *The Inter-American Commission on Human Rights* (1970), Chapter III, The Structure, Powers and Procedures of the Commission; L.B. Sohn and T. Buergenthal, *International Protection of Human Rights* (1973), pp. 1011-1099; 1284 ff.

undertake to submit reports on the measures they have adopted which give effect to the rights recognized in the Covenant and on the progress made in the enjoyment of those rights. Rule 66 of the rules of procedure adopted by the Committee repeats this requirement. There is no indication in the rules as to what the periodicity of reports will be. Paragraph 2 of rule 66 simply states that whenever the Committee requests States Parties to submit reports under article 40, paragraph 1 (b) of the Covenant, it shall determine the dates by which such reports shall be submitted.

It may be recalled that in the Third Committee in 1966, some representatives envisaged regular reports by States Parties. The Canadian representative "hoped that Governments would be reporting frequently" (A/C.3 SR. 1435, para. 15). The Pakistani representative "expected that . . . the Committee would request at least one report per year".

As to the form of reports, paragraph 3 of rule 66 states that the Committee may, through the Secretary-General, inform the States Parties of its wishes regarding the form and contents of the reports to be submitted under article 40 of the Covenant. In this connexion, it is worth noting that in the Third Committee in 1966 the Canadian representative referring to the guidelines concerning the reports which the States Parties were to furnish, believed that the Parties should be told what their reports should contain and should be encouraged to furnish information that was meaningful and not meaningless generalities. The object should be to secure information which was useable and manageable. As regards the function of the Committee to consider the reports the Canadian representative felt that the article gave the Committee the authority "to examine, analyse, appraise and evaluate the reports, and it should do so in a searching and critical fashion".[60]

The word "measures" in Article 40 of the Covenant was meant to have "very broad connotations and to comprise all spheres of activity".[61] It covers legislative, judicial or other actions.[62] When this question was discussed at the 1426th to 1427th meetings of the Third Committee in 1966, Mrs. Harris (USA) "to remove any ambiguity connected with the word 'measures'" proposed that the reports of parties should relate to "legislative, judicial or other action".[63] This proposal gave rise to some discussion in the Committee. Mr. Nasinovsky (USSR) thought that this formulation was too narrow. It "minimized the vitally important matter of practical

---

[60] A/C.3/SR.1426, para. 22.
[61] Mr. Sanon (Upper Volta), A/C.3/SR.1427, para. 40.
[62] *Ibid.*, paras. 39-41.
[63] A/C.3/SR.1426, para. 18.

compliance with the letter and spirit of the Covenant".[64] Mr. Saksena (India) said that "the question of the type of action, legislative, judicial or otherwise, had been thoroughly considered by sponsors of the article. They had considered it was preferable not to specify the contents of the reports."[65] Mrs. Ould Daddah (Mauritania) felt that "specifying the type of action which was to constitute the subject-matter of the reports might limit the scope of such reports".[66] Miss Tabbara (Lebanon) felt that the United States proposal had the drawback of specifying the measures which were to form the subject-matter of the reports and consequently limiting the scope of such reports.[67] The United States representative stated "that she would be satisfied . . . if she were sure that the sponsors intended the word "measures" to cover legislative, judicial or other actions" whereupon Mr. Sanon (Upper Volta) replied in the affirmative.[68]

The Human Rights Committee discussed this question at its 17th and 18th meetings. Sir Vincent Evans " . . . believed that the initial reports from States parties should be as comprehensive as possible and should contain the type of information desired by the Committee . . . It was therefore now desirable to indicate to States what material the Committee wished to see included in their reports. For example, under the relevant articles of the Covenant, those reports should include information on (a) legislative, administrative and other measures adopted to give effect to the rights recognised in the Covenant; (b) measures taken that might impose limitations on the exercise of those rights, (c) effective remedies, referred to in article 2, paragraph 3 of the Covenant, available for alleged violations of rights; (d) difficulties which a State party might have in implementing the provisions of the Covenant; (e) the progress made in the enjoyment of the rights recognised in the Covenant."[69] However, the view prevailed that the Committee should wait until it had gained more experience in examining reports before attempting to formulate guidelines. Nevertheless, a letter which the Committee agreed to send to States Parties informing them of the work of the Committee at its first session and the tasks to be undertaken at the second session indicated that most of the heads of information referred to above should be contained in the reports to be submitted by States Parties. At its second session, the Committee adopted a set of

---

[64] *Ibid.*, para. 26.
[65] *Ibid.*, para. 38.
[66] A/C.3/SR.1427, para. 19.
[67] *Ibid.*, para. 23.
[68] *Ibid.*, para. 39.
[69] CCPR/C/SR.17, para. 51.

general guidelines regarding the form and contents of reports.[70]

4. Progress made

In a recent case involving a State Party to the Covenant the Supreme Court of the country took the view that although the Covenant had been ratified by the State concerned it had "not been promulgated as a law of the Republic and for that reason could not serve as a legal precedent" before the courts.[71] A working group of the Commission on Human Rights charged with examining the situation of human rights in the country concerned raised the question as to how it was possible to give effect to the rights recognized in the Covenant, if courts deny it any legal effect in the internal order. It advanced the view that in order to fulfill its obligations under article 2, paragraph 2, of the Covenant a Party had an obligation to take the necessary steps to adopt such legislative or other measures as may be necessary to give effect to the rights recognized in the Covenant. It was the firm opinion of the Group that, having entered into force, the Covenant established an obligation for any State that had ratified it to respect and to ensure to all individuals within its territory and subject to its jurisdiction the rights recognized in the Covenant (see article 2, para. 1, of the Covenant). No omission of the executive, no decision of the judiciary can diminish the extent of the international commitment of a Party to abide by the provisions of the Covenant.[72]

This problem was foreseen when the Third Committee adopted the implementation provisions of the Covenant 1966. At the 1427th meeting of the Committee on 18 November 1966 the representative of New Zealand referring to the terms "progress made in the enjoyment of . . . rights" which now features in paragraph 1 of article 40, felt that this concept seemed to imply that civil and political rights might be implemented on a progressive basis. Such a concept, she felt, was juridically unsound "since the practice well-established in international law, of many countries . . . was not to ratify an international agreement until their domestic law was brought into harmony with the provisions of the agreement."[73] The representative of Iraq thought that while it was true that some countries could not ratify an agreement until their laws were brought fully into

---

[70] See the report of the committee on its first and second sessions, A/32/44, Annex IV.
[71] E/CN.4/1221, paras. 223-224.
[72] *Ibid.*
[73] A/C.3/SR.1427, para. 2.

harmony with it, it was equally true that ratification, in the case of other countries, was accompanied by a process of progressive adaptation of domestic law.[74] The representative of Ireland stated that she would not request a separate vote on the words "the progress made" "if it was clearly understood that they meant the progress which had been made as a result of the measures adopted by States and which was to be incorporated in their reports."[75] Mr. Mohammed (Nigeria) on behalf of the sponsors of the article confirmed that interpretation.[76]

It may be recalled that in 1948, at the suggestion of the United Kingdom representative the Chairman of the Drafting Committee of the Commission on Human Rights requested the Legal Department for an opinion on the following question: "Is it proper and permissible for a State which accedes to, and ratifies an International Convention to state that it will subsequently adapt its municipal (domestic) law to the provisions of the Convention, or is it necessary that the adaptation of the municipal law precede the ratification of the Convention?". In response to this request the Legal Department submitted the following comments: "I. . . . The question presented related to Article 2 of the Draft Covenant on Human Rights tentatively adopted by the Drafting Committee on 14 May 1948 which included the following passage: 'Each State Party to the Covenant undertakes to ensure (a) through adequate laws and procedures to all individuals within its respective jurisdiction, whether citizens or nationals, persons of foreign nationality or stateless persons, the rights and freedoms set forth in Part II of this Covenant and further undertakes that such rights and freedoms where not now provided under existing laws and procedures be given effect in their domestic laws through the adoption of appropriate laws and procedures: . . . '

"The question is whether it is necessary that a State 'adapt' its municipal law to comply with these provisions before that State may become a party to the Covenant. In the first place, it is clear that under international law a State may enter into a treaty which requires it to make certain changes in its municipal law. It is in fact frequently the case that a State assumes an international obligation which necessitates new domestic legislation or modification of its existing legislation. In some such cases the treaty provisions expressly require a change in domestic law; in other cases the obligation assumed in the treaty involves domestic legislation because of the constitu-

---

[74] *Ibid.*, para. 3.
[75] A/C.3/SR.1427, para. 45.
[76] *Ibid.*, para. 46.

tional or statutory requirements in the particular country. Even though such changes in domestic legislation may be required they need not take place before ratification or accession – unless of course the treaty itself so provides. Thus, as far as international law is concerned, the adaptation of municipal law is not a condition precedent to a State binding itself internationally. A State may properly undertake an international obligation and then subsequently take the necessary domestic legislative measures to ensure the fulfilment of the obligation undertaken.

"The principles set forth in the foregoing paragraph have been accepted by the Permanent Court of International Justice, expressly or by implication, in several cases. . . .

"In considering this matter a clear distinction must be made between international law and the requirements of municipal law. It is recognized that under the municipal law of many countries an international convention or treaty does not become binding in domestic law or enforceable by the courts until it has been 'incorporated' or 'transformed' by legislative action into the municipal law and thus made a part of the law of the land. . . . Nevertheless, the fact that this requirement exists under municipal law does not affect in any way the international obligation of the State to carry out the treaty. In other words, even though the necessary enabling legislation is not enacted the treaty is binding internationally and there would clearly be a duty to make reparation for any resulting breach of the obligation. . . .

"The question of the Drafting Committee also presents implicitly another question, namely: If a State has not adapted its municipal law to the provisions of the Covenant prior to, or at the time of, its ratification or accession, has it failed to carry out its obligations under the Covenant? Or, in other words, what is the legal situation during the interval between the date on which a treaty enters into force for a particular State and the enactment of the necessary municipal legislation? In the light of the principles discussed above the answer to this question is quite clear. A State is under a duty to execute the provisions of a treaty from the date at which the treaty becomes binding upon that State. The fact that there may be omissions or deficiencies in municipal law would not, in international law, justify the failure of the State to fulfil its treaty obligations. The only exception to this arises, of course, where the treaty itself contains a provision that there shall be no duty to carry out the obligation prior to the enactment of the required municipal legislation. But where this exception does not exist a party is under a duty to enact such legislation as may be necessary to carry out the treaty obligations; consequently it may not rely on the absence of such legislation to avoid responsibility for carrying out the requirements of the treaty. As a corollary to this it may be noted that the obligation is not discharged by a mere recommendation by the Executive to the Legislature requesting the necessary legislative action. In short, the obligation of a State arises at the moment it becomes a party to the treaty regardless of what its municipal law may require.

"There is ample support for the foregoing principles in the jurisprudence of the Permanent Court of International Justice."[77]

5. Arrangements for the consideration of reports

As regards arrangements for the consideration of reports, the Committee has followed the arrangements of the Committee for the Elimination of Racial Discrimination. Essentially, the Committee for the Elimination of Racial Discrimination has drawn up guidelines which Governments are requested to follow in submitting reports. A representative of the Government is invited to be present when the report is discussed. He answers questions put by the members of the Committee for the Elimination of Racial Discrimination and provides supplementary information. The Committee for the Elimination of Racial Discrimination seeks to establish a dialogue with the Government rather than to have a confrontation with it.

Rule 68 of the rules of procedure adopted by the Committee provides that the Committee shall, through the Secretary-General, notify the States Parties (as early as possible) of the opening date, duration and place of the session at which their respective reports will be examined. Representatives of the States Parties may be present at the meetings of the Committee when their reports are examined. The Committee may also inform a State Party from which it decides to seek further information that it may authorize its representative to be present at a specified meeting. Such a representative should be able to answer questions which may be put to him by the Committee and make statements on reports already submitted by his State, and may also submit additional information from his State.

At each session the Secretary-General is called upon to notify the Committee of all cases of non-submission of reports or additional information requested under rules 66 and 70. In such cases the Committee may transmit to the State Party concerned, through the Secretary-General, a reminder concerning the submission of the report or additional information. (Rule

[77] E/CN.4/116.

69). If, after this reminder the State Party does not submit the report or additional information required, the Committee shall so state in the annual report which it submits to the General Assembly of the United Nations through the Economic and Social Council.

Rule 70 states that when considering a report submitted by a State Party under article 40 of the Covenant, the Committee shall first satisfy itself that the report provides all the information required under rule 66 of the rules. If a report of the State Party to the Covenant, in the opinion of the Committee, does not contain sufficient information, the Committee may request that State to furnish the additional information which is required indicating by what time the said information should be submitted. If, on the basis of its examination of the reports and information supplied by the State Party, the Committee determines that some of the obligations of that State Party under the Covenant have not been discharged, it may make, in accordance with article 40, paragraph 4, of the Covenant, such general comments as it may consider appropriate.

Rule 71 states that the Committee shall, through the Secretary-General, communicate to the States Parties for their observations the general comments it has made under article 40, paragraph 4, of the Covenant on the basis of its examination of the reports and information furnished by States Parties. The Committee may, where necessary, indicate a time-limit for the receipt of observations from States Parties. The Committee may also transmit to the Economic and Social Council the comments referred to in paragraph 1 of this rule, together with copies of the reports it has received from the States Parties to the Covenant and the observations, if any, submitted by them.

6. Role of the specialized agencies

Rule 67 of the rules of procedures, repeating paragraph 3 of article 40, states that the Secretary-General may, after consultation with the Committees, transmit to the specialized agencies concerned copies of such parts of the reports from States members of those agencies as may fall within their field of competence. The Committee may invite the specialized agencies to which the Secretary-General has transmitted parts of the reports to submit comments on those parts within such time-limits as it may specify. When this rule was being drafted in the Committee, the view was expressed that "if the Committee invited the specialized agencies to submit their comments, it would be departing from the provisions of the Covenant, which merely provided that the Secretary-General might . . .

transmit . . . copies . . . of the reports . . .''.[78] However, it was pointed out that the wording of the rule gave the Committee every latitude regarding co-operation, which it might or might not institute as it desired.[79]

At its first session the Committee discussed the participation of specialized agencies in meetings of the Committee which are of interest to them and several members were in favour of such participation.[80] The Committee returned to this question at its third session, when a discussion took place of the issues that were involved regarding co-operation with specialized agencies. Among the issues which were mentioned were: (i) Should specialized agencies simply be present at meetings of the Committee or should they be formally granted the status of observers? Does the Covenant allow for the granting of observer status? (ii) Can representatives of specialized agencies participate in closed sessions of the Committee? (iii) Can the specialized agencies submit comments on reports of States parties or parts thereof as are transmitted to them by the Committee? (iv) What arrangements can be established for providing the Committee with the studies and documents of the specialized agencies? (v) What measures are necessary to ensure that similar rights contained in the Covenant and in instruments of the specialized agencies are not interpreted differently? (vi) What arrangements should be established to minimize the possibility of conflicts between the work of the Committee and the work of the specialized agencies in examining petitions alleging violations of human rights?

In view of the complexity of some of the issues involved the question was entrusted to a working group of the Committee for study and the representatives of the specialized agencies, particularly ILO and UNESCO, were asked to submit written comments to the Committee on this question.[81] At its 73rd meeting on 2 February 1978, the Committee took the following decisions based on the proposals of the working group:

1. With a view to establishing close co-operation with the specialized agencies of the United Nations, the Human Rights Committee requests the Secretary-General of the United Nations to inform the specialized agencies concerned, including ILO, UNESCO, FAO and WHO, that it would welcome the attendance of their representatives at its public meetings.

2. The Committee requests the Secretary-General of the United Nations, in

---

[78] Mr. Graefrath, CCPR/C/SR.10, para. 3. See also similar comments by other members of the Committee at its 56th meeting, CCPR/C/SR.56.

[79] Mr. Uribe Vargas, CCPR/C/SR.10.

[80] CCPR/C/SR.10 and 18. See also CCPR/C/L.3 in which the specialized agencies re-stated their interest in co-operating with the Committee.

[81] CCPR/C/SR.56, 73.

accordance with article 40 (3) of the Covenant, to determine, in consultation with the Committee at each session, the parts of the State's reports that should be transmitted to the specialized agencies concerned, it being understood that this relates only to reports emanating from a State which is also a member of the specialized agency concerned.

A decision on the following additional proposal of the working group was postponed to the fourth session:

3. Written statements by the specialized agencies concerned providing information on their practice with regard to the interpretation and implementation of the provisions of international instruments within their competence similar to the provisions of the Covenant shall be distributed by the Secretary-General of the United Nations to the members of the Human Rights Committee.

7. Role of the Economic and Social Council

Paragraph 4 of article 40 of the Covenant provides that: "The Committee shall study the reports submitted by the States parties to the present Covenant. It shall transmit its reports, and such general comments as it may consider appropriate, to the States parties. The Committee may also transmit to the Economic and Social Council these comments along with the copies of the reports it has received from States parties to the present Covenant." Paragraph 2 of rule 71 of the rules of procedure repeats this provision. In the Third Committee in 1966 the Pakistani representative stated his understanding that "once the Human Rights Committee had transmitted the reports with its comments to the Economic and Social Council it would be up to the Council to take whatever action it might deem necessary and to consult whatever subsidiary organs it might wish".[82] On this interpretation it would be possible for the Council to transmit the reports which it receives to the Commission on Human Rights for its information. This would be an advisable course to follow and it would be a way of co-ordinating the work of the Human Rights Committee with that of the Commission on Human Rights.

Article 45 of the Covenant provides that "The Committee shall submit to the General Assembly of the United Nations, through the Economic and Social Council, an annual report on its activities." Rule 63 of the rules of procedure repeats this provision. When Article 45 was adopted in the Third Committee in 1966, the representative of Hungary envisaged an active role for the Economic and Social Council in considering these reports.[83] The representative of India stated that "The intention was that the Council should be able to examine the report and transmit it together

[82] A/C.3/SR.1426, para. 15.
[83] A/C.3/SR.1435, para. 13.

with any comments it might have to make. The report itself would describe the work of the Human rights Committee and include in particular that Committee's views on the general position regarding the enjoyment of the human rights set out in the Covenant; the Council's comments would also be general with no specific reference to particular countries".[84]

The first report of the Committee was considered by the Economic and Social Council on 17 October 1977.[85] The Council decided, at the suggestion of its President, to take note of the report of the Committee and transmit it to the General Assembly at its thirty-second session. It was apparent that the Council was not clear as to what its role should be and it was suggested that some consideration be given to this matter during coming sessions.

8. The Optional Protocol

Under article 1 of the Optional Protocol, "A State party to the Covenant that becomes a party to the Protocol recognizes the competence of the Committee to receive and consider communications from individuals subject to its jurisdiction who claim to be victims of a violation by that State party of any of the rights set forth in the Covenant. No communication shall be received by the Committee if it concerns a State party to the Covenant which is not a party to the present Protocol".

Article 2 provides that "Individuals who claim that any of their rights enumerated in the Covenant have been violated and who have exhausted all available domestic remedies may submit a written communication to the Committee for consideration".

Under Article 3, any communication which is anonymous, or which is an abuse of the right of submission of such communication or is incompatible with the provisions of the Covenant, is inadmissible.

Under Article 4, paragraph 1, "Subject to the provisions of article 3, the Committee shall bring any communications submitted to it under the present Protocol to the attention of the State party to the present Protocol alleged to be violating any provisions of the Covenant; Paragraph 2 provides that within six months, the receiving State shall submit to the Committee written explanations or statements clarifying the matter and the remedy, if any, that may have been taken by that State".

Under Article 5, "1: Committee shall consider communications received under the present Protocol in the light of all written information made

[84] A/C.3/SR.1435, para. 17.
[85] E/SR.2087.

available to it by the individual and by the State Party concerned; 4. The Committee shall forward its views to the State Party concerned and to the individual.''

Under Article 6, ''The Committee shall include in its annual report under article 45 of the Covenant a summary of its activities under the Protocol''.

The procedure for the consideration of communications received under the Optional Protocol is dealt with under rules 78-88 of the rules of procedure. As regards the transmission of communications to the Committee, rule 78 provides that the Secretary-General shall bring to the attention of the Committee, in accordance with the present rules, communications which are or appear to be submitted for consideration by the Committee under Article 1 of the Protocol. The Secretary-General, when necessary, may request clarification from the author of the communication as to his wish to have his communication submitted to the Committee for consideration under the Protocol. In case doubts remain as to the wish of the author, the Committee will be seized of the communication.

Under rule 79, the Secretary-General is required to prepare a list of communications submitted to the Committee in accordance with rule 78 above, with a brief summary of their contents, and to circulate this list to the members of the Committee at regular intervals. The Secretary-General must also maintain a permanent register of all such communications. The full text of any communication brought to the attention of the Committee will be made available to any member of the Committee upon his request.

Under rule 82, meetings of the Committee or its subsidiary bodies during which communications under the Protocol are examined shall be closed. Meetings during which the Committee may consider general issues such as procedures for the application of the Protocol may be public if the Committee so decides.

Under rule 83, the Committee may issue *communiqués,* through the Secretary-General, for the use of the information media and the general public regarding the activities of the Committee at its closed meetings.

As regards procedures to determine the admissibility of communications rule 89 provides that the Committee may establish one or more Working Groups of no more than five of its members to make recommendations to the Committee regarding the fulfilment of the conditions laid down in articles 1, 2; 3 and 5 (2) of the Protocol. The rules of procedure of the

Committee shall apply as far as possible to the meetings of the Working Group.[86]

Rule 86 states that the Committee may, prior to forwarding its final views on the communication to the State Party concerned, inform that State of its views whether interim measures may be desirable to avoid irreparable damage to the victim of the alleged violation. In doing so, the Committee shall inform the State Party concerned that such expression of its views on interim measures does not imply a determination on the merits of the communication.

This rule occasioned some discussion in the Committee. Some members felt that interim measures were important to avoid irreparable damage to a petitioner.[87] However, the view was expressed that there were no provisions in the Optional Protocol which gave the Committee the competence to request measures of a State. Under Article 5 of the Protocol the Committee was merely to consider and forward its views to the States concerned.[88] To this it was replied that "while there was no reference in either the Covenant or the Protocol to the possibility of recommending interim measures, it was a commonly accepted notion that bodies had such implied powers as were necessary to enable them to perform their functions in a reasonable manner."[89] "A human rights committee established to guarantee the implementation of the Universal Declaration of Human Rights could not wait for the implementation of a rule of procedure when humanitarian questions were involved. The rule must therefore be viewed in the light of all the articles of the Protocol rather than just article 5."[90]

9. The role of the secretariat

Rule 80 provides that the Secretary-General may request clarification from the author of a communication concerning the applicability of the Protocol to his communication, and in particular regarding: (a) the name, address, age and occupation of the author and the verification of his identity; (b) the name of the State party against which the communication is directed; (c) the object of the communication; (d) the provision or provisions of the

[86] At its 18th meeting on 1 April, 1977, the Committee appointed a Working Group of Five to meet three days before its second session to examine communications transmitted to the Committee. The members of the Working Group were Messrs. Graefrath, Kelani, Lallah, Mora Rojas and Opsahl. Alternate members were Sir Vincent Evans, Messrs. Ben Fadhel, Ganji, Hanga and Prado Vallejo. This Working Group, with varying membership has met before each session of the Committee thus far.

[87] See CCPR/C/SR.13, 17.

[88] Mr. Graefrath, CCPR/C/SR.13, para. 28. Mr. Koulishev, *ibid.*, para. 30.

[89] Mr. Espersen, *ibid.*, para. 39.

[90] Mr. Uribe Vargas, CCPR/C/SR.17, para. 21.

Covenant alleged to have been violated; (e) the facts of the claim; (f) steps taken by the author to exhaust domestic remedies; (g) the extent to which the same matter is being examined under another procedure of international investigation or settlement.

When requesting clarification or information, the Secretary-General must indicate an appropriate time-limit to the author of the communication with a view to avoiding undue delays in the procedure under the Protocol. The Committee may approve a questionnaire for the purpose of requesting the above-mentioned information from the author of the communication. The request for clarifications referred to above will not preclude the inclusion of the communication on the list provided for in rule 79, paragraph 1.

Under rule 81, for each registered communication the Secretary-General shall, as soon as possible, prepare and circulate to the members of the Committee a summary of the relevant information obtained. Presumably, this article refers to the information obtained under rule 80, as under rule 79 the Secretary-General is already required to submit brief summaries of communications received.

The discussions in the Committee make it clear that it is for the Human Rights Committee, not the Secretary-General, to decide on the admissibility of a communication.[91]

10. The Human Rights Committee in practice

The first report of the Committee shows evidence of seriousness, independence, courage and dedication.[92] Some salient features of the Committee's approach are outlined below. The Committee has underlined its independence by pointing out, in its first report, that it is not a subsidiary United Nations body but a conventional organ established by the States parties to the Covenant.[93] It recognizes that it is not a court but, rather, an expert body which should be mindful of judicial, diplomatic, fact-finding and conciliation elements in its functions. At the first session of the Human Rights Committee the question arose whether the Committee is a judicial

---

[91] CCPR/C/SR.11. For an indication of the roles of the secretariats of the European Commission on Human Rights and the Inter-American Commission, respectively see J.E.S. Fawcett, *The Application of the European Commission on Human Rights* (1969), pp. 324-325. A.P. Schreiber, *The Inter-American Commission on Human Rights* (1970), pp. 62-63.

[92] Official records of the General Assembly, 32nd session. Supplement No. 44, A/32/44.

[93] *Ibid.,* para. 90.

body. Mr. Uribe Vargas considered that its "work was of a judicial nature".[94] Other members also referred expressly or impliedly to judicial elements in its functions. However, Mr Graefrath "did not share the view that the work of the Committee could be compared with that of a court . . . Unlike a court, the Committee was not required to make any judgements,[95] but simply to consider and comment on reports and to act as a conciliatory body[96] in dealing with complaints and communications".[97] Mr Suy, (United Nations Under-Secretary-General, the Legal Counsel) "believed that the Human Rights Committee was neither a legislative nor a judicial body and that every expert body was *sui generis*".[98]

The approach which appears to have prevailed in the Committee is a pragmatic one. Issues will be faced as they arise, and approaches and techniques adopted which are likely to produce the best results. The Committee is an expert body which needs to be mindful, *inter alia,* of political, judicial, fact-finding and conciliation elements present in its functions. The hope expressed by Under-Secretary-General Buffum in opening the first session of the Committee, was that "in examining reports submitted by States Parties . . . the Committee would establish a continuing and constructive dialogue with . . . States with a view to fulfilling the obligations set out in the Covenant".[99]

The approach of the Committee in its relationship with governments is "to develop a constructive dialogue with each State party in regard to the implementation of the Covenant and thereby contribute to mutual understanding and peaceful and friendly relations among nations in accordance with the Charter of the United Nations" (Report, Annex IV).

A very heartening feature of the Committee is its recognition of the need

[94] CCPR/C/SR.6, para. 72.

[95] Cp. Mrs. Harris (USA), A/C.3/SR.1417, para. 53: "The role of the Human Rights Committee was essentially to act as a conciliation body available to the States concerned; however, it was not competent to determine whether a State Party had failed to fulfil its commitments". Similarly, Mr. Paolini (France), A/C.3/SR.1418, para. 7, "The Committee should not make any findings or any recommendations to the Parties direct but should limit itself to general comments".

[96] Cp. Mr. Hanga, CCPR/C/SR.13, para. 11: "he wondered whether it was possible to compare the Committee to a conciliation body". Mr. Suy, the Legal Counsel, replied "that conciliation was only aspect of the Committee's work". *ibid.,* para. 15.

[97] CCPR/C/SR.7, para. 1. Cp. Mr. Saksena (India), A/C. 3/SR. 1428, para. 10, who drew attention to the non-judicial character of the Committee. Mr. Nasinovsky (USSR), A/C.3/SR.1425, para. 53, felt that "the Committee was not a judicial body". However, Mr. Egas (Chile), *ibid.*, para 57, envisaged the possibility that the Committee might exercise judicial functions.

[98] CCPR/C/SR.13, para. 6.

[99] CCPR/C/SR.1, para. 4.

to be in close rapport with the public. The Committee has agreed that its reports, formal decisions and all other official documents shall be documents of general distribution unless the Committee decides otherwise. In paragraph 170 of its report, members of the Committee expressed the opinion that, although the principle of confidentiality should govern their deliberations when dealing with complaints, a minimum of information should be made available in the report of the Committee without divulging the contents of the communications, the nature of the allegations, the identity of the author and the name of the State party against which the allegations were made. It was felt that the general public had a legitimate interest in knowing the main trends in the approach of the Committee in its consideration of communications. This is in line with the intention of the drafters of the Covenants who envisaged them "generating information and focussing public opinion on human rights matters".[100]

As regards the Committee's approach to the examination of reports it generally agreed that the main purpose of such examination should be to assist States parties in the promotion and protection of the human rights recognized in the Covenant (Report, paragraph 105). The examination of reports considered thus far has been detailed. For each of the reports numerous questions were asked of the represenlive of the government concerned, who was present at the examination. Typical questions were:

- What was the legal technique of incorporation of the Covenant into domestic law?
-   Whether, and if so under what conditions, an individual could request the courts or administrative authorities to apply the Covenant against a law or regulation contrary to its provisions.
- For what offences was the death penalty inflicted?
- Are there people not convicted of crime who are detained for political reasons?

In several instances the government representative was requested, and undertook, to provide supplementary information to the Committee. The Committee's intention, after the completion of its study of each State's report is to call for subsequent reports. The aim of such further reports will be to bring the situation up-to-date in respect of each State. The Committee has drawn up a set of general guidelines regarding the form and contents of reports to be submitted by States parties in the future. Among the questions in which it is interested is whether the provisions of the Covenant

---

[100] Mrs. Harris (USA), A/C.3/SR.1399, para. 2.

can be invoked before, and directly enforced by, the courts, other tribunals or administrative authorities, or whether they first have to be transformed into internal laws and administrative regulations. The Committee is also interested to know of derogations, restrictions or limitations.

Details of the Committee's consideration of communications received under the Protocol are contained in Chapters VI and VII of its first report which show that the Committee transmitted some communications to the State parties concerned requesting information and observations relevant to the questions of admissibility. In some cases it also decided to request additional information from the authors of communications. Two communications were declared inadmissible. The Committee has decided that, as a rule it will only consider an alleged violation of human rights which occurred on or after the date of entry into force of the Covenant and the Protocol for the State party concerned unless it is an alleged violation which is continuing or has continuing effects.

Five significant legal questions may be singled out in the report of the Committee. First, as to the role of lawyers in representing complainants the Committee has decided that normally complaints should be submitted by the individual himself or by his representative but that it may consider a communication submitted on behalf of an alleged victim by others when it appears that he is unable to submit the communication himself (Report, para. 67). Second, as to the exhaustion of prior remedies, the Committee adopted the view that it may, under Article 5 (2) of the Protocol, consider a communication where the application of remedies is unreasonably prolonged either at the national or international level (Report, paras. 68-72). Third, Rule 86 of the Committee's rules of procedure provides for the indication of interim measures to avoid irreparable damage to the victim of an alleged violation. Fourth, the Committee has decided that individual opinions may be appended to its views on complaints submitted to it. Fifth, the consideration of the question of reservations is interesting. In considering the report of one State party some members expressed the view that some of the reservations made by the country in question were not really necessary and feared that too many reservations may distort the meaning of the Covenant. They stressed that under the Vienna Convention a State may not make reservations incompatible with the essential object and purpose of a treaty. Other members, however, were of the view that ratification and implementation of the Covenant with reservations is better than its non-ratification. In their opinion, the making of reservations may usefully clarify the legal situation wherever there was an obvious discrepancy between the Covenant and existing domestic legislation. In their view reservations should be judged according to whether they are in accordance with international law as elaborated in the Vienna Convention on the Law of Treaties. This is a question which deserves to be watched closely as the practice of the Committee develops.

The foregoing brief résumé of the first and second sessions of the Human Rights Committee shows that a good basis has been laid on which to build. The Committee has also set a good example for the Working Group of the Economic and Social Council in its examination of reports under the Covenant on Economic, Social and Cultural Rights.

The real challenges, however, lie ahead. It is to the credit of the Committee that in its examination of reports, members asked questions such as:
– On what subject matters would it be impossible to bring national legislation into full conformity with the Covenant and to withdraw relevant reservations?
– How could freedom of information be implemented by persons who dissented from government policies?
– What in the context of freedom of expression is meant by the right to "constructive criticism in a manner that will safeguard the soundness of the domestic structure and strengthen the socialist system?"[101]

How will the Committee react if the answers are unsatisfactory? How will the Committee ensure that assurances given to it are not merely routine commitments? These are the challenges that lie ahead.

The Third Committee of the General Assembly considered the first report of the Human Rights Committee at seven meetings from 17 October to 2 November 1977. The Third Committee considered the wish expressed by the Human Rights Committee in paragraph 185 of its report that its Chairman be invited to present the annual report of the Human Rights Committee to the General Assembly. At the request of the Third Committee, the Director of the Division of Human Rights made a statement explaining the reasons for this wish of the Human Rights Committee. He stressed in particular the Committee's desire to establish direct contacts from the outset with the General Assembly in view of the role which it was called upon to play in the promotion and protection of human rights. He also indicated that the Chairman would be able to reply to any questions which might be put to him and provide any necessary clarifications concerning the work of the Committee. Members of the Third Committee were, however, of the opinion that there was not sufficient precedent to justify the sending of an invitation to the Chairman of the Human Rights Committee.   They felt moreover, that the Human Rights Committee was

[101] See A/C.3/32/SR.20 and 24.

independent of, and not responsible to, the General Assembly. This independence should be safeguarded.

During the discussions of the report all speakers expressed their satisfaction with the report and praised the achievement of the Committee during its first two sessions.[102] In its resolution 32/66 adopted on 8 December 1977 upon the recommendation of the Third Committee, the General Assembly noted the report of the Committee with appreciation and expressed its satisfaction at the serious manner in which the Committee was undertaking its functions. The Assembly also appreciated that the Committee strived for uniform standards in the implementation of the provisions of the Covenant and of the Protocol thereto. The Secretary-General was requested to keep the Human Rights Committee informed of the activities of the Commission on Human Rights, the Sub-Commission on Prevention of Discrimination and Protection of Minorities and of the Committee on the Elimination of Racial Discrimination.

C. CONCLUSION

Writing in 1967, one year after the Covenants were adopted by the General Assembly, the late Wilfred Jenks stated that "the entry into force of the Covenants can be an epoch-making advance in the international protection of human rights, but their immediate practical value will depend on the extent to which they are promptly and widely ratified without reservations which detract significantly from the obligations which they embody and on how far the procedures of implementation are applied . . . with the highest standards of thoroughness and objectivity.[103] These words retain their full force at the present time.

---

[102] For a summary of the discussion, see A/C.3/32/SR.30, 31, 32, 33 and 37.

[103] C.W. Jenks, "Human Rights, Social Justice and Peace. The Broader Significance of ILO Experience", in *Nobel Symposium* 7, *op. cit.* in note 5 above, pp. 246-247. Cf. W. Buffum, United Nations Under-Secretary-General, "The thoroughness and thoughtfulness with which the Committee approached its tasks could have a major impact on the future role of the United Nations in the vital area of human rights". CCPR/C/SR.1, para. 3.

CHAPTER IX

UNESCO AND THE CHALLENGES OF TODAY AND TOMORROW: UNIVERSAL AFFIRMATION OF HUMAN RIGHTS*

UNESCO SECRETARIAT

A. CONSPECTUS

The universal assurance of human rights is not only a major necessity of our time, but its very hallmark, distinguishing it from earlier ages. People today, in their attitudes towards the recognition and application of human rights, are no longer prepared to accept without question a universality which represents no more than an ideal, abstract principle to be put into effect in the unforeseeable future and the mere affirmation of which would be sufficient to sanction the existence of privileged enclaves of achievement and vast areas of darkness, stagnation and despair. Effective universality is now the yardstick for measuring the conditions of human existence, and by that standard the public conscience cannot fail to be shocked by the fate of part of mankind. This awakening consciousness and this demand of our times are reflected in the fact that the international community has proclaimed the principle that all are entitled to the same rights, and has pledged itself collectively to work together to achieve those rights for all, "without distinction of any kind, such as . . . colour, sex, language, religion, political . . . opinion, . . . birth or other status". and without acceptance of any special circumstances, historical, social, or other, as warranting or excusing any violation of those rights, disregard of them, or failure to make resolute efforts to secure their gradual achievement.

1. Effective universality of human rights —a fundamental necessity

Immediately after the end of a world war which, with all its train of suffering, had sprung from denial of human rights and had itself carried that denial to the extreme, the pressing need to reaffirm those rights in all their aspects was seen to be essential as the only possible foundation for the building of a just and lasting peace. From then on, an all-embracing con-

*Reproduced with the permission of UNESCO from the UNESCO publication, "Thinking Ahead" (1977).

ception of human rights began to emerge: civil and political rights, economic, social and cultural rights gained recognition and demanded action to
sustain them as interrelated components of a single whole, transcending the
level at which their requirements might appear to compete with one another.

The struggles of various peoples for their liberation, the emergence of
new independent nations, the establishment, gradually covering the whole
of the planet, of an international community pledged to the pursuit of
common ideals, the revolt, or the clamant sufferings, of oppressed or exploited minorities, all combined to complete this process of developing
awareness and to give this demand its full impact, from the three stand-
points of effective universality in the application of human rights; indis-
solubility of civil and political rights and economic, social and cultural
rights; and the necessary rôle of men and women themselves – individually
and in groups – in the struggle for human dignity, and in the development
and building up of a world order and a social order in which their rights
and those of others would be guaranteed. For it is a mockery to grant
explicit freedoms to those who are prevented, by destitution, from exercis-
ing them; but, on the other hand, to improve the material well-being of the
people at large while they are kept in bondage and in ignorance, excluded
from the community of human relations and the mainstream of history,
would also be a denial of the dignity of man.

Recent decades, then, have seen a decisive advance in the full affirmation, for the whole of humanity, of that respect for man without which
there can be no public morality; and in the recognition of the fact that
human rights are necessarily indivisible: their violation in the case of a
single human being implies the flouting and denial of the very principle
from which they spring; if only certain rights are recognized and guaranteed, the denial or disregard of others is sufficient denunciation of the
illusory character of such partial observance.

2. Realities that fall far short of aspirations

And yet, in comparison with this clear need, what blemishes mar the
picture that the actual situation presents! Not only are human rights still
not effectively assured in practice in most of the world's countries, but
there is nothing to suggest that any steady, undeviating progress is being
made towards improvement: clashes of interest, overriding reasons of
State, sudden, sharp changes in the economy and in social relationships,
the vicissitudes of national and international policy, inter-group antago-

nisms, fluctuations in power relationships, the pressures of egoism, intolerance or obscurantism, the pretexts afforded by circumstances – all these are continually responsible for shameful retreats which may well produce indignation and alarm. It would indeed be disastrous if, in the end, these retreats were to be met by the false wisdom or illusory realism of resigned acceptance.

Specific violations of human rights take many different forms in our present-day world: deliberate violations that State authorities, claiming to be the sole judges of their legitimacy, justify on the grounds of particular circumstances of political or social crisis, the need for the maintenance of order or the safeguarding of national unity; flagrant violations (although there is often an attempt to conceal these beneath a travesty of the very principles that are being trampled underfoot) such as those revealed in exceptional, localized situations – apartheid, vestiges or upsurges of colonialist or neo-colonialist oppression, foreign occupation; less obvious violations, embodied in the structures or the functioning of unjust societies which, under the veneer of formal democracy, engage in forms of oppression and exploitation that bear particularly heavily on underprivileged groups or on certain categories of individuals, including the great mass of women; interference with freedom of thought, conscience or religion, or with the possibility of seeking, receiving or spreading information or ideas; violations of which the community has more recently become conscious, such as those involved in the unjustified appropriation of natural and cultural resources or the despoiling of the environment or, again, those that may, for individuals and nations, attend the consequences of scientific and technological progress; violations arising from contempt for or rejection of cultural identity, or from the tensions present in multi-ethnic societies; and so on. The problem of the protection and application of human rights is immense, since it covers every aspect of the life of individuals and groups.

3. The full achievement of human rights and its implications

The determination to promote human rights is at the basis of all the great purposes by which mankind is motivated at this point in its history; it gives them their significance, sets their trends and likewise imposes certain criteria for the action to which they give rise. The assurance of human rights and the *construction of peace* are tasks that go hand-in-hand, no doubt because any war irremediably compromises the exercise of rights of all kinds, while denial of rights, in itself, inevitably ends by engendering violence: and because a peace based on inequality, domination and exploitation, even if it could be maintained by compulsion, would be peace in name only. But an ever deeper reason is that the universal application of human rights coincides with the building up, both materially and spiritually, of a genuine human community taking in all mankind. The achievement of human rights on the scale of mankind as a whole also implies that all should enjoy living conditions that will not expose them to hunger, destitution, apprehension for the future, the extremes of ignorance and social exclusion, or condemn them to distress and despair. It accordingly implies the *development of all nations;* it further implies their independence in co-operation, and mutural recognition of their dignity. At the same time, it is by his very efforts in the cause of development, in the achievement of independence and in the practice of discussion on equal terms, that man, with his inherent rights, gains stature, and fulfils his potential. Springing from the dialectic of development taken in its fullest sense, the desire for *balance* and *harmony between man and his environment* (both natural and socio-cultural), the striving after *communication* which will provide the foundation for a real life in common, the determination to establish a *new economic and social order* on a world scale that will be an order based on justice and co-operation for common purposes – all these reflect at different levels the demand for the full and universal implementation of human rights.

While, then, the fate of men and women is in their own hands, no international organization is better placed than UNESCO to appreciate the vital and fundamental importance of the promotion of human rights, to bring it home to people, and to translate it into practical programme terms. Indeed UNESCO, by appealing to men's minds and calling upon intellectual resources, seeks to help in giving all men the means for their own liberation, their accession to a better life, and the building up of a real community among them. The problem of the promotion of human rights is naturally in the forefront of those on which the Organization intends to focus its action, as a reference to the ultimate purpose of such action. But at the same time, the promotion of human rights takes a practical form *vis-à-vis* the specific problems with which mankind is confronted today. Ultimately it involves the whole range of UNESCO'S activities directed to achieving a host of particular objectives; conversely, concern to secure the observance and achievement of human rights is bound to qualify and determine, in various specific contexts, the way in which UNESCO deals with the other problems claiming its attention. It is no accident that, in listing the aspects of our present human problems with which the question of the full exercise of human rights is linked, we should have come back to the main lines of the schedule of problems that UNESCO has resolved to tackle. Alone among all the organizations belonging to the United Nations system, UNESCO can lay claim to a dual mission: it has to work for the promotion of human rights in the particular fields of its competence, and it must have a place at the very centre from which particular rights emanate, clarifying them, ensuring their recognition, and promoting them, and the principles behind them, as a whole.

It is none the less true that, while the full achievement of human rights presupposes patient efforts in the furtherance of development, the dissemination of knowledge and the equalization of opportunities for acquiring it, the humanizing of the environment and the background to life, the enhancement of cultures and communication between them and the promotion of a genuine mutual communication system among people, this does not mean that active measures for the protection, achievement and extension of human rights can be put off until tomorrow except at the cost of an intolerable abdication. It is one thing to take into account, as we must, the fact that circumstances are difficult, the need for patient improvement of the conditions determining the life of every society and the extent and level of what it can achieve, the limited amount and precarious nature of the resources that can be mobilized for this purpose, and the need for a determined and prolonged effort to build a better and a juster world. It would be quite another to disregard the obligation, admitting of no compromise, to tackle without further ado all the clear denials of human rights which are already such a scandal. In the first case, what is involved is a question of degree – a more or less satisfactory position as regards the possible achievement of rights. In the second instance, a question of principle is at stake: the question of respect for man, which is indivisible. The difficulties of the times do not remove the scandal of inequality – rather the reverse; the requirements of public order and safety – not to mention the will to power – can neither justify nor excuse arbitrary arrest and the use of torture, any more than concern for growth – not to mention the lure of gain – can make the subjection and exploitation of human labour acceptable, or than the desire to build up an intellectual elite can warrant keeping the mass of the people in ignorance. Without prejudice to the persistent efforts needed to build a world more conducive to the full enjoyment of human rights, the protection, consolidation and extension of those same rights call urgently for resolute, specific, direct action.

The first aspect of the programme relates to research: research directed to increasing our knowledge about human rights, their content and interrelations, studying the necessary conditions for their achievement, and identifying and denouncing violations of those rights in the day-to-day functioning of societies; research of a more formal, legal nature, which relates to the methods of official recognition, institutional measures calculated to guarantee the protection of rights by the public authorities and to ensure that individuals whose inherent rights may be endangered have the possibility of remedy at law.

The second is concerned with respect for cultural identity as the basis of the free self-determination and self-fulfilment of individuals and groups. It draws on experience of two kinds: favourable, in the appreciation of the values inherent in each culture and the importance for individuals and groups of unfettered participation in the values of their own particular culture; and unfavourable, in the case of peoples or groups who have been under domination and deprived of that culture, and of individuals, excluded from society, with the impoverishment and far-reaching disturbances that result from such alienation, and the forms of protest and cultural metamorphosis that go with it. A definition must, however, be given of the purposes for which cultural identity is to be defended and promoted: not introspective withdrawal but increased participation in larger communities, mutual appreciation of the values of all peoples, fuller integration in development and, in the case of communities that are today rejected or in a marginal position, the right to existence and dialogue on a footing of equality.

A third aspect relates to a part of humanity that has for too long been subject to discrimination, or even exploitation: women. It combines the vital need to ensure that women can exercise human rights to the full, with the requirement that there should be a far-reaching improvement of their status. The programme is designed to bring to light, so that they can be eliminated, the factors which have led to the inferior status of women and still jeopardize the full exercise of their rights, and is also concerned with the positive definition and application of measures designed to bring about a change for the better in the status of women in various societies, which is linked up with the need to promote active participation by women in the work of development.

Special attention is to be given to the defence of the rights of a category of human beings who are particularly wronged or threatened – refugees and members of national liberation movements. The right to eduation, in particular, as an instrument of emancipation, is especially important in this context, as well as the right to cultural identity. This is a particular, and specially acute, instance of the denial of human rights.

The last aspect deals with the mobilization of the means afforded by education and information for spreading awareness of the vital need for universal observance of human rights, explaining the content and inter-relations of those rights, and giving people the means and the desire to go more deeply into the conditions required to secure human rights and to work for their achievement.

B. UNDERSTANDING AND ENSURING HUMAN RIGHTS

With perhaps greater vigour than ever, the international community is at present manifesting its resolve to promote the universal consummation of human rights, understood in the widest and fullest sense of the term. How-ever, it finds itself today, in a manner of speaking, at a crossroads.

1. Work achieved since 1945

Normative work was undertaken on an international scale in 1945 fol-lowing a war which was, first and foremost, a fight for man. This work, of which the linchpin is the 1948 Universal Declaration of Human Rights, is, to a certain extent, complete. It takes the form of an apparently all-em-bracing series of international standards defining human rights, set out either in declarations or in the fity or so treaties and conventions on human rights, and backed by an impressive number of public bodies (intergovern-mental bodies like the United Nations Commission on Human Rights and also independent bodies such as, in the case of UNESCO, the Conciliation and Good Offices Commission set up in connection with the Convention against Discrimination in Education) as well as several private non-govern-mental organizations. These various bodies or organizations have been given the task, or have taken it upon themselves, not to penalize but simply to identify by a very varied range of methods (judicial, semi-judicial, consul-tative, administrative, political) the most serious violations of human rights in the world.

The feeling that a stage in the international protection and promotion of human rights is coming to an end, is further strengthened by the entry into force of the International Covenants on Economic, Social and Cultural Rights (3 January 1976) and on Civil and Political Rights (23 March 1976). These two instruments have for the international community the value of constitutional texts inasmuch as they provide, with the Universal Declara-tion, a universally valid set of criteria which must henceforth be used to guide all action or evaluate every situation.

2. Recurrent infringements of human rights

Nevertheless, the "peoples of the United Nations" in whose name the San Francisco Charter was drawn up and adopted, all feel the need for new measures which would make it possible for human rights to become a reality generally observed. The truth is that deeds and practices still fall far short of ambitions and declared intentions. Violations of human rights remain a common event, whether they are open and deliberate or more covert. To begin with, particular situations still exist which provide an opportunity or pretext for a radical denial of human rights, as in southern Africa where racial discrimination is systematic. In other places, the exercise of civil and political rights is hamstrung by infringements of the freedoms normally accorded to individuals and groups. On other occasions still, there are forms of discrimination which affect people's place of residence or access to employment. Finally, there is evidence of the practice of torture, so much so that the General Assembly of the United Nations was led, at its 30th session, unanimously to adopt a resolution condemning torture in all its forms.

The recurrence of these situations has recently led the majority of worldwide or regional international organizations to take a variety of steps, such as the adoption by the United Nations General Assembly of resolution 3221 (XXIX) which urges the desirability of exploring alternative approaches and ways and means in the field of human rights.

3. Towards a focusing of activities

At the start of this new move in favour of human rights, one concern in everybody's mind is that these rights should not be devalued by a multiplicity of declarations conveying false hopes and ill able to mask the sad facts. What is rather needed is a *deepening of the knowledge of human rights and a consolidation of what has been achieved in the way of standards and institutions* during the period which has only just ended. The task first of all is to protect man as he is, man with a situation and a place in history, through the rights provided for by the declarations in force, and only then to consider new rights for man in the abstract.

The task is first of all to enlarge the legal, indeed too legal, notion of human rights through contributions from other disciplines, chief of which must be the social sciences, before proposing new legal standards for adoption by States. The main aim of work in the social sciences in this connexion is to throw light on the specific circumstances in which individuals and groups can effectively enjoy their rights. The social sciences essentially attempt to analyse social relationships and practices, including those that determine the way in which the machinery and institutions for guaranteeing the exercise of human rights actually function. The sociological examination of violations of human rights, and more generally, of situations in which these rights are denied, is thus of crucial importance. It is in the light of this work that the functioning of existing machinery and procedures for the international protection of human rights should be consolidated before recommending States to adopt new measures.

This period of study and consolidation provides UNESCO with a real opportunity for illuminating and focusing more effectively the various international activities undertaken on behalf of human rights. The work which has just been completed is in fact somewhat fragmentary: the instruments adopted by various international and national organizations contain a number of contradictions and liaison is awkward between the different world-wide or regional bodies set up to secure the recognition of, or respect for, human rights; accordingly public opinion frequently has difficulty in grasping the necessarily global character of the efforts made to promote these rights by the United Nations agencies and by other organizations.

UNESCO, by the very nature of its tasks, is ideally suited to assume responsibility, during the period of study and consolidation for advancing the cause of human rights taken in their entirety, by encouraging and assisting the international community to use, in the service of this cause, whatever educational, research and information resources it can muster.

4. The institutional framework

Research into human rights and into the best ways of enforcing them is indissociable from the principle of an organized international community.

International organizations with responsibility for human rights have sometimes entrusted this work to a specialized body. In the case of the United Nations, it is the Commission on Human Rights – and more especially its Sub-Commission on Prevention of Discrimination and Protection of Minorities – and the Commission on the Status of Women. In the case of the League of Arab States, it is the permanent Arab States Commission on Human Rights; with the Organization of American States it is the Inter-American Commission on Human Rights and with the Council of Europe, its Committee of Experts on Human Rights. Other organizations, like the International Labour Organisation and UNESCO, have relied more on the appropriate units in their secretariats. The United Nations has combined both methods.

The research conducted by these bodies or administrative departments was hitherto concerned with defining rather than enforcing the legal standards of human rights.

The studies and investigations directed towards the guaranteeing of human rights are entrusted preferably to specialized bodies set up on an *ad hoc* basis or according to the terms of particular provisions made in an international human rights convention. In the United Nations for instance there are the Special Committee on Apartheid, the Special Committee on Decolonization, the Committee on the Elimination of Racial Discrimination and the Committee on Human Rights. In ILO, there are the bodies provided for under its Constitution, and also its Governing Body's committee on Freedom of Association. The Organization of African Unity has its Liberation Committee while the Council of Europe has the bodies set up under the European Convention on Human Rights, the Commission and the Court, as well as those associated with the European Social Charter. Lastly, there are the bilateral methods employed by the socialist States for the international promotion of human rights, particularly cultural rights.

Whether directed towards setting standards for the promotion of human rights or ensuring their enforcement, international studies and investigations have always been supported and sustained and sometimes even initiated by a host of national and international movements, organizations, groups and institutes, most frequently of a private nature. And it will be to their eternal honour to have originated the Universal Declaration of Human Rights.

5. UNESCO'S *action and the contribution of the social sciences*

This proliferation of instruments and institutions none the less gives to even the most optimistic an impression of confusion and weakness, and to others a feeling of failure. The excessive dispersion of effort will thus have to be overcome by means of an overall approach to all the aspects and implications of the problem of human rights in order that this feeling of failure shall not become the acknowledgement of a reality.

In so far as regards UNESCO, which by its very purpose has always been dedicated to the cause of human rights and peace, its most recent activities extend in two directions. First it operates a major *programme of social studies* devoted to the elucidation of certain general factors conducive or inimical to the advance of human rights and to the analysis of certain specific social situations entailing serious violations of human rights, particularly in connexion with colonialism and racial oppression, and especially to unmasking and condemning the social institutions and practices which perpetuate these grave injustices. The first group of studies has borne mainly on ways of eliminating racism and racial discrimination and has led to meetings of experts and to studies and publications either of general significance or applying to particular situations, especially those found in southern Africa. Other questions studied have been inter-group relations in multi-ethnic societies, the role played by the various factors making for discrimination and inequality and ways and means of establishing more equitable social relationships which are more in conformity with human dignity and human rights.

The second direction in which UNESCO'S activities have been turned in recent years has been towards *defining in greater depth the rights existing within its fields of competence* and examining the optimum conditions for their enforcement. The Organization has attempted to improve the working of existing legal instruments, particularly the Convention against Discrimination in Education, and to prepare new instruments concerning education, access to culture and the protection of the cultural heritage. A start has also been made on examining problems not all of whose aspects are as yet fully explored, and particular mention may be made of a meeting of experts on "Human Rights and Population" and a symposium on biology and ethics. Akin to this work to clarify and illustrate human rights and ways of implementing them, particularly at international level, is the encouragement given by UNESCO to furthering the advanced study of these rights, either through surveys concerning the organization of university research and teaching on these subjects, or through the development and dissemination of methodological guides, handbooks, etc.

The two broad series of activities just described have been supplemented over the last two years by UNESCO'S *increased participation in the work of the United Nations bodies with responsibilities for human rights*.

6. Overall approach and specific studies

Under its Constitution, UNESCO has special responsibility for everything involving prevention of the various forms of discrimination and promotion of the rights to education, science, culture and information in the service of peace. With the passage of time, however, extra tasks have been entrusted to it, either by its own General Conference or by the United Nations'

General Assembly or Economic and Social Council (ECOSOC), in regard to the race problem, apartheid, the preparation of textbooks on human rights for higher education, or surveys on particular issues.

In the coming years, UNESCO'S action should be guided by three principles.

First, in the light of UNESCO'S particular responsibilities, an *overall approach* to human rights will have to be encouraged in order to gather together the fragmentary components – as regards both international standards and their implementation – so that they can be better known and more effectively taught. Without abandoning the search for solutions to the eternal conflict between the individual and the State, it is also necessary to promote knowledge and recognition of human rights as an arena affording the possibility of co-operation between the individual and the State when faced with the abuse of private power (e.g. by multinational corporations) or within the framework of a new economic order. Finally, only this overall approach will enable human rights to be made personal by adapting their requirements to particular situations relating, for example, to multi-ethnic or multi-racial societies, socially excluded groups or groups which have been relegated to an inferior position.

Secondly it will be necessary to further the *specificity of cultural rights,* taken in the broad sense of the term, since these are rights for which UNESCO bears particular responsibility. As cultural rights denote inherent qualities of man *vis-à-vis* organized society and at the same time reflect man's beliefs as to the nature of that society, they are both individual and collective in character, culture truly deserving its name only if it belongs to everyone and if it is expressed for the benefit of all: in short, only if it is shared. This will be the principle which must for example govern UNESCO'S contribution to the human rights activities of the United Nations, and primarily with regard to implementation of the world code of human rights formed by the two Covenants of 1966.

Thirdly, there must be a redoubling of vigilance and of the spirit of accuracy and objectivity in the *scientific* study of the complex problems raised by the effective implementation of human rights, which must include an analysis of the underlying reasons why they are so frequently flouted. Knowledge of the social structures which provide the backcloth for any ethical assertion and any formulation of human rights, as for any attempt to promote them, requires to be taken further and also extended to cover other societies and other aspects. Elucidation of the philosophical and cultural attitudes subtending acceptance or refusal or standard-setting activities is also of major importance. UNESCO is here again fulfilling a task specific to it. In the final analysis, the effort called for will have to be directed, on the one hand, to adopting a rigorous scientific approach to all UNESCO'S fields with the concern to illuminate and to serve human rights. Human rights are neither a new morality nor a lay religion and are much more than a language common to all mankind. They are requirements which the investigator must study and integrate into his knowledge using the rules and methods of his science, whether this is philosophy, the humanities or the natural sciences, sociology or law, history or geography. In a word, the task is gradually to build up or promote a genuine scientific formulation of human rights.

These three principles of action should guide UNESCO in the two aspects of its practical activities on behalf of human rights which are defined in the above analysis: deepening the knowledge of human rights and consolidating what has been achieved.

Deepening . . .

Action in favour of *deepening the knowledge of human rights* should thus be centred on an analysis of the violations of these rights and the manifestations, causes and effects of these violations, with particular reference to racism, colonialism, neo-colonialism and apartheid. It should also form part of the Decade for Action to Combat Racism and Racial Discrimination and have recourse particularly to the social sciences in which important research work has been carried out. Sociological examination is also very much needed for the necessary study of the socio-economic phenomena which affect the exercise of human rights, particularly those of groups and especially socially excluded groups such as minorities and migrant workers.

Between now and 1982, appropriate programme action will be directed specifically towards:

Acquiring a better understanding of the main socio-economic processes at work in situations of racial discrimination, apartheid, colonialism and neo-colonialism.

Building up a body of knowledge which will throw light on the functioning of the principal types of multi-ethnic societies and the ideological and cultural aspects of ethnic awareness, thus encouraging the adoption of social policies better able to guarantee the exercise of human rights in the societies in question.

Shedding light on the relationships existing between certain socio-economic and cultural phenomena (especially those associated with rapid technological change and accelerated urban development) and the exercise of human rights in general and the rights of socially excluded groups in particular. This additional knowledge will have been put to use more especially in connection with the efforts to establish a new international economic order.

. . . *consolidating*

Action to *consolidate what has been achieved in the way of standards and institutions* should be aimed at developing a specialized study of human rights, along lines directed towards the guaranteeing of such rights in a manner which will have to be, if not integrated, at least co-ordinated among all international organizations. UNESCO intends, within its fields of competence, to improve existing legal instruments, having regard to the appropriate articles of the Universal Declaration of Human Rights and the Covenants. At the same time, it will participate in systematic development of the various research activities relating to human rights at international level, both as regards improving the conceptual framework and the matter of establishing a network of institutions.

UNESCO will seek to initiate a wide-ranging debate at international level on the problems raised by the right to communication and ways of promoting it.

. . . *through teaching*

Between now and 1982 efforts will be made to encourage the development of courses and research programmes on human rights, the setting up or enlargement of specialist departments in university and scientific establishments and the training of teachers and research workers in this field.

UNESCO'S action will also be aimed at developing methods for the advanced study of human rights and preparing the necessary teaching material and reference works.

. . . *and co-operation*

Steps wil be taken to make the Organization's standard-setting activity more effective and to secure better co-ordination with similar activities carried out by the other agencies of the United Nations system, particularly by participation in the implementation of the International Covenant on Economic, Social and Cultural Rights, under the auspices of the Economic and Social Council, and by the study of reports and in information provided by governments on measures adopted, progress made and obstacles encountered in securing the rights which fall within UNESCO'S purview.

CHAPTER X

THE ROLE OF THE ILO: PRESENT ACTION AND FUTURE PERSPECTIVES

DR. NICOLAS VALTICOS*

It is always a perilous honour to have played a pioneering role: after being in the vanguard, there is a danger of finding one day that one has become a venerated ancestor and a somewhat outdated model. What is the position today of the International Labour Organisation, which has often been considered a pioneer in the international protection of human rights? This is an appropriate moment to ask this question for at the present time the Organisation is facing serious problems, and it has moreover just reviewed the whole body of its standard-setting work and adapted its supervisory procedures to present needs, and it is in the process of drawing up a standard-setting programme which should be valid for the next 20 years and more.

Over the years, numerous voices have testified to the contribution made by the ILO to the launching of action for the international protection of human rights. An authoritative voice is that of René Cassin, whose name is closely linked with this international action, and who has written that the general protection of human rights first took shape in the ILO, whose work has provided the foundation for a system of universal customary common law protecting the essential individual freedoms.[1] René Cassin laid particular emphasis on the exemplary value of the supervisory procedures built up by the Organisation, whose experience, he wrote, can and should be used to improve the situation of the whole of humanity. A multiplicity of similar references could be cited and over a time span of 30 years international lawyers of such distinction as George Scelle,[2] Lord MacNair[3] and more recently – as will be seen below – the late lamented Chief Justice Earl

---

* Assistant Director-General, Adviser for International Labour Standards, International Labour Office; Associate Professor in the Faculty of Law at the University of Geneva; Associate of the Institut de droit international. The views expressed in this chapter are those of the author.
[1] René Cassin, *Human Rights Journal,* Vol. IV-4, 1971, pp. 684-685.
[2] *Précis de droit des gens.* Vol. II, 1934, p. 521.
[3] "The International Labour Conventions" in *The expansion of International Law,* Jerusalem, 1962, p. 45.

Warren – have suggested that the ILO procedures should be more widely resorted to by other international institutions.

What, then, are the reasons for which these procedures have been taken as a model?

First, because the ILO has introduced a quasi-legislative procedure for the international regulation of human rights by precise international instruments designed to be the subject of formal undertakings by States. Secondly, because the ILO has sought to ensure the effective implementation of these instruments through a developed system of supervision which comprises in particular an objective evaluation and the participation of non-governmental elements.

These two major aspects deserve closer study.

A. THE DRAFTING OF INTERNATIONAL STANDARDS

The drafting of international standards is the logical point of departure for international action designed to protect human rights, since there must be initial agreement, with at least a minimum of precision, on the scope of the rights to be protected.

1. The International Instruments

It has been by drawing up progressively, year by year, a total of some 150 Conventions and 160 Recommendations that the ILO has been able to establish a solid and authoritative base for systematic action designed to ensure the implementation of this body of standards in the different countries of the world.

It is true that the "standards" of the ILO do not consist only of the Conventions and Recommendations.

Thus the Organisation's constitutional instruments have been drawn on as a legal basis for certain important standards. This has been the case for two passages, now well known, in the Declaration of Philadelphia of 1944, which has been incorporated into the ILO Constitution. One of these affirms that "all human beings, irrespective of race, creed or sex, have the right to pursue both their material well-being and their spiritual development in conditions of freedom and dignity, of economic security and equal opportunity"; the other, that "freedom of expression and of association are essential to sustained progress". These are no empty phrases. They have provided the legal framework for concrete action on a large scale, both to safeguard trade union freedom and to combat racial discrimination. They have made possible an evaluation of the behaviour, the law and the practice of States, and they have permited recommendations to be made, where necessary, for corrective action or even a change in social policy.

At the other end of the standard-setting spectrum will be found standards which are less formal than Conventions and Recommendations, such as resolutions adopted by the Conference, some of which, on trade union freedom and human rights, have often been used as a basis for decisions of the ILO supervisory bodies, and for the case law of these bodies.

It is however principally the Conventions – and Recommendations – which have formed the foundations of ILO action for the protection and promotion of both economic and social rights (employment, conditions of work and life, social security, employment of women, children and special categories of workers, social institutions etc.), and certain fundamental rights and freedoms such as freedom of association, the abolition of forced labour and the elimination of discrimination in employment.

At this stage, certain essential questions must be clarified.

2. Universality of Standards

One of the main effects of the standards adopted by the ILO has been to underline the universal validity of human rights. There has sometimes been a tendency to voice doubts as to the possibility of having universal standards in view of the diversity which exists between countries in the economic, social and political fields. Nothing could be more dangerous for the protection of human rights than this sceptical relativism. Reasoning of this kind would lead to a denial of the recognition by mankind of certain common values which transcend differences of race, faith, political structure, culture and economic development and which are based on the equality, freedom and solidarity of all men. It would be equivalent to dividing up the world with sealed partitions and admitting that there should be – to recall an often quoted phrase – "sub-standards for sub-humans".[4]

This does not mean that there is no room for regional instruments alongside the universal standards. Such instruments could supplement the existing universal standards on subjects of particular interest to a given

---

[4] Report of the African Advisory Committee on its Third Session, Dakar, October 1957. *Minutes of the Governing Body of the ILO,* November 1967, p. 82, para. 156.

region, or even open the way to subsequent universal action. It can also be useful to examine at the regional level the problems which arise in the implementation of universal standards in a given region. This has been done by the ILO since 1970.

The standards themselves, however, in a world which has to live as one and meet the universal aspirations of its peoples, must in their essentials be uniform.[5] Recent consultations undertaken by the ILO resulted in a massive affirmation of this principle.

3. Flexibility of Standards

It is however undeniable that there are great differences between countries. It would therefore be illusory to seek to reach the same level of protection for each human right everywhere at the same time. It is for this reason that, in the first place, it is ILO practice to adopt separate instruments for each subject matter, so that States may ratify the Conventions separately in the light of their state of development and the evolution of their legislation.

Secondly, in the wording of the instruments themselves care has been taken to introduce a degree of flexibility, and this to an increasing extent with the growth in the number and diversity of the Member States. However, in the field of fundamental human rights it has been felt that there is no room for any form of flexibility which would impair the protection which the Convention is designed to ensure. The purpose of the flexibility devices used in Conventions – and they are numerous and very varied[6] – is to avoid at one and the same time excessive detail (which would not be appropriate in instruments designed for very different states) and excessive generalisation (which would be liable to make the Conventions devoid of substance).

4. Future Perspectives

What is the future outlook for the adoption of international labour standards? Must it be considered, first of all, that the present body of standards, consisting of over 300 instruments, now covers the essential

---

[5] See Valticos, "Normes universelles et normes régionales dans le domaine du travail", in *Régionalisme et universalisme dans le droit international contemporain,* Société française pour le droit international, Colloque de Bordeaux, Paris, 1977, pp. 289-307; Wolf, "Y a-t-il un droit social régional?", *eod. loc.,* pp. 309-312.

[6] See Valticos and Wolf, "L'OIT et les pays en voie de développement: techniques d'élaboration et mise en oeuvre de normes universelles", in *Pays en voie de développement et transformation du droit international,* Société française pour le droit international, Colloque d'Aix en Provence, Paris, 1974, pp. 127-146.

labour problems and that the task of drawing up international standards is practically complete? This is far from being the case.

First of all, needs and conceptions change with the years at the international as well as at the national level, and the older instruments thus often have to be reworked to adapt them to contemporary needs. Already some 40 of the 150 odd Conventions adopted over almost 60 years represent the adaptation of older instruments to the test of time and the lessons of experience. Whether it be a question of the earlier concept of social insurance which has developed into social security, or of the employment of women where the concern for their protection is progressively giving way before the striving for equality, standards are steadily being brought up to date and there is no doubt that this will continue, perhaps even at an accentuated pace, in the years to come.

A second consequence of the evolution of needs and concepts will be that new questions will arise which will call for the adoption of international labour standards. The very history of international labour law – like that of national labour law – is made up of the emergence of new questions as a result of social progress and of needs which make themselves felt in modern societies – the need for greater material security and welfare but also the need for freedom, equality and participation. Thus when the first ILO Convention on holidays with pay was adopted in 1936 the idea was a recent one and was considered revolutionary. Its development since is well known. And what is to be said of the Convention against discrimination in employment, which was adopted in 1958, in response to relatively recent developments in ideas and awareness, and which rapidly came to be regarded as one of the fundamental instruments of the ILO? In the field of occupational safety and hygiene, which affect workers' lives and health, rapid technological change makes necessary the constant adoption of measures against new or newly-identified risks. This trend will certainly continue. Thus, problems of the environment will no doubt require action on a broader scale than the classical questions of occupational health and safety. Thus, again, a question which, although it is not new, has become more acute in modern societies has already been included in the agenda of the International Labour Conference for 1979, namely that of older workers.

These predictions are more than mere suppositions. Following a recent "in depth review" of international labour standards, a working party of the ILO Governing Body is in the process of examining all these standards so as to identify, in particular, the instruments which are in need of revision and the subjects on which the preparation of new standards should be considered. This work is still under way, but it is already apparent that the subjects which, at first sight, would seem to come into these two categories are so numerous that they would fully engage all the ILO's legislative capacity for the next 25 years or more, irrespective of the questions to which future developments will give rise. A huge area thus remains to be covered by international labour law, which will continue to make a major contribution to social policy in the world as long as it is able to anticipate and channel the new needs of societies in constant evolution.[7]

This continuing legislative activity gives rise to a further problem: that of the growing number of international instruments. Is there not a danger that the existence of several hundred instruments will embarrass, if not paralyse, countries (governments as well as occupational organisations)? Reference has sometimes been made to "dead wood" that needs eliminating. This approach has given rise to objections. Quite apart from the legal difficulties which would be involved in abrogating instruments most of which have been the subject of formal undertakings, it has been observed that it would be unlikely that everybody would agree that a given Convention has lost all interest. While it may have become out of date for some countries, an instrument may still be of value or even premature for others.[8] The problem is now approached from another angle, in that the working party has decided to place in a distinct category the instrument whose ratification and application should be promoted on a priority basis, and attention will be primarily concentrated on these instruments.

A final point on which it is possible to make a prediction without fear of error relates to the way in which future instruments will be drafted. There is no doubt that the use of flexibility devices will be continued and even intensified, especially for conventions laying down general principles which are supplemented by Recommendations providing guidance on methods of implementation, and for Conventions containing provisions for their progressive application, such as those which can be ratified with the initial acceptance of only certain parts.

B. THE IMPLEMENTATION OF STANDARDS

The drawing up of standards is only the first stage in the international protection of human rights. The essential stage is their implementation, and

---

[7] See Jenks, *The World Beyond the Charter,* London, 1969, p. 180.

[8] See Wilfred Jenks, "ILO standards: Are they Obsolete, Premature, Marginal or Important?", in *Social Policy in a Changing World,* ILO, Geneva, 1976, p. 86.

this is a difficult task in this paradoxical world in which countries' growing interdependence is paralleled by an often touchy susceptibility concerning national sovereignty. In this area new paths have been opened up by the ILO.

1. Ratification of Conventions

The legal effect of ILO Conventions is governed by the traditional rule according to which they are binding only on the States which ratify them. It is therefore important, as a first step, to obtain ratification from States. It is to be observed that the ILO Conventions have received an impressive number of ratifications, at present around 4.500 by some 140 States. The Conventions which deal with fundamental human rights have each received an average of 99 ratifications.

This achievement is largely the result of a rule, an innovation in international law, which is contained in the ILO Constitution and which requires the States Members of the Organisation to submit Conventions and Recommendations, within 12 or 18 months of their adoption, to the competent national authority, generally the legislative authority.[9] This rule, which leads the government services concerned to examine carefully the ILO Conventions and the effect to be given to them, has resulted in a generally high number of ratifications. It has even been suggested that an analogous procedure be envisaged for the Conventions adopted under the auspices of the United Nations.[10]

2. Supervision of implementation

In order to ensure that the standards it adopts have the greatest possible impact, the ILO has built up over the years a diversified system of supervision which remains the most advanced on the international level both as regards the variety of methods it uses – whether these are aimed at fact-finding[11] or based on the examination of written communications – and by reason of the fact that it makes it possible to examine the effect given even

---

[9] See Valticos, "The International Labour Organisation and National Parliaments", in *Inter-parliamentary Bulletin,* 1969, No. 1, pp. 16-31.

[10] See R. Ago, "La codification du droit international et les problèmes de sa réalisation", in *Recueil d'études de droit international en hommage à Paul Guggenheim,* Geneva, 1968, p. 120.

[11] See Valticos, "L'inspection internationale dans le droit international du travail" in *L'inspection internationale,* Etudes réunies et introduites par G. Fischer et D. Vignes, Brussels, 1976, pp. 379-437.

to non-ratified Conventions and to promote, even in cases of non-ratification, the implementation of the essential principles of the Organisation, in particular freedom of association. In the search for effectiveness, the various procedures built up have gone as far as it has been possible to go without clashing with national sovereignties.

This is not the place to go in detail into the ILO supervisory procedures. They have often been described.[12] It will suffice here to draw attention to their most significant aspects.

3. The Participation of Non-Governmental Elements

The most characteristic feature of the over-all activities of the ILO is the participation, alongside governments, of representatives of employers and workers. This is "tripartism". This principle makes it possible to break into the monopoly role which States play in international law and which sometimes turns discussions on human rights into essentially political debates or results in obscure compromises. The participation of non-governmental elements is not limited to ensuring the direct representation of those who are immediately concerned; it also provides additional sources of information, gives greater vitality to international action and makes it possible for an informed and free public opinion to introduce a breath of fresh air. In the cases which most shock world conscience, this participation makes it easier to bring into play the ultimate moral weapon which has been called "the mobilisation of shame"[13] and which can be an effective means of inducing States to comply with the obligations which they have entered into.

4. Resort to Independent Bodies

A second significant element in the ILO system is that it has resort to independent persons when a legal evaluation of the application of international standards has to be made. This is a point of fundamental impor-

---

[12] See Valticos, "Un système de contrôle international: la mise en oeuvre des conventions internationales du travail", in *Recueil des Cours de l'Académie de droit international,* 1968-I, pp. 311-407: by the same author, "Les méthodes de protection internationale de la liberté syndicale", *ibid.,* 1975-I, pp. 79-138: Wolf, "Aspects judiciaires de la protection internationale des droits de l'homme par l'OIT", in *Human Rights Journal,* Vol. IV-4, 1971, pp. 773-830; Wolf, "ILO experience in the Implementation of Human Rights", in *The Journal of International Law and Economics.* August-December 1975, pp. 599-625.

[13] A. Zimmern, *The League of Nations and the Rule of Law;* 1919-1935, London, 1936, p. 460.

tance and the reasons for it are self-evident.[14] These independent bodies provide the surest guarantee of integrity, impartiality and objectivity in the exercise of the quasi-judicial function of evaluating the conformity of national situations with international standards. When, as is often the case elsewhere, the supervisory bodies are in effect composed of government delegates, their members cannot entirely erase from their minds the concerns of their countries. In any event, their composition will give rise to doubts in people's minds, and may even be invoked to call the results of their work into question.

Thus, this rule is also inspired by concern for the credibility and effectiveness of supervision. Once all those concerned – including the international organisation as a whole – have confidence in the integrity of the supervisory bodies, their intervention will be the more readily accepted by the States concerned and their conclusions will be more likely to meet with general acceptance.

What exactly is involved in this concept of independence? The essential criterion is that the persons concerned do not hold any position in which they are subject to the directions of the authorities of a given country. It is true that independence is also a question of character. There is thus also an individual element which may depend to a certain extent on the background and traditions which form the intellectual and moral "environment" of each individual. This element can only be taken into account by choosing persons whose personality and past activities provide appropriate indications.

The process of choosing the persons is also a matter of considerable importance. If it is left to States, there would be a lesser guarantee that the person chosen is independent, or his independence might be challenged. It is for this reason that it is the ILO practice for the members of these bodies to be appointed by the Governing Body on the proposal of the Director-General of the ILO, who of course undertakes the necessary consultations.

The independence of the supervisory bodies is only the first prerequisite for the full performance of their functions. It is also necessary that the questions submitted to them be examined in depth. These bodies are therefore assisted by thorough staff work undertaken by a qualified secretariat

[14] On the importance of independent bodies see Jenks, "The International Protection of Trade Union Rights" in *The International Protection of Human Rights,* ed. by Evan Luard, London, 1967, pp. 237 *et seq.:* Valticos, "Un système de contrôle international", op. cit., pp. 384-385. The late lamented Pierre Juvigny wrote on this subject that it was in the ILO's honour that it had created conditions which secreted a genuine tradition of objectivity ("L'OIT et les droits de l'homme"), in *Revue française des affaires sociales.* April-June 1969, p. 94.

made available to them by the ILO. More generally, the spirit in which they fulfil their task has been described as combining a striving for exactitude in appraising situations, firmness on the principles and obligations at issue, boldness combined with a sense of proportion and realism, and the will to achieve positive results through constructive mutual discussion.

5. Independent Bodies and Representative Bodies

At the present stage of international organisation, the intervention of independent bodies, essential though it may be, is not sufficient, particularly in the most important cases, to ensure the satisfactory implementation of international standards. If this objective is to be more closely approached, the international organisation itself must add the weight of its representative bodies. Thus various ILO tripartite bodies take over from the independent bodies and seek to persuade the governments concerned to ensure a more satisfactory application of the Conventions. This process is seen most strikingly in the work of the tripartite committee which is set up each year by the International Labour Conference to examine the application of Conventions and Recommendations.

It is worth spelling out the differing roles of these two types of body. The independent bodies, such as the Committee of Experts on the Application of Conventions and Recommendations, the essential mainspring[15] of supervision, are called on to undertake the examination, on a legal basis, of the degree of application of international labour standards. This they do principally through their reports, which are autonomous and do not require the approval of another body. Their quasi-judicial role derives from their terms of reference as well as from their composition. The essential role of the Committee of Experts in the supervisory process is illustrated by the fact that the Committee each year examines thousands of reports supplied by governments, makes some 1,200 comments on them (in the form of published observations and of requests addressed directly to the governments concerned) whereas the Conference Committee, for lack of time, only examines about 120 of these cases (some 10 per cent) though these are the most important.

The fact is that the role of the Conference Committee differs from that of the Committee of Experts. It consists in the search, with the governments concerned and by means of dialogue, for solutions to the imperfections noted by the Committee of Experts. There is no question of proceeding to a

---

[15] Juvigny, *loc. cit.*

new legal evaluation - which the Conference Committee would not be equipped to undertake - nor is it in any way a second instance. At this stage, it is essentially a question of seeking to give effect to the conclusions which have previously been reached by the legal body.

Following its exchanges of views with the representatives of the governments concerned, the Conference Committee sums up these discussions in its report which also contains its own conclusions. For the last 20 years or so, it has drawn attention more particularly to the cases, among those in which the application of Conventions is not satisfactory, which it considers the most serious. The inclusion of a case in this "special list" sometimes gives rise to heated discussions. In more recent years, since 1975, the Committee has also included in its report a series of special paragraphs in which it sets out the essence of certain cases - they related to seven countries in 1977 - which gave rise to significant discussions.

Finally, the Committee's report is presented to the plenary Conference where it is the subject of a more general discussion, which normally concludes with the adoption of the report by the Conference itself. Sometimes (in 1966 and 1967) the Conference has considered it sufficient simply to take note of the report, since it describes the work undertaken by the Committee. The most common practice has been for the Conference to adopt the report formally, and this has not given rise to problems except on two recent occasions, in 1974 and 1977, when, following disagreements on cases of particular political significance, the report was not adopted by the Conference through lack of a quorum. This was in part due to the special rules of the ILO governing the quorum,[16] and the lack of a quorum does not mean that the report was rejected but simply that it was not adopted, while remaining a Conference document giving an account of the work of the Committee in question. This did not in any way block the working of the supervisory machinery since the Committee of Experts and the Conference Committee meet each year and take account of their previous discussions. It nonetheless remains true that this non-adoption constituted a serious incident, and this type of problem might well be examined at a forthcoming session of the Conference.

---

[16] By virtue of article 17, paragraph 3 of the ILO Constitution, "the voting is void unless the total number of votes cast is equal to half the number of the delegates attending the Conference" and abstentions are not considered as "votes cast". This led in 1977 to the result that the Conference Committee's report which, in plenary sitting, received 137 votes in favour and none against, with 197 abstentions, was considered as not having been adopted by the Conference.

6. The Role of "Quiet Diplomacy"

Alongside the formal procedures, in particular those originating in complaints, and parallel to them the Director-General of the ILO and, under his directives, representatives appointed by him, have engaged, in delicate cases, in a sort of "quiet diplomacy"[17] designed to assist the supervisory bodies and to undertake with the governments concerned the informal consultations which, without encroaching in any way on the judicial independence of these bodies, were necessary to obtain the fullest co-operation of the States concerned and to reach a satisfactory solution. Another group of cases in which recourse to this sort of diplomacy has been increasingly and successfully used in the course of the last 10 years in some 30 States is a relatively new device of "direct contacts", designed to help in the solution of long-standing discrepancies or more generally of difficulties relating to standards.

7. Diversity of supervisory techniques, regular supervision, supervision on the basis of complaints, special studies and inquiries

On the basis of the general principles already described, the ILO supervisory procedures comprise a great variety of techniques. Broadly speaking, these techniques make use of two different methods.

The first, which is also the most used, involves the supply by States, at periodic intervals, of reports, based on report forms drawn up for this purpose, setting out the way in which they give effect to international standards. Thousands of these reports are examined each year and the original rule, which provided for the supply of annual reports on each ratified Convention, has had to be relaxed (most recently in 1976), so as to provide for reports at less frequent intervals, subject to a number of safeguards designed to maintain the effectiveness of supervision.

The second method consists of the examination of complaints of various kinds which can be made not only by governments but also by occupational organisations or their delegates. The major forms of this type of proceeding, which are provided for by the ILO Constitution, relate to the application of Conventions by countries which have ratified them and may involve the establishment of independent commissions of inquiry. This

---

[17] See N. Valticos, "Diplomacy in an Institutional Framework: Some Aspects of ILO Practice and Experience", in La Comunità Internazionale, 1974-3, pp. 8-13.

procedure has been followed in relation to such issues as forced labour (as regards Portugal – in respect of Angola and Mozambique – in 1961 and Liberia the following year), trade union freedom (for Greece in 1968 and a number of Latin American countries recently), hours of work and discrimination in employment on the basis of political opinion (in Chile, in 1974). In some of these cases the independent commissions of inquiry undertook on-the-spot investigations for which solid guarantees were given.

In the field of discrimination, representations (a simpler form of complaint), were made in 1977 against Czechoslovàkia on the one hand and a number of western European countries on the other.

In addition, a procedure was introduced in 1950 under an agreement between the ILO and the Economic and Social Council of the United Nations for the examination of complaints alleging violations of freedom of association even against countries which have not ratified the relevant Conventions. These complaints are examined by a tripartite committee of the Governing Body (the Committee on Freedom of Association) and they may, generally in important cases, be referred in addition to a Fact-Finding and Conciliation Commission if the government concerned agrees. This requirement of the consent of the State concerned was at first a stumbling block, the first governments approached having refused, but since 1964 several governments have given their consent, thus making it possible to undertake a detailed examination, with an on-the-spot investigation, of a number of very different cases such as those against Japan in 1964 and Chile in 1974.

Finally, in several cases, the ILO has undertaken inquiries and studies which were either general in scope or related to a particular country, sometimes at the country's own request. The most recent such case was the study of the labour and trade union situation in Spain, undertaken in 1968-69 by a group composed of independent persons, which met freely with people from all sides of the spectrum, including detained trade unionists. Studies of this kind, which take the ILO standards as their point of departure, are designed to clarify controversial questions and to help governments to solve the problems which face them on important issues of social policy and human rights.

New procedures are thus frequently established to take account of new needs and situations. In 1972 the Governing Body approved proposals for special surveys on national situations in cases which raise questions of discrimination in employment. No such studies have yet been undertaken.

8. The results of supervision

How effective is this system?[18] Over-all figures for the procedure based on
the examination of Government reports show that over the last 14 years
more than 1,100 cases concerning some 150 countries have been noted, in
which governments have taken the measures recommended by the supervisory bodies. As to the procedures based on the examination of formal
complaints, the governments concerned have almost always given effect, in
part at least, to the recommendations of commissions of inquiry.

To give a number of more concrete examples, the lives of some scores of
trade unionists in Africa and Latin America have been saved, and
hundreds of others have been freed as a result of the intervention of the
bodies responsible for safeguarding freedom of association. In Asia,
noticeable improvements have been obtained in Japan in respect of trade
union rights in the public sector and minimum wages in the private sector,
while in Indonesia the Government undertook, in 1976-77, to free – or
bring to trail at an early date – tens of thousands of detainees, and has
already freed a number of them. In eastern Europe, provisions considered
incompatible with the freedom of association and forced labour Conventions are regularly discussed and some of them have been repealed or
amended. In western Europe progress has been made in implementing
equality of remuneration in several countries following the ratification of
ILO Convention No. 100: in Spain where, as has already been said, an independent body had visited the country in 1969, the trade union legislation
was profoundly modified in April 1977 after the changes which had taken
place in the country, and this was done on the basis of the ILO's freedom
of association Conventions which Spain was then in a position to ratify
shortly afterwards. In general, one is struck by the extent to which ILO
standards, and the procedures for their follow-up, produce regular results.

9. The difficulties of supervision

The results obtained should not be used to conceal the difficulties, and
sometimes even the failures, which are also encountered on occasion.

In relation to the States concerned, the first problem is to establish a
dialogue with them. This has already been achieved to a very large extent,
since a very high proportion (80 per cent) of the reports due are received
from governments, and almost all the States requested to do so (generally

---

[18] See in particular *The impact of International Labour Conventions and Recommendations,* ILO, Geneva, 1977.

around 50) participate in the discussions of the Conference Committee on the Application of Conventions in their country. The response which has been registered to the procedure of "direct contacts" initiated in 1968 provides further testimony. The cases in which a dialogue cannot be established are the exceptions. Moreover, they are most often due to administrative inadequacies rather than intentional. Whatever the reason, the ILO seeks, by a variety of means, to establish contact.

However, dialogue is no more than a precondition for reaching the desired goal, which is the fuller implementation of international standards, and there remain many cases in which the application of standards is defective and in which divergences, some of them major, have persisted for a long time. The causes may be varied: poor administrative organisation, difficulties of an economic or a political nature, etc. In all these cases, the supervisory bodies – and the ILO as a whole – seek, first by persuasion and discreet action, then by public discussion and pressure, to bring the States concerned closer to the international standard. It is in the field of human rights – freedom of association, forced labour and, to some extent, discrimination – that some of the most difficult problems are met, no doubt because these questions are sometimes closely linked with important aspects of the political institutions of the country concerned, or are considered as affecting vital interests of the State (for example, the question of free choice of trade union or non-discrimination in employment on grounds of political opinion). On these questions, as on some more technical questions which are covered by other ILO Conventions, supervision is a long-term task, which does not always meet with success, but in which examination and discussion at the international level are in themselves of undisputed value. Insistence, year after year, sometimes leads to results. When the time for change arrives – as has been seen in certain recent cases – the problems raised by the ILO bodies are among the first to receive the attention of the authorities, and the international standards and comments then form a major element in the new orientation of government policies. Supervisory action is thus carried on with perseverance and without discouragement.

It has however sometimes been asked – and the question was raised expressly when the United States gave notice of withdrawal from the ILO in November 1975 – whether the same standard is applied to all States in the supervisory process. Is not the ILO more severe with certain groups of States than with others, more especially at the level of the International Labour Conference? In short, are there not sometimes double standards? In fact, it is to be generally noted that the most differing States are equally the subject of comments by the supervisory bodies and that they are called on to answer for the situation in their country on the same footing. There have sometimes been discussions of whether it was right to take account of the economic and social conditions in each country in assessing the application of Conventions, but on this point the Committee of Experts – followed by the Conference Committee – was unanimous in recalling in 1977 that "its function is to determine whether the requirements of a given Convention are being met, whatever the economic and social conditions existing in a given country. Subject only to any derogations which are expressly permitted by the Convention itself, these requirements remain constant and uniform of all countries. In carrying out this work, the Committee is guided by the standards laid down in the Convention alone, mindful, however, of the fact that the modes of their implementation may be different in different States. These are international standards, and the manner in which their implementation is evaluated must be uniform and must not be affected by concepts derived from any particular social or economic system".[19]

A glance at the list of observations made by the Committee of Experts is, moreover, sufficient to confirm that no countries or groups of countries are favoured. This is clearly shown by the statistics relating to these observations. The same general comment can be made as to the next stage, the discussion by the tripartite Conference Committee. The most differing States are regularly called on to answer before the Committee, and it has often made critical comments even to very important countries.

There have, it is true, been certain temporary pauses in the working of the machinery when, in cases of deadlock, the discussion – which had been heated and lengthy on an important question – was not renewed each year and the supervisory bodies simply indicated that there had been no developments and that the parties' positions remained unchanged. But detailed discussions were renewed some years later as a result of new elements affecting the situation.

It has also happened that during its final phase, in the Conference plenary, the machinery has run into difficulties. As indicated above, such situations are clearly exceptional and do not affect the system as a whole. However, it is essential that every effort be made to avoid their recurrence in future, in order to ensure the normal functioning and continued credibility

---

[19] International Labour Conference, 63rd Session, 1977, Report III, Part 4A, *Report of the Committee of Experts on the Application of Conventions and Recommendations,* ILO, Geneva, 1977, pp. 10-11, para. 31.

of the ILO supervisory machinery.

The problems which arise in connection with the procedures founded on complaints are of a different order. It is true that these procedures have not been used equally in respect of the various regions – or of countries with differing systems – of the world, but they can only come into play if a complaint is made by a government or by an employers' or workers' organisation. This situation is compensated to some extent by the parallel functioning of the procedure based on periodic reports from governments.

On this issue it is worth quoting the authoritative opinion of the late Earl Warren, former Chief Justice of the United States, who was a member of the Committee of Experts, and who said in 1973: "I have been impressed at the extent to which the basic features of effective implementation are built into the constitutional structure of the ILO: fact-finding, exposure, conciliation and adjudication. The handling of complaints, which is the heart of meaningful enforcement of human rights, has been carefully structured in a precise procedural manner. What is still more important, there is a record demonstrating that these arrangements have produced concrete results. Though there may be limits to the use of ILO as a precedent, there is experience there that can be applied effectively to the entire range of human rights concerns."[20]

The problems, it is true, have arisen at the level of the International Labour Conference, where another type of difficulty has also arisen in relation to resolutions, even though few in number, by which the Conference, swayed by the political tensions which shake the world, has condemned the policy of certain member States without there having been recourse to the normal supervisory procedures which contain guarantees of due process. The purpose of these resolutions is clearly not so much to evaluate precisely the position in the country concerned (a task for which precise and objective machinery exists) but to express the feelings of the Conference – or at least its majority – in the face of a situation which it views with particular concern. It is none the less true that strong differences of view have resulted, particularly in relation to a resolution adopted in 1974 concerning the situation of Arab workers in the territories occupied by Israel. There have been no more such resolutions since then, and it is envisaged that the questions to which texts of this kind give rise, and in particular their receivability, will be examined within the framework of the more general problems of the structure of the ILO.

[20] Earl Warren, "It's time to implement the Declaration of Human Rights", in 59 *American Bar Association Journal,* 1973, p. 1259.

10. Future perspectives

How is the future of supervision to be envisaged in these circumstances?

Based as it is on the provisions of the ILO Constitution itself, and on practice characterised by continuing growth over the years,[21] the supervisory machinery now seems, in spite of the incidents which have sometimes marked its progress, to be solidly rooted in written provisions and generally accepted. With this firmly laid foundation, it may be considered that evolution is still possible in several directions.

In the first place, while the role of employers' and workers' organisations is already considerable – and indeed essential for the thoroughness of supervision – by reason of their capacity to make complaints, to comment on government reports, to present evidence and their participation in the Conference Committee and the Governing Body, it may be expected that the measures taken in recent years to inform and train them so as to better equip them to fulfil their functions in this area will be further developed. It is, moreover, significant that a resolution adopted by the International Labour Conference in June 1977 is aimed at the strengthening of tripartism in ILO supervisory procedures of international standards. At the national level, more systematic co-operation may also be expected between these organisations and their countries' governments following the adoption in 1976 of Convention No. 144, which provides for tripartite consultations on matters affecting international labour standards.

A second question is whether a further simplification of the supervisory procedures is to be expected. After the decisions reached in 1976 as to the periodicity of the reports to be requested from governments, it will be difficult to go further without compromising the effectiveness of supervision. There is one respect, however, in which it would be possible to continue in this direction without any major drawbacks: if it is decided, as it has been stated is the intention, to classify a number of Conventions as of priority interest, it would then be logical for the other Conventions to be the subject of less frequent reports.

On the other hand, the concern for increased effectiveness in the human rights field will certainly continue to influence the development of the supervisory procedures and no doubt more generally the over-all means of action of the Organisation. At the present stage of development of the

---

[21] For the essential aspects of this growth, see Valticos, "Fifty Years of Standard-Setting Activities by the ILO", in *International Labour Review,* September 1969, pp. 227-236.

supervisory procedures major improvements no longer seem possible: the fundamental principle of complementary resort to independent bodies and tripartite bodies is firmly established and can hardly be called into question. In addition, two relatively recent trends will no doubt develop in the years to come: in the first place, the use of discreet methods of discussion between the governments concerned and the representatives of the Director-General in an attempt to overcome difficulties encountered; in the second place, in serious cases – and possibly in cases in which the discreet attempts at settlement have failed – resort to the formal procedures of complaint and representation, the number of which has for a series of reasons substantially increased in the course of the last ten years.

In the area of complaints alleging violations of freedom of association, it has sometimes been suggested that the consent of the government concerned should no longer be required for the referral to the Fact-Finding and Conciliation Commission of a case concerning a government which has not ratified the relevant Conventions. It is true that at the outset this requirement prevented the referral of a number of important cases to the Commission. However, the problem is now of diminished importance because the freedom of association Conventions have been ratified by a very large number of States and, in their case, the government's consent is not required for the complaints procedure to be set in motion. For other countries, the work of the Committee on Freedom of Association already makes it possible to examine the substance of complaints. It is nevertheless possible that the suggestion, which raises questions of principle as well as of a practical nature, will be examined in the near future.

Finally, it would be a logical step, following the difficulties which have been met with recently, to seek to define more precisely the respective roles of the different supervisory bodies, so as to ensure that they shall not encroach on one another's functions.

However, independently of the actual methods followed under these procedures, the future of the ILO supervisory system will depend, above all, on the spirit in which it is operated. Will it continue to be characterised by the synthesis of vitality and realism and the concern for objectivity which have left their imprint on the system as a whole, and, at the level of the representative bodies, by the sense of community interest and of "common responsibility for common welfare"[22] which – apart from certain

[22] See Valticos, "Diplomacy in an Institutional Framework", *op. cit.*, pp. 12-15; Jenks, *The World Beyond the Charter, op. cit.*, p. 137. *Social Justice in the Law of Nations* – The ILO Impact after Fifty Years, London, 1970, pp. 67-68; Jessup, *A Modern Law of Nations,* New York, 1950, pp. 446-447.

exceptions, serious, it is true, but which should not lead to generalisations – have for the most part infused the attitude of all concerned? The long history of supervision gives grounds for hope that, even if the voyage is sometimes stormy, the direction will remain the same.

The ILO system of supervision is, moreover, not of interest only to the Organisation itself. A growing role is entrusted to it in the implementation of instruments adopted by other organisations, both universal and regional. It is sufficient to mention here that it has been envisaged as a major element in the implementation of the International Covenant on Economic, Social and Cultural Rights, which provides for a specific contribution from the specialised agencies. Arrangements for this co-operation were worked out following the entry into force of the Covenant in 1976, and the ILO may well, by reason of its body of standards, the working of its procedures and the work it has already done in this field, become "the most effective executing agency of the Covenant",[23] just as it may play a useful role in the implementation of certain provisions of the Convenant on Civil and Political Rights which deal with questions within the ILO's competence.

On a more general level, the ILO's supervisory system has to a large extent been a prototype for international supervision. This has already been indicated above. An affirmative reply can now be given to the question of whether the model still remains valid. Thus, in 1974, a Subcommittee of the United States House of Representatives stated:

The ILO methods of protecting human rights should be emulated by other international organizations. The development of international labor law through adopting Conventions and Recommendations, and the implementation of these standards through effective complaint and reporting procedures, are the ILO's principal achievements in human rights. The Subcommittee commends the ILO for this record.[24]

Finally, at the regional level, the ILO system (more particularly supervision based on the examination of periodic reports from governments) directly inspired the procedure established in 1961 for the supervision of the European Social Charter, which was also drafted – and whose imple-

---

[23] See Wilfred Jenks, "Human Rights, Social Justice and Peace – the Broader Significance of ILO Experience", in *Nobel Symposium, International Protection of Human Rights,* ed. by A. Eide and A. Schou, Stockholm, 1968, p. 251.

[24] *Human Rights in the World Community. A Call for US Leadership.* Report of the Subcommittee on International Organizations and Movements of the Committee on Foreign Affairs, House of Representatives, 24 Mar. 1974, 93rd Congress, 2nd Session, Washington, 1975, p. 45.

mentation is supervised – with the active participation of the ILO.

To end with a general conclusion, which should also be taken as an indication for the future and which does not concern only the ILO but also all the other international procedures such as those of the United Nations and the Council of Europe, it must be stressed that the true effectiveness of the methods of implementing instruments on human rights will depend in large part on the setting aside of political considerations so as to permit an objective, quasi-judicial examination of cases. As has already been said, representative bodies have a role, and even an important role, to play, but they must do this so as to contribute together to a fuller observation of human rights and not – and this concerns governments especially – by showing mutual indulgence or engaging in a form of diplomatic warfare.

On the new page which has been turned for the international protection of human rights by the Covenants, what will matter – whatever the organisation concerned – will be not so much the procedural rules – although they are of undeniable importance – as the spirit in which they are implemented. This means that States – old as well as new – must recognise more and more completely that the concepts of co-operation and interdependence and the principles of community interest in human rights and the welfare of mankind are in the process of replacing the traditional concept of national sovereignty in its absolute and exclusive sense. It also means that the international organisations, and more particularly the bodies responsible for following up the implementation of the relevant international instruments, must be able to carry out their functions with the combination of thoroughness, objectivity, common sense and diplomacy but firmness which is necessary to the realisation of these standards. The international community would have a heavy burden of responsibility to bear if it did not prove equal to such a task.

CHAPTER XI

THE ROLE OF REGIONAL, NATIONAL AND LOCAL INSTITUTIONS: FUTURE PERSPECTIVES

DR. B.G. RAMCHARAN*

A. REGIONAL ARRANGEMENTS

1. Regional arrangements under the Charter of the United Nations

Article 52 of the Charter of the United Nations envisages the existence of regional arrangements or agencies for dealing with such matters relating to the maintenance of international peace and security as are appropriate for regional action, provided that such arrangements or agencies are consistent with the purposes and principles of the United Nations. Professor Inis Claude Jr. has commented thus on the Charter's provisions: "The . . . Charter conferred general approval upon existing and anticipated regional organizations, but contained provisions indicating the purpose of making them serve as adjuncts to the United Nations and subjecting them in considerable measure to the direction and control of the central organization. The Charter reflected the premise that the United Nations should be supreme, and accepted regionalism conditionally, with evidence of anxious concern that lesser agencies should be subordinated to and harmonized with, the United Nations".[1] Professor Claude also "stressed that the suitability of regionalism depends in the first place upon the nature of the problem to be dealt with. Some problems of the modern world are international in the largest sense and can be effectively treated only by global

---

* All views expressed in this paper are those of the author in his purely personal capacity.
[1] Inis L., Claude, Jr., *Swords into Ploughshares* (1964), p. 106. See generally, T. Buergenthal, "International and Regional Human Rights Institutions: Some examples of their interaction", *Texas International Law Journal* (1977), R.C. Lawson (Ed.), *International Regional Organizations* (1962); C.V. Narasimhan, *Regionalism in the United Nations* (1977); F.V. Garcia-Amador (Ed.), *Basic instruments of economic integration in Latin America and in the Caribbean* (1975 - 2 vols); M. Haas (Ed.), *Basic documents of Asian regional organizations* (1974 - 4 vols); L.B. Sohn (Ed.), *Basis documents of African regional organizations* (1971-73 - 4 vols); R.J. Yalem, *Regionalism and World Order* (1965); *Société française pour le droit international, régionalisme et universalisme dans le droit international contemporain* (1977); B.G. Ramcharan, *The International Law Commission* (1977), Chapter 7: A comparative analysis of the codification and progressive development of law at the universal and regional levels; B.G. Ramcharan, "Human Rights in Africa: Whither Now", *University of Ghana Law Journal* (1975), pp. 88-105.

agencies. Others are characteristically regional and lend themselves to solution by correspondingly delimited bodies; still others are regional in nature, but require for their solution the mobilization of extra-regional resources . . .

"The nature of a problem is significant not only for the determination of the most appropriate means of solution, but also for the measurement of the range of its impact. A problem may be regional in location, and susceptible of regional management and yet have such important implications for the whole world as to make it a fit subject for the concern of the general organization. The world at large cannot be disinterested in such regional matters as the demographic problem in South Africa or the status of the forced labourers in the Soviet bloc. Thus, the question of the ramification of a problem as well as that of its intrinsic quality affect the choice between regional and universal approaches."[2]

In considering arrangements at the regional level there are certain imperatives which need to be borne in mind. The first of these is the provision in Article 52 (1) of the United Nations Charter that regional arrangements must be "consistent with the purposes and principles of the United Nations". The thrust of this principle in the human rights field is that regional standards on human rights should not be lesser than those contained in the universal standards laid down by the United Nations. Secondly, it should be remembered that "the underlying basis of the actual working balance between regionalism and universalism which has evolved in the twentieth century has been the conception of regional agencies as concomitant supplements to" universal organizations. "In this conception, regional institutions may function as subordinate pieces of international machinery, sharing the load, diverting some of the tensions of international relations from the central world organization and serving as agents of the larger community in handling problems which pertain primarily to their own regional localities. This conception gives no theoretical priority to the principle of universalism and concedes no inherent superiority to the institutions based upon the principle, rather it assumes the compatibility of regional and general approaches, in minimising their competitive aspects, and looks toward the development of a pragmatic sharing of the tasks of international organizations."[3]

The relevance of the foregoing two points has been noted by Robertson: " . . . (I)t can", he said, "be argued that human rights appertain to human beings by virtue of their humanity and should be guaranteed to all human

---

[2] *Op. cit.* in note 1 above, p. 95.
[3] Claude, *op.cit.,* in note 1 above, p. 105.

beings on a basis of equality, without distinction, wherever they may live. Discrimination on grounds of race, sex, religion, or nationality is forbidden both in the United Nations texts and in the regional conventions. Equally there should be no distinction based on regionalism. The African and the Asian should have the same human rights as the European or the American."

" . . . Human rights should be the same for all persons everywhere, at all times. In other words, the normative content of different international instruments should be, in principle, the same . . . Here the touchstone or the yardstick, is the Universal Declaration, which sets out, in the words of its Preamble, 'a common standard of achievement for all peoples and all nations'. No regional system should be allowed to exist which is not consistent with the norms and principles set out in the Universal Declaration" the essential aim of regional arrangements should be "to secure greater respect for the norms established by the United Nations in the Universal Declaration and other relevant texts".[4]

2. Regional arrangements in the field of human rights

Regional arrangements in the field of human rights exist presently in the Arab, American and Western European regions.[5] In the Western European region there is a European Convention on Human Rights which provides for a European Commission and a European Court of Human Rights. In the American region there is an Inter-American Commission on Human Rights and an American Convention on Human Rights. In the Arab region there is, within the League of Arab States, a Permanent Arab Commission on Human Rights.[6] In the European region as a whole, including Western and Eastern Europe, the European Conference on Security and Co-operation in Europe may be considered as a regional arrangement which also embraces human rights matters. In the African region, although there is no specifically human rights institution, the Charter of the OAU does set out among the aims of the OAU "to promote international co-operation, having due regard to the Charter of the United Nations and the Universal Declaration of Human Rights".

Outside of the specifically human rights regional organizations

---

[4] A.H. Robertson, *Human Rights in the World* (1972), pp. 158-161. See also N. Valticos, "Normes universelles et normes régionales dans le domaine du travail," in *Société française pour le droit international* (1977), pp. 289-312.

[5] See A.H. Robertson, *Human Rights in the World* (1972).

[6] An Arab Declaration on Human Rights is currently in preparation - see E/CN.4/1283, p. 29.

mentioned above, there are other regional organizations whose work is related to the promotion of human rights. Among these may be mentioned the United Nations regional economic and social commissions and other regional economic and social organizations such as the EEC, CMEA, ASEAN, etc.

For many years now, there have been efforts to encourage the establishment of further regional human rights commissions, particularly in the African and Asian regions. At its twenty-third session in 1967 the Commission on Human Rights by its resolution 6 (XXIII) set up *Ad Hoc* study group to study in all its aspects the proposal to establish regional commissions on human rights within the United Nations family, in the light of the Commission's discussion of the subject.

The *Ad Hoc* Study Group submitted its report (E/CN.4/966 and Add.1) to the Commission at its twenty-fourth session in 1968. The views of the members of the *Ad Hoc* Study Group were divided but there was agreement that if further regional commissions are to be created this should be done on the initiative of the States in the region and not be imposed by the United Nations.

After a discussion of this report, the Commission in its resolution 7 (XXIV) of 1 March 1968 requested the Secretary-General to transmit the report to Member States and to regional intergovernmental organizations for their comments and further requested the Secretary-General to consider the possibility of arranging suitable regional seminars under the programme of advisory services in the field of human rights in those regions where no regional commission on human rights existed, for the purpose of discussing the usefulness and advisability of the establishment of such commissions (Commission resolution 7 (XXIV) of 1 March 1968).

In September 1969, at the invitation of the Government of the United Arab Republic, a seminar on the establishment of regional commissions on human rights with special reference to Africa was held in Cairo. The participants at the seminar agreed unanimously to request the Secretary-General of the United Nations to communicate the report of the seminar to the Secretary-General of the Organization of African Unity and the Governments of its member States so that the Organization of African Unity might consider appropriate steps, including the convening of a preparatory committee representative of Organization of African Unity membership, with a view to establishing a regional commission on human rights. The participants appealed to all Governments of Member States of the Organization of African Unity to give their support and co-operation in establishing a regional commission on human rights for Africa. They further requested the Secretary-General of the United Nations to offer all assistance under the programme of advisory services in the field of human rights in an effort towards establishing a regional commission on human rights for Africa and to draw the attention of the United Nations Commission on Human Rights to the report of the seminar and to arrange for full consideration and exchange of information between the Commission on Human Rights and the Organization of African Unity concerning the establishment of a regional commission on human rights for Africa. They also expressed the hope that the specialized agencies and regional organizations would, upon its request, offer their co-operation to the Organization of African Unity in connexion with the establishment of a regional commission on human rights for Africa.

At its twenty-sixth session in 1970 the Commission had before it the report of the *Ad Hoc* Study Group as well as comments by 29 Member States and three regional intergovernmental organizations. The report of the Cairo Seminar (ST/TAO/HR.38) was also made available to the Commission. In the resolution it adopted on the question (resolution 6 (XXVI), the Commission noted the report and the conclusions of the Cairo seminar and in particular the request addressed by the seminar to the Secretary-General to draw the attention of the Commission to the report and to arrange for full consideration and exchange of information between the Commission and the Organization of African Unity concerning the question of the establishment of a regional commission on human rights for Africa.

At the thirty-second session of the General Assembly a resolution was adopted by consensus on regional arrangements for the promotion and protection of human rights (resolution 32/127). In this resolution, the General Assembly, aware of the importance of encouraging regional co-operation for the promotion and protection of human rights and fundamental freedoms, appealed to States in areas where regional arrangements in the field of human rights do not yet exist to consider agreements with a view to the establishment within their respective regions of suitable regional machinery for the promotion and protection of human rights. It also requested the Secretary-General, under the programme of advisory services in the field of human rights, to give priority to the organization, in areas where no regional commissions on human rights exist, of seminars for the purpose of discussing the usefulness and advisability of the establishment of regional commissions for the promotion and protection of human rights. The Secretary-General was further requested to submit a progress report on the implementaton of this resolution to the General

Assembly at its thirty-third session for further consideration.

The representative of Nigeria, in introducing the draft resolution, said that the purpose of the draft resolution was to urge States to seize the initiative within their own geo-political environment in devising local arrangements concerning human rights which would reflect the character-istics of the regions themselves. The resolution was intended to encourage them to exchange ideas and exercise their freedom to establish such machinery as they deemed suitable. The Secretary-General, he felt, could play a useful part in efforts to achieve this purpose by assisting regional bodies to sponsor regional seminars on human rights or by organizing such seminars himself.[7]

The resolution received wide support. It was sponsored by Italy, Kenya, Lesotho, Nigeria, Oman, Panama and Swaziland. Countries expressly speaking in favour included Belgium, Brazil, Costa Rica, Cuba, Egypt, Iran, Ireland, Madagascar, Morocco, New Zealand, Nigeria, Norway, Syria, Union of Soviet Socialist Republics, the United Kingdom and the United States of America.

The objective of the resolution, as stated by one delegate, was "to encourage other regions to adopt human rights machinery tailored to their own needs".[8] However, caution was expressed that the existence of regional machinery should not reduce or replace the part played by the United Nations in the area of human rights. On the contrary, it was said, the United Nations and the regional bodies should work in harmony so that the international community can defend human rights at the world, as well as the regional levels.[9] It was stressed that any regional system established must be based on the contractual agreement of the countries of the region concerned and should conform to the interests of the countries in question.[10] The representative of Yugoslavia also gave useful advice when she stated that "while the question of regional arrangements for the promotion and protection of human rights was extremely important, it was also very sensitive and must be approached in different ways and in the dif-ferent regions."[11]

Some debate took place on the use of the word "machinery" as com-pared to "arrangements" in operative paragraph 1 of the resolution. While the sponsors emphasized that the objective was the establishment of regional commissions, it was pointed out that consideration should not be

[7] A/C.3/32/SR.74, paras. 83-85.
[8] Mr. Tyson (USA), A/C.3/32/SR.77, para. 23.
[9] *Ibid.,* para. 24, Miss Ilic (Yugoslavia), *ibid.,* para. 33.
[10] Mr. Alfonso (Cuba), A/C.3/32/SR.77, para. 35.
[11] Miss Ilic (Yugoslavia), A/C.3/32/SR.77, para. 32.

restricted to such commissions. Alternative arrangements should also be kept in mind.

The draft resolution was subjected to some "toning down"[12] during the course of passage. The original resolution (A/C.3/32/L.63) would also have recommended to the Economic and Social Council to request the United Nations regional economic and social commissions to study ways and means by which they could contribute to the promotion and protection of human rights within their respective regions, and would have invited the Council, if necessary, to expressly include in the terms of reference of the regional commissions the promotion and protection of human rights. It would also have requested the Executive Secretaries of the regional economic commissions to disseminate information on human rights within their respective regions: to organize regional seminars, training courses, symposia, panel discussions and other similar activities in the field of human rights and, for these purposes to appoint or designate within their respective secretariats a human rights officer responsible, under the advice of and in collaboration with, the Division of Human Rights, for the performance of these and other tasks in the field of human rights.

However, curiously, it was thought that these proposals would "give rise to serious constitutional problems within the United Nations system which might make it difficult to adopt . . . " them.[13] It was also felt that they could contradict the "criterion with regard to the powers currently exercised by the regional commissions and their Executive Secretaries".[14] It is unfortunate that this attitude led to the withdrawal of these provisions from the draft resolution. There has, quite rightly, been great emphasis placed recently on the realization of economic, social and cultural rights, and on an integrated approach to development. In line with these approaches it would have been fitting for the regional economic and social commissions to consider integrating the human rights factor in their work in the economic and social fields.

The resolution of the General Assembly comes at a particularly appropriate time. There has, in recent years, been growing recognition of the need for regional activities for the promotion and protection of human rights. The International Commission of Jurists has been organizing a series of regional seminars in various parts of the world with this objective in mind. It has already held such seminars in East Africa and the Caribbean. Further seminars are planned in the future for West Africa and for the

---

12 Mr. Ayeni (Nigeria), A/C.3/32/SR.77, para. 13.
13 Mr. Alfonso (Cuba), A/C.3/32/SR.76, para. 109.
14 *Idem,* A/C.3/32/SR.77, para. 34.

countries of the Andean region. The International Institute for Human Rights is sponsoring a seminar in Caracas in July/August 1978 on "Universalism and regionalism in the field of international protection and promotion of human rights".

At the thirty-fourth session of the Commission on Human Rights in 1978, several delegations favoured the establishment of further regional commissions. The Commission by resolution 24 (XXXIV) once again requested the Secretary-General to consider the possibility of arranging suitable regional seminars under the programme of advisory services in the field of human rights in those regions where no regional commission on human rights exists at present for the purpose of discussing the usefulness and advisability of the establishment of regional commissions on human rights. The Commission further requested the Secretary-General to take appropriate steps to give the Organization of African Unity, if it so requests, such assistance as it may require in facilitating the establishment of a regional commission on human rights for Africa, and decided to give due attention to this question at its thirty-fifth session.

3. Strategies for future regional action

Recent efforts for further regional action in the field of human rights have focused mainly on the establishment of regional human rights machinery in Africa and Asia. This is a goal that certainly deserves to be pursued with full vigour. However, action should not be restricted to it. A policy for regional action in the future should encompass:

(a) The establishment of further regional commissions.
(b) The establishment of arrangements at sub-regional levels.
(c) The establishment of less formal, more consultative arrangements such as standing conferences or consultative committees.
(d) The establishment of human rights committees or task forces in existing regional political, economic or social organizations.
(e) The establishment of human rights desks, task forces or committees in the Secretariats of existing regional organizations.
(f) The assignment of a role in the promotion of human rights and in the dissemination of information thereon by the United Nations regional economic and social commissions.
(g) The establishment of regional institutes on human rights.
(h) The holding of more regional seminars and training courses on human rights.
(i) Encouraging and assisting non-governmental organizations such as

regional bar associations, trade unions and church organizations to contribute to the promotion of human rights. The major non-governmental organizations should aim at appointing regional field officers for human rights.

(j) The appointment of United Nations field officers for human rights in the various regions of the world.

(a) The establishment of further regional commissions, and
(b) Arrangements at the sub-regional level
While work should certainly continue for the establishment of an African Commission and an Asian Commission on human rights, due attention should be paid to the possibilities for action at the sub-regional level. Professor Boutros-Ghali has drawn attention to the existence in Africa of "des groupements régionaux concurrents . . . formés sur une base linguistique, tantôt sur une base idéologique".[15] Each regional sub-system, he points out "constitue une petite Europe ou une petite Amérique latine du XIXe siècle qui co-existe avec des autres sous-systèmes. Ils constituent ensemble le système africain".

Leopold Senghor has identified three regional sub-systems in Africa: "L'Afrique du Nord, l'Afrique occidentale, l'Afrique orientale, en attendant que soit libérée l'Afrique du Sud. Chacune de ces Unions pourrait à son tour se diverser en unions plus petites . . .".[16]

As Professor Claude has observed, "one of the basic dilemmas of international organization (is) the disparity between *needs* for organization and *capacity* for organization. The unanswerable question is whether institutional endeavours should be geared to the requirements posed by the objective situation or to the possibilities offered and limited by the political situation".[17] This point is relevant both for the African and Asian regions. Professor Boutros-Ghali has noted even of the regional sub-systems in Africa that "Les ensembles régionaux demeurent extrêmement faibles et inefficaces. Les Etats africains manifestent une répugnance évidente et généralisée à s'engager sérieusement dans des processus d'intégration ou à élaborer des institutions supranationales structurées. Ils préfèrent créer des groupements régionaux très souples qui constituent, en dernière analyse, des groupes de pression dirigés vers l'extérieur plutôt que des institutions

---

[15] B. Boutros-Ghali, "Le système régional Africain", in *Société française pour le droit international, Régionalisme et universalisme dans le droit international contemporain* (1977), pp. 61-72.
[16] *Ibid.,* p. 64.
[17] Claude, *op. cit.* in note 1, above, p. 96.

dotées de pouvoirs réels en vue de promouvoir la solidarité à l'intérieur du Sous-système".[18] This would seem to suggest the following conclusions which may be applicable both to the African and the Asian continents.

(1) Efforts should certainly be pursued to establish regional arrangements at the pan-continental level.

(2) However, it may be necessary to aim, at the pan-continental level, for arrangements which are more flexible than those suggested by the European and Inter-American models.

(3) While striving for pan-continental arrangement, particular sub-regions should be examined to ascertain whether (a) arrangements might be established therein while pan-Continental arrangements are still being worked out; (b) sub-regional arrangements can eventually lead to pan-continental arrangements; (c) more elaborate arrangements are possible at the sub-regional level than are possible at the pan-continental level.

In sum, therefore, attention should be paid to the prospects both at the regional and sub-regional levels.

Attention should also be paid to sub-regions even in regions which already have regional machinery in the field of human rights. The Caribbean region, for example, falls within the Inter-American region and can therefore undoubtedly profit from the Inter-American machinery. However, there are forms of action that can still be taken at the Caribbean level to promote and protect human rights in addition to the possibilities offered by the Inter-American machinery: consultative arrangements by Caribbean governments, a role for the Caribbean integration organization, the CARICOM, and roles for the Caribbean Bar Association, the Caribbean Conference of Churches and the Caribbean Trade Union Organizations.[19] Great emphasis should, in our view, be placed on action at the sub-regional level in the future.

(c) The establishment of less formal, consultative arrangements
Experience thus far with the African and Asian Continents ought to temper our optimism as regards the possibilities of establishing formal regional commissions or regional arrangements in the field of human rights. Proposals for the establishment of an African Commission on Human Rights have been on the table since the 1960s. Requests have been made to the Organization of African Unity to initiate action for the establishment of such a commission. Yet, today there has not been much progress in the

---

[18] Boutros-Ghali, *loc. cit.,* p. 64.
[19] See, I.C.J., Human Rights and Development, Report of a Seminar on Human Rights in the Caribbean, held in Barbados in September 1977.

establishment of an African regional commission. Efforts are just in their embryonic stages for the establishment of a regional commission for Asia. A strategy for regional action should, therefore, contemplate the establishment of less formal, more consultative arrangements in the field of human rights, such as regional standing conferences or consultative committees on human rights. These would provide opportunities for exchange of views, identifying regional problems, and taking action in areas where regional co-operation is possible.

At the I.C.J. seminar on human rights and their promotion in the Caribbean held in Barbados in 1977, the suggestion was made that if a regional commission was not possible because of governmental reluctance, an institutional consultative process on a regional basis could be established.[20]

(d) The establishment of human rights committees or task forces in existing regional, political, economic or social organizations

A policy for regional action in the field of human rights should take into account the fact that in most regions or sub-regions of the world there exist regional institution in the political, economic or social fields. These institutions have established structures and, sometimes, permanent secretariats.

It is agreed on all sides today that human rights must be promoted and protected in their entirety and that economic, social and cultural rights and civil and political rights are indivisible and interdependent. It is also agreed that there should be an integrated approach to development in which the human rights element should be a central factor. If the foregoing principles are to be translated into meaningful action, it is essential that the human rights component should be promoted within regional organizations in the political, economic or social fields. Existing regional organizations should be encouraged to establish permanent task forces or committees charged with the functions of integrating human rights into their work programmes and also with following developments in the field of human rights in their respective regions.

(e) The establishment of human rights desks, task forces or committees in the Secretariats of the existing regional organizations

Following the same reasoning as under the previous heading, it is suggested that the permanent secretariats of existing regional bodies should be encouraged to establish human rights desks, task forces or committees to integrate the human rights component into their work programmes and

[20] *Ibid.*, 1977.

also to follow developments in the field of human rights within their respective regions. These committees, task forces or officers would act discreetly. The idea is not that they should become involved in collecting accusations against member Governments. Instead, they should systematically study ways and means of integrating the human rights factor into the work of their organizations and also systematically follow developments in the field of human rights with a view to making recommendations for action to their respective bodies.

(f) The assignment of a role in the promotion of human rights and in the dissemination of information thereon by the United Nations regional, economic and social commissions

If the United Nations is to be faithful to the integrated approach to development the human rights component should feature, to a greater extent, in the activities of bodies in the economic and social fields. This is especially true of the regional economic and social commissions which operate "in the field", nearer to the problems faced by Governments. The regional economic and social commissions have permanent secretariats which can be utilized for promotional purposes. As a minimum, the regional economic and social commissions should disseminate within their respective regions, information and material on human rights. Special attention could be paid to human rights in the process of development.

(g) The establishment of regional institutes on human rights

If formal regional arrangements are difficult to establish in the outstanding regions, regional institutes on human rights could perform a useful role in educating the opinion of leaders, government officials, university professors, teachers and the public at large. They can study regional problems in the field of human rights and prescribe measures for dealing with them. They can act to sensitize public opinion in the region at large on the need for the establishment of regional institutions in the field of human rights. They would serve initially to prepare the ground for regional institutions and after these institutions have been established, as adjuncts to such institutions. Regional institutes may also be established in regions where there already exists regional machinery, for example, in Latin America, Western Europe and in the Arab World.

(h) Regional seminars and training courses

The United Nations, as well as organizations such as the ILO, UNESCO, and the International Commission of Jurists already have a policy of holding regional seminars on human rights questions, at which Government officials and academic personnel are exposed to the international standards of human rights. There is an urgent need for the intensification of such regional seminars and training courses. They can perform a valuable role in moulding opinion in the various regions on the need for regional institutions and can also serve as channels for elaborating blueprints for such institutions.

(i)   Action by non-governmental organizations

At the seminar on Human Rights and their Promotion in the Caribbean, the view was advocated that if a formal regional commission was difficult to establish on account of governmental reluctance a conference or association of national non-governmental organizations involved in human rights should be established to discharge a promotional and protectional function throughout the region. The proposal was also made for the creation of an institutional consultative process on a regional basis.

Pending the establishment of regional arrangements by governments, non-governmental organizations bear a major responsibility for taking action to promote human rights at the regional level. Organizations such as regional bar associations, trade unions, and church organizations can contribute in an invaluable manner to the promotion of human rights. In the Caribbean region, the Caribbean Conference of Churches and the Caribbean Bar Association have provided the lead in pointing to regional human rights problems. They have experimented with innovative approaches such as the establishment of a Caribbean Human Rights and Legal Aid Fund designed to provide legal assistance to persons whose human rights are violated.

International non-governmental organizations should develop conscious strategies for action at the regional level. Assistance and encouragement should also be given to local regional organizations to take promotional action within their respective regions.[21]

(j)   Human rights field officers

One of the aims of the United Nations and of the larger international non-governmental organizations should be to emulate the practice of the International Committee of the Red Cross in employing field officers in the various regions of the world. These field officers can disseminate infor-

[21] Cf. O. Paliwal, "Areas of co-operation between the United Nations and the Afro-Asian Peoples' Solidarity Organization" in *Twenty Years of the Afro-Asian Peoples' Solidarity Organization* (1977), pp. 51-58.

mation, gather information on human rights problems in their respective regions, and act as channels for the provision of expert assistance to governments in the human rights field.

B. NATIONAL OR LOCAL INSTITUTIONS

As early as in resolution 9 (II) of the Economic and Social Council of 21 June 1946, the Economic and Social Council invited Member States to consider the desirability of establishing information groups or local human rights committees within their respective countries to collaborate with them in furthering the work of the Commission on Human Rights. The question of national advisory committees on human rights was, subsequently, repeatedly considered by the Commission on Human Rights, by the Sub-Commission on Prevention of Discrimination and Protection of Minorities and by the Economic and Social Council. A series of resolutions on this question was adopted, including Economic and Social Council resolutions 772 B (XXX) of 25 July 1960 and 888 F (XXXIV) of 24 July 1962, and in regard to proposals to establish national committees to assist in the development of information media in the less developed countries and to appoint national commissions on the status of women, Council resolutions 819 (XXXI) of 28 April 1961 and 961 (XXXVI) of 12 July 1963 respectively. The General Assembly also considered the advisability of the proposals for the establishment of national commissions on human rights or the designation of other appropriate institutions in conjunction with the adoption of the International Covenants on Human Rights (General Assembly resolution 2200 C (XXI) of 16 December 1966).[22]

It would be fair to say that: (1) The previous efforts of the United Nations have not significantly increased the number or effectiveness of such national or local institutions. A greater impact has come from non-

[22] See ECOSOC resolution 9(II); E/CN.4/115; E/CN.4/166; ECOSOC resolutions 772 B (XXX), 819 (XXXI), 888 F (XXXIV); GA resolutions 1961 (XVIII), 2081 (XX), 2200 C (XXI) and 2217 (XXI); A/C.3/L.1334, A/C.3/L.1407, A/C.3/L.1408, A/C.3/SR.1452, 53, 55, 56; E/CN.4/932. Report of the Commission on Human Rights (1970), paras. 106-108. E/CN.4/SR.1063-1066. International Convention on the Elimination of All Forms of Racial Discrimination, Article 14 (2). Programme of the Decade for Action to Combat Racism and Racial Discrimination, para. 12; GA Resolution 32/123; ST/TAO/HR/33: Effective realization of civil and political rights – selected studies. ST/TAO/HR/19: Remedies against the abuse of administrative authority – selected studies. ST/TAO/HR/25: Seminar on participation in local administration as a means of promoting human rights. ST/TAO/HR/28: Seminar on the effective realization of civil and political rights. ST/TAO/HR/15: Seminar on judicial and other remedies against the abuse of administrative authority with special emphasis on the role of parliamentary institutions.

governmental organizations. (2) Some information has been obtained on the more well-known institutions such as the Ombudsman, the Conseil d'Etat or the Procurator, but little information has been forthcoming on more novel types of institutions, for example, legal aid institutions and legal defence committees.

At the thiry-second session of the General Assembly in 1977, the idea of national or local institutions came to the fore again. The Secretary-General, in a note containing suggestions for the commemoration of the thirtieth anniversary of the Universal Declaration of Human Rights advanced the idea that the General Assembly, on the occasion of the thirtieth anniversary of the Universal Declaration of Human Rights, could examine national or local institutions for the promotion and protection of human rights. It was also suggested that a seminar could be organized on this subject in 1978. The General Assembly, in resolution 32/123 on the commemoration of the thirtieth anniversary of the Universal Declaration accepted the proposal for a seminar on this topic and requested that the report of the seminar be forwarded to it for its consideration.

At the thirty-fourth session of the Commission on Human Rights in 1978, several delegations supported the idea that measures should be taken to strengthen the role of national or local institutions in the field of human rights. The experience of some countries in utilizing such institutions was examined. On 8 March 1978, the Commission adopted resolution 23 (XXXIV) in which it invited Member States, within the framework of their national legislation and policy and according to their available means, to set up national institutions for the promotion and protection of human rights, having such structures, composition and recommendatory or other powers as the Government of the Member States concerned may wish to give them, bearing in mind the legal, judicial, executive and other systems of the country as well as the goal of the realization and effective achievement of all human rights and fundamental freedoms.

The seminar on national and local institutions in the field of human rights, to be held in July 1978, was requested to suggest guidelines for the structure and functioning of national institutions, bearing in mind the following possible functions of such institutions:

(a) Acting as a source of relevant information for the Government of a Member State and for the people of that country regarding matters connected with human rights;

(b) Assisting in the education of public opinion towards an awareness and respect for human rights;

(c) Considering, deliberating upon and making recommendations, within their specified terms of reference, regarding any particular state of affairs that may exist nationally that the Government may wish to refer to them;

(d) Advising on any questions regarding human rights referred to them from time to time by their national Government;

(e) Studying and keeping under review the status of legislation, judicial decisions and administrative arrangements for the promotion of human rights, and preparing and submitting, in this connexion, periodic reports at prescribed intervals to the appropriate authorities designated by the Government of the Member State concerned;

(f) Performing any function which the Government of a Member State may wish to assign to them in connexion with its duties under those international conventions in the field of human rights to which it is a State party.[23]

The Secretary-General of the United Nations was requested to circulate the Commission's resolution as well as any guidelines suggested by the United Nations seminar to Member States for their comments and suggestions, regarding future guidelines which could be made available to Governments for their assistance in setting up national institutions in the field of human rights.

Member States were also requested to communicate to the Secretary-General all relevant information on that subject, with a view to facilitating an exchange of information. The Secretary-general was requested to submit to the Commission a report containing the information received from Member States.

[23] This list of functions was extracted from proposals made during previous consideration of this question in the Commission on Human Rights and in the General Assembly.

CHAPTER XII

PROGRESSIVE TRANSNATIONAL PROMOTION OF HUMAN RIGHTS

PROF. ANTONIO CASSESE*

A. THE PRESENT DISSATISFACTION WITH UNITED NATIONS ACTION IN THE FIELD OF HUMAN RIGHTS

Discontent with the action of international intergovernmental organizations and particularly with that of the United Nations in the field of human rights is so widespread that it is not necessary to press the point. The criticism levelled at United Nations action in the field of *implementation* of human rights has been particularly harsh. This criticism has been formulated mainly in the west. In my opinion, it is largely unfounded, for these critics would like to see the United Nations do things that it is not capable of doing. They fail to realize that promoting the effective implementation of human rights does not mean transferring the British constitutional model to all or nearly all the States of the world, but, rather, confronting complex social, economic, political and institutional problems. The grave violations of human rights so widespread today do not arise only from the whim of despots or the desire for power of select oligarchies. They may *also* arise from these phenomena, but the essential reasons for these grave violations lie in the 'structural violence' so widely diffused in the world, in the existence of socio-political structures that are incapable of guaranteeing respect for human dignity. The United Nations does not have instruments of direct action against this 'structural violence'; hence one cannot expect it to rapidly and effectively intervene against oppressive Governments. That the United Nations intervenes with the limited instruments at its disposal, in relation to certain particularly grave and flagrant situations such as those of South Africa and Chile, is in itself a notable achievement. Admittedly, this can only be a "selective" intervention, conditioned by the orientation of the majority of member States.

Some of the criticisms levelled at the United Nations in the field of *standard setting* seem more well-founded, even though this is the very field

---

* Professor of International Law, University of Pisa.

where United Nations action has been more meritorious. It cannot be denied that the World Organization has achieved momentous results in this field. Although the adoption of resolutions and of conventions has been in itself of major importance, the United Nations' greatest success consists in spreading the essential human values that underlie those instruments, on a universal level; making Governments, peoples, groups and individuals realize that certain values exist which *should be* achieved. As has been rightly observed,[1] the United Nations which was created *mainly* to safeguard peace and to end or control tensions and conflicts – has not been afraid of exciting tensions and conflicts by spreading ideals which, when compared with reality, could only provoke deep indignation and, as a result, a strong sense of rebellion. Nevertheless, the "normative" action of the United Nations in the field of human rights is bound by various limits which considerably diminish its effect on the international state of affairs.

First of all, in spite of the presence of a strong group of progressive States, one sometimes has the impression (at least in certain fields, like that of minorities) that, at the heart of the United Nations, the tendency to protect the interests of Governments sometimes outweighs the need to consider the aspirations of peoples. Perhaps those States which are more directly involved are not sufficiently active or committed; or perhaps they themselves are sometimes conditioned by internal problems. The fact is that, on more than one occasion, a sort of convergence of interests or of reticences has arisen among governmental apparati, in that they have refrained from confronting certain grave problems of peoples or of minorities. Too often, one has the impression that the voices of peoples and individuals who suffer and struggle against an oppressor reach the United Nations filtered and deformed by the screen of sovereignty.

Another factor limiting the resolutions and declarations of the United Nations is that, in more than one case, they are not formulated with the aim of operating as true guidelines or, at any rate, they are not able to create a strong impetus for action. Too often, those who formulate these standards do not bother to translate them into concrete action in the single States. Thus these resolutions and declarations sink into oblivion.

A third factor limiting United Nations standards derives from the procedure with which they are usually adopted, namely, "consensus".

[1] B.V.A. Röling, "International Law and the Maintenance of Peace", IV *Netherlands Yearbook of International Law,* 47 ff. (1973).

This procedure admittedly certifies the will to avoid splits between the majority and the minority, and therefore to further a spirit of broad co-operation. In particular, it means that the Afro-Asian majority must realistically admit that to "deliberate" anything without the agreement of the great western powers and the socialist block would be altogether sterile and illusory. However, the practice of "consensus" is too often a source of ambiguous compromises. As a matter of fact, in order to avoid divergences and conflicts, the United Nations often chooses vague and polyvalent formulas whose broad generalities prevent the individuation of a sure line of action.

Another factor limiting international standards on human rights elaborated by the United Nations lies in the fact that these standards (the United Nations Covenants on Human Rights, for instance) often contain many "safeguard clauses" designed to authorize, in certain circumstances, restrictions on or curtailments of human rights. These clauses are sometimes so broad that they actually constitute loopholes for Governments.

B. THE SPREAD OF NON-GOVERNMENTAL ORGANIZATIONS AND TRANSNATIONAL GROUPS IN THE FIELD OF HUMAN RIGHTS

All of the abovementioned incapacities and deficiencies of the United Nations were soon perceived by non-governmental groups, individuals and organizations who considered it useful and important to make up for the shortcomings of the World Organization with their own direct action. In this way there arose numerous initiatives by groups which derive their origin and justification not from intergovernmental action, but directly from the social fabric of the international community. Two phenomena must be taken into consideration in order to fully explain this proliferation of centers of action. First of all, the circumstance (pointed out above) that the United Nations, in thirty years of action in the field of human rights and the rights of peoples, has disseminated such an intense consciousness of, and acute responsibility for, the respect of a few essential values that – having realized the failure of Governments to achieve these values – private groups, non-governmental organizations and national political movements have felt the need to actively strive to contribute to their effective realization.

The second phenomenon that may help understand the spread of non-governmental or transnational initiatives and actions in the field in question is that which some scholars define the "vertical expansion of the international community".[2] In recent years, in fact, the "horizontal" expansion of the international community (the increase in the number of States due to the newly-won independence of numerous territories previously subject to colonial domination) has gone hand in hand with the entrance onto the world scene of bodies and subjects other than States which have begun to play an important role in international life. These include peoples, national liberation movements, international intergovernmental organizations, individuals and private groups (such as the "international non-governmental organizations" or multinationals). Their presence has shattered the traditional structure of international society. This structure rested essentially on sovereign and independent States and it tended to legitimize the monopoly of each State over groups, individuals and other bodies within its political and territorial sphere. At the same time, it tended to recognize the authority of each State to "filter" the international protection of the interests of persons and bodies under its dominion. Today this "confinement" of groups, individuals and peoples within the structures of States has broken down. Consequently, new "protagonists" and new points of reference which bring together needs and interests different from those of States, and which express them forcefully on the international plane, have enriched international life. As a matter of fact, some of these new "subjects" (mainly peoples, national liberation movements, "non-governmental organizations" and transnational groups for the protection of human rights) are among the more dynamic factors of the international community, for they bring to the fore demands for renewal and progress which numerous States, by contrast, tend to ignore.

Even the less conspicuous category of these new participants in international life, the "non-governmental organizations", contributes appreciably to the development and implementation of a new international law on human rights. This contribution is made on various levels. Some organizations operate "in the field", in relation to specific situations which call for concrete solutions in the light of existing international laws or of new, emerging principles (examples of this kind include Amnesty International, the International Commission of Jurists and the Interparliamentary Union, which has recently instituted a special procedure for the protection of the rights and liberties of members of parliaments). Others, by contrast, seek to elaborate new international rules which can sub-

---

[2] W. Friedmann, *Law in a Changing Society,* London, 1959, at 419; B.V. Röling, *International Law in an Expanded World,* Amsterdam 1960, pp. XXI-XXII, 15 ff.

sequently be used by States or from which States can at least draw inspiration (for instance, the International Association of Penal Law recently elaborated an international draft convention on torture as an international crime).[3] Other non-governmental organizations, instead, endeavor to stimulate States to put into practice the international treaties that they have accepted (for example, the group of people who elaborated the text known as "Charter 77" and who hope to obtain respect for the United Nations Covenants on human rights on the part of the country in which they live, operates in this way).

C. COMMON FEATURES OF PROGRESSIVE TRANSNATIONAL GROUPS ACTING IN THE FIELD OF HUMAN RIGHTS

All of the organizations and private groups to which I have referred in the preceding paragraph can be distinguished on the basis of the following criterion: whether or not they operate within the framework of the United Nations, in addition to acting autonomously in international society. The better known organizations that also operate within the framework of the United Nations include Amnesty International, the International Commission of Jurists, the International Association of Democratic Lawyers, and others. These organizations have acquired a great deal of credit for the work they have done, urging Governments to consider problems that are normally neglected, calling the attention of the UN to situations that it is unacquainted with, and proposing suitable initiatives and actions for protecting human rights more effectively.

Other organizations which – at least until now – have not collaborated with the United Nations are less well known. I believe it appropriate to focus on one or two of them. These groups, organizations and initiatives should be viewed in historical perspective. They are integral parts of a trend which emerged toward the end of the '60's. Until then, only pro-western organizations and groups in the liberal tradition had concerned themselves with human rights at the universal level. But, beginning in the late '60's, pro-socialist groups and organizations also began to show concern for this

---

[3] For a case study of non-governmental participation in the development of international norms see V. Leary, "A New Role for Non-Governmental Organizations in Human Rights", in A. Cassese (editor), *Modern International Law: Problems and Prospect,* Sijthoff 1978.

More generally, for the growing role of private persons and unofficial groups in international dealings see M.R. Berman and J.J. Johnson (editors), *Unofficial Diplomats,* New York 1977.

area of problems.[4] The groups I shall discuss share the following features: they are inspired by a *progressive vision* of international society; they try to link themselves to the actions both of the *Third World Governments* (reinforcing these actions and making up for shortcomings and omissions which limit their influence at present) and of *national liberation movements,* in an effort to associate these countries and movements to the western workers' movement; above all, they favour *groups and peoples* more than single individuals whose fundamental rights are trampled on; they realize that it is not enough to call situations of grave and flagrant violations of the rights of individuals or peoples to the attention of international public opinion, but that it is also and above all necessary to investigate and understand *the historical causes and socio-political roots of those violations,* if one wants to systematically eradicate oppression and abuse; finally, they share an *ideological mould* which leads back to an anti-imperialist attitude and, more generally, criticizes the hegemony of the great economic, industrial and military powers and every form of neo-colonialism.[5]

D. THE PASSING OF VERDICTS ON BEHALF OF THE CONSCIENCE OF PEOPLES AND IN THE INTEREST OF MANKIND

The first level on which the groups I would like to discuss operate is *judicial.* During the war in Vietnam, a group of philosophers, jurists, writers, political scientists and politicians of different nationalities believed that, in the face of the silence of Governments with regard to the Vietnam

---

[4] Weissbrodt, "The Role of International Non-governmental Organizations in the Implementation of Human Rights", 10 *Texas International Law Journal* 301 (1977), stresses that in late 1971 NGO's "traditionally associated with socialist countries began actively to participate in international non-governmental conferences on issues of common concern".

[5] One of the basic texts adopted by the transnational groups under discussion, namely the Algiers Declaration of the Rights of Peoples (see *infra,* para. 4), stresses, however, that the main adversary of all those fighting for the protection of the rights of peoples is imperialism. It is said in the preamble of the Declaration: " . . . We live at a time . . . of frustration and defeat, as new forms of imperialism evolve to oppress and exploit the peoples of the world. Imperialism, using vicious methods, with the complicity of governments that it has itself often installed, continues to dominate a part of the world. Through direct or indirect intervention, through multinational enterprises, through manipulation of corrupt local politicians, with the assistance of military regimes based on police repression, torture and physical extermination of opponents, through a set of practices that has become known as neo-colonialism, imperialism extends its strangehold over many peoples." I have tried elsewhere (see my paper "La portée politico-juridique de la Déclaration d'Alger", in A. Cassese and E. Jouve, editors, *Pour un droit des peuples,* Paris, Berger-Levrault, 1978) to show that the whole spirit of the Declaration warrants a broader interpretation, to the effect that, according to the Declaration, peoples are oppressed not only by imperialist powers but also by some authoritarian governments belonging to other areas of the world, including the socialist area.

tragedy (motivated by reasons or Realpolitik or by membership in international groups or international political alignments), world public opinion must intervene to do that which Governments would not or could not do: to determine if crimes against humanity were being committed in Vietnam and, if so, to condemn the Governments and other bodies responsible for those crimes. Thus the First Russell Tribunal was set up in 1966, on the initiative of the philosopher B. Russell. Naturally, it did not have the juridical authority of national or international courts and it could not deliver juridically binding and executive decisions. It did, however, have a different and, perhaps, greater authority, it acted as expression and spokesman of the conscience of peoples, a supreme moral presence which passed verdicts in the name of all humanity. The founding declaration, approved in London on 15 November 1966, reads:

Although this task has not been entrusted to us by any constituted authority, we have taken the responsibility upon ourselves in the interest of mankind and for the defence of civilization. Our action is based on a private understanding. We are absolutely independent of every government whatever and of whatsoever official or semiofficial organization. We firmly believe that we are giving expression to the profound anxiety and remorse of all those who, throughout many nations, are our brothers. We firmly believe that our action will contribute to reawakening the world's conscience.

The President of the Tribunal, Jean-Paul Sartre, again insisted on the moral legitimization of the Tribunal's action in his opening speech at the first session, in Stockholm, on 2 May 1967. He observed,

We are perfectly well aware that we have not received any mandate from anyone. If we have taken the initiative of convening, we have done so because we knew that no one *could* give us this mandate. Certainly our Tribunal is not an institution (Il est certain que notre Tribunal n'est pas une institution). But it does not replace any established power. It has arisen rather from a *lack* and from an *appeal* (il est plutôt né d'un *vide* et d'un *appel*).

As a matter of fact, the trial which took place in 1967 and the condemnation of the USA which resulted[6] had considerable effect on world public opinion and perhaps contributed in some measure – even though indirectly – to the progressive change of mind of the American ruling class, regarding strategy in Vietnam and the advisability of a withdrawal from South East Asia. The Tribunal's verdict certainly influenced American public opinion greatly.

---

[6] For interpretation and documentation fo the Russell proceedings see John Duffett (editor), *Against the Crime of Silence: Proceedings of the International War Crimes Tribunal,* New York, Simon and Schuster, 1970.

A few years later, the same people who had conceived the First Russell Tribunal thought of instituting another international tribunal to judge the grave and flagrant violations of human rights in some Latin American countries. Thus the Second Russell Tribunal was set up in 1973. The Second Russell Tribunal met in three sessions, in 1974, 1975 and 1976. At the end of these sessions, it condemned several Latin American Governments (Brazil, Chile, Bolivia, Uruguay and the Dominican Republic) and appealed to world public opinion to work to end the grave violations of the rights of peoples encountered in those countries.

In this second phase, the Russell Tribunal reitereated some of the questions of principle that it had already confronted in the first phase and it more clearly specified the grounds for its authority,[7] as well as the profound motivations of its actions.[8]

Two dominant elements characterized this second phase of the Russell Tribunal. First of all, the Tribunal did not limit itself to denouncing violations of fundamental rights committed by the Governments, as was the case with Vietnam. It also investigated the historical causes and the general social, economic and political context of those violations. Secondly, a network of supporting committees grew up in several countries which worked

---

[7] As soon as it was officially constituted, on 6 November 1973, the Russell Tribunal II made the following statement concerning its own investiture: "It does not reject the idea that a tribunal is necessarily the emanation of an authority. A society as little organized as international society is governed by an authority that is diffuse, embodied not in juridical persons or in governments but residing in those peoples themselves. The only rational and real foundation of international law is the desire for peace of men and women who share the conviction of their mutual solidarity". Furthermore in its 1974 verdict it pointed out that "Governments have always claimed to be the only institutions qualified to represent the international community. Such a claim is patently unjustified, especially when it is considered that the action of governing bodies at the international level has impeded rather than encouraged the development of law and the growth of international solidarity. The Russell Tribunal II will do its best to express the aspirations of the international community. It needs the active support of public opinion; if it is to help men and women everywhere to develop a more active and enlightened awareness of world problems and to obtain the support and assistance that legitimize its activities".

[8] In the verdict that the Russell Tribunal II issued in the 1975 Session, it stated the following: "the power to pass judgement is one of the most formidable powers that exists. But the members of the Russell Tribunal decided that silence would make them accomplices, should they, out of excessive juridical scruples, hesitate to investigate. To declare that one must not get involved in politics is to give support to those in power, and thereby to collaborate in their policies. To refrain from passing judgement on injustices, when whole peoples are the victims, and when one is sufficiently apprised of the facts, is, by that very silence, to stand on the side of hangmen and torturers.

"There is no officially established international tribunal to hear the case of these oppressed peoples. The judges in their own countries, in Brazil and in Chile for example, have collaborated in destroying the rule of law – step by step in Brazil, brutally in Chile. The Russell Tribunal exists not only to fill a gap in the international juridical system, it must redress the injustices committed by those whose first duty should have been to refuse to minister to an authority which is all the more brutal because it is aware of the precarious nature of its power, in order to uphold the laws."

alongside and in connection with the Tribunal. The aim of these committees was to sensitize national and international public opinion regarding the problems that the Tribunal was investigating and to mobilize political groups, union movements and, more generally, all public opinion, to take action against those responsible for the violations of human rights and the rights of peoples ascertained by the Tribunal.

The positive results of the organization's activity are attested by the press coverage given to the Tribunal throughout the world, the presence of representatives of African and Asian national liberation movements at its more solemn ceremonies, the requests by political movements to set up new sessions on the problems of other countries[9] and the widespread request to make the Tribunal permanent.

Notwithstanding these unquestionably positive aspects, one must not neglect or pass over in silence the limits of the Russell Tribunal or, for that matter, of any such judicial body. To begin with, the trials are conducted against Governments that do not accept the Tribunal's authority. Consequently, as in the case of all trials *in absentia,* they cannot count on proof, facts, testimonies or documents, produced by the defendant, which would be invaluable to the ascertainment of the truth. In addition, the principle *audiatur et altera pars* cannot be applied in full. This makes it particularly difficult for the tribunal to come to objective and exhaustive conclusions. Secondly, the Tribunal must lend itself to the facile criticism of being motivated by political considerations, both in the choice of Governments and authorities brought to trial and in certain aspects of the concrete development of the trial. This is, perhaps, an inevitable criticism which, however, should be attenuated by the consideration of the high moral quality of the members of the Tribunal. Thirdly, the paucity of financial means available to the Tribunal, the lack of cooperation by Governments and institutions and, perhaps, the incapacity of or impossibility for the organizers to mobilize greater energies have sometimes had a negative effect on the Tribunal's activity. One has the impression that, in some cases, its inquiries and investigations are not as thorough and exhaustive as they should be. Finally, there does not seem to have been a suitable connection between the results of the First and Second Tribunals, in that the Tribunal was unable to develop a coherent and thorough jurisprudence on the themes it dealt with.

---

[9] The Venezuelan paper *El Nacional* (Caracas) of 10 January 1976 carried an article stating that "Dr. José Herrera Oropeza, President of the National Movement for the Defense of Panama, and of the Committee for the Independence of Puerto Rico, sent a letter to the President of the II Russell Tribunal, Senator Leslie Basso, urging that the Tribunal give special consideration to the plight of Panama and Puerto Rico".

We can only hope that some of these limits will be overcome with the creation, in the near future, of a permanent Tribunal of the rights of peoples sponsored by a body instituted following the dissolution of the Second Russell Tribunal, namely, the International Foundation for the Rights and the Liberation of Peoples. It is worthwhile to note that the action of this tribunal will not be limited to the areas of imperialism and neo-colonialism, but will also be extended to "military dictatorships based on police repression" or, more generally, to all "political ideologies and practices that disregard the needs and rights of peoples, minorities and individuals".[10] The permanent nature of the tribunal, the various ways of selecting judges and, in broader terms, its functional characteristics, also leave hope that its action can be authoritative, incisive and universal.

E. THE DEVELOPMENT OF PROGRESSIVE INTERNATIONAL STANDARDS
ON THE FUNDAMENTAL RIGHTS OF PEOPLES, MINORITIES AND
INDIVIDUALS

The groups that gave rise to the Russell Tribunal also operated on another level, that is, the *normative plane*. Already in the course of the Russell

[10] I deem it useful to quote the preambular paragraphs of the Statute of the International Permanent Tribunal of the Peoples, adopted by the International Foundation for the Rights and the Liberation of Peoples in 1978 (the original text is in French):

"Considérant que les peuples, les minorités et les individus sont de plus en plus exposés à des violations flagrantes et systématiques de leurs droits fondamentaux, en raison de la prolifération de régimes militaires dictatoriaux fondés sur la répression policière, de l'emprise toujours plus pénétrante de groupes néo-colonialistes sur de vastes zones du monde, de l'existence d'idéologies et de pratiques politiques qui n'attachent pas de valeur aux exigences et aux droits des peuples, des minorités et des individus;

"Considérant que ces violations des règles essentielles de la communauté internationale, tels que notamment les crimes d'apartheid, de génocide, d'exploitation néo-colonialiste des peuples et des minorités, d'oppression systématique des peuples et d'autres groupes humains, sont perpétrées sans que la communauté internationale organisée soit à même de se dresser contre de tels crimes et violations et de leur mettre un terme;

"Considérant en particulier que les organes de la communauté internationale organisée, s'ils ont réussi à élaborer des règles fondamentales de conduite visant à proclamer les droits fondamentaux des peuples, des minorités et des individus, ne sont pas encore à même de mettre en oeuvre ces règles, notamment par des mécanismes internationaux capables de garantir qu'elles soient respectées par les gouvernements et les groupes privés;

"Considérant qu'il est nécessaire en même temps d'approfondir les causes économiques, politiques et sociales de ces phénomènes néfastes que sont les crimes et les autres infractions contre les peuples, les minorités et les individus, et de tâcher d'y mettre un terme;

"Considérant que jusqu'à ce que les gouvernements progressistes réussissent à mettre en place des organismes internationaux capables de faire cesser lesdits phénomènes, il incombe aux groupes politiques et syndicaux avancés et à l'opinion publique éclairée de créer des structures internationales qui soient à même d'attirer l'attention des gouvernements, des mouvements politiques et syndicaux et de l'opinion publique mondiale sur les violations flagrantes et systématiques des droits des peuples, des minorités et des individus, ainsi que sur leurs causes économiques, politiques et sociales."

Tribunal proceedings, the members of the Tribunal became aware of the lacunae, inadequacies and reticences of international law. Hence they sought, among other things, to fill these lacunae and to make up for these inadequacies, clarifying and developing a few general principles of international law (the principle of self-determination of peoples, for instance) and the United Nations resolutions on the new international economic order.[11] Following the termination of the Russell Tribunal's activities, the two institutions which became its heirs – the abovementioned Foundation and the International League for the Rights and Liberation of Peoples – maintained that the elaboration of a new judge-made law was not enough; that it was also necessary to solemnly proclaim, in a normative text, new lines of action in which States and other subjects of the international community could find inspiration. As the most urgent task was considered that of sanctioning the fundamental rights of peoples, it was decided to elaborate an international "charter" on this subject which takes up, explores, renders explicit and gathers together the numerous starting points on the matter contained in the resolutions of the United Nations

---

[11] The Russell Tribunal II touched upon problems of international law in the verdict it delivered in 1975. It pointed out, *inter alia,*

"Classic international law is beset by a fundamental contradiction. It is made up of laws which are binding on States, laws which the States themselves, through their governments, have recognised as binding in their dealings with one another. But the formality of the representatives of governments which, in fact, exercise authority in a regular manner in the territorial space belonging to them, makes impossible any control by an international organ of the manner in which governments exercise that authority. While by no means negligible, the contemporary values of the international legal order are purely formal. The prohibition of wars of aggression implies a territorial *status quo* which ends up by freezing national frontiers. On the other hand, certain forms of economic and cultural aggression escape the control mechanisms of classic international law. Nor does classic international law encourage the active cooperation of peoples to reduce injustices flowing from the present uneven distribution of wealth and knowledge.

"Such is the aim of the new international law which may, by contrast, be described as the 'peoples' international law. The most noteworthy achievement of this new dynamic law has been political decolonisation, today almost complete, economic and cultural decolonisation, on the other hand have yet to be achieved. Numerous resolutions of the United Nations General Assembly, as well as the very recent Charter of the Economic Rights and Duties of States, include many interesting suggestions for reducing the flagrant economic and cultural inequalities in the world today . . .

At the level of law, the Tribunal notes elements of conflict between the liberal framework of international economic law, the more 'socialist' tendencies in law as reflected in resolutions voted by the General Assembly of the United Nations, and finally the formalism of classical international law which recognises only states represented by governments having effective control over their territory. It will be necessary in the future to make adjustments between these three trends: in international economic law, in peoples' law, and in classic international law governing relations between States.

"The Russell Tribunal supports the notion that both classical international law governing relations between States and, even more, the liberal framework of international economic law have an outdated air, whilst peoples' law is the new and progressive element in international law. Consequently if there is need to overcome contradictions between these differing aspects, these must be resolved in favour of the 'peoples' law'."

General Assembly. An international conference held in Algiers in 1976, in which representatives of national liberation movements, politicians, union leaders, jurists, political scientists and economists participated, formally adopted the Universal Declaration of the Rights of Peoples.

It would not be fitting to examine this Declaration in detail here.[12] I shall thus limit myself to two general observations. First of all, the Declaration, like the verdicts of the Russell Tribunal in the past, represents a break with the deeply-rooted positivist conception of law. This conception is based on an unacceptable premise and produces unacceptable consequences. The premise is that only the formal law created by the "official" sources of law exists. The consequence to which this premise leads is that jurists who want to influence the evolution of law in some way must do so only through "official channels" – in our case, through the foreign ministries of States – to make their influence on the elaboration of international laws felt. By contributing to the elaboration of the decisions of the Russell Tribunal and the Algiers Declaration, and by discussing these texts critically and making them available to a wider audience, jurists and political scientists have chosen another road. They have created a *"non official"* law which is aimed at *supplementing* (rather than *replacing)* interstate law, which is capable of expressing the needs of individuals and groups more directly and more generally and which, at the same time, acts as a stimulus for Governments (at least the more progressive ones). Naturally, this "non official" law operates in a different sphere than that of "formal law". Nevertheless, by gradually penetrating the involucre of States' interests, it can even end up being translated into *"jus positivum"*. One must not forget that, since 1907, when the preamble of the IV Hague Convention on the Laws and Customs of War on Land was adopted, States recognized that the principles of the law of nations may result from "the laws of humanity" and "the dictates of the public conscience". In 1977, States reiterated this principle, incorporating it in Art. 1 para. 2 of the I Protocol Additional to the 1949 Geneva Convention on War Victims. In this way, States have clearly admitted that pressures exerted by the "conscience of humanity" can play an important role in the formation of international

---

[12] The Algiers Declaration has aroused great interest in the international legal literature. See e.g. A. Uribe, "Légitimer les droits des peuples", *Le Monde diplomatique,* September 1976; P. Fois, "La dichiarazione universale dei diritti dei popoli di Algeri", 31 *La Comunità internazionale,* 491 (1976); R. Falk, "The Algiers Declaration of the Rights of Peoples and the Struggle for Human Rights", in A. Cassese (Editor), *Modern International Law: Problems and Prospects,* cit. *supra* at note 31; F. Rigaux, "The Algiers Declaration of the Rights of Peoples" *ibid.* A. Cassese and E. Jouve (Editors), *Pour un droit des peuples,* cit., *supra* at note 5.

law. The Algiers Declaration – like other, similar texts – gives concrete form to the demands of the conscience of peoples, of the more advanced political movements and of enlightened public opinion. It can thus legitimately aspire to become one of the elements that gradually give rise to new principles of international law. Even before turning into rules and principles of positive law, however, the Algiers Declaration can accomplish the important task of orienting world public opinion and creating parameters of judgement for critically evaluating the action of Governments. Furthermore, it can become a point of reference for the action of all those involved in the struggle against authoritarianism.

My second general observation is that the Algiers Declaration, like State constitutions or the "constitutions" of international organizations (the United Nations Charter, for example) is not and is not intended to be a "petrified" text which consecrates the fundamental rights of peoples in a final, *ne varietur* way. Rather, it is intended to be a *"living"* text, a working tool to be enriched and modified with the evolution of international relations. It is in this way that it was conceived by the "founding fathers" and in this way it has been interpreted by those people who have committed themselves to disseminating and implementing it.

F. RESEARCH, DISCUSSION AND DISSEMINATION OF IDEAS IN THE FIELD OF THE FUNDAMENTAL RIGHTS OF PEOPLES, MINORITIES AND INDIVIDUALS

The groups and persons who operate in the two ways outlined above also act *on a third level:* that of the discussion and study of general and particular problems regarding the fulfilment of human rights and the rights of peoples and of the adoption of concrete initiatives (round tables, conferences, debates, mass demonstrations, etc.) designed to sensitize public opinion to these problems and to mobilize ever-growing groups. In this sector, the International League for the Rights and Liberation of Peoples, mentioned above, plays a considerable role. Art. 2 of the Statute of the League states:

The League proposes to fight for a new political, economic and juridical order based on the right of peoples to self-determine their own future, against every form of dependence and subjugation and against imperialism.

The League's objectives are the full development of the values common to the whole people, the promotion of a real equality among all citizens, the effective respect of fundamental human rights and the building of an international community based on peaceful relations, reciprocal respect and friendship of all peoples.

Art. 3 continues:

The League thus will establish contacts with all liberation movements which are fighting for the same end. It will help denounce, before world public opinion, by way of the press and of political fora, violations of the rights of peoples as well as to forge instruments for the cultural and political struggle against imperialistic oppression and any form of domination.

To achieve the objectives which these rules set, the League, together with the Foundation, has organized various initiatives, among them a conference on cultural imperialism and numerous meetings and debates on the Algiers Declaration and on its applicability to certain concrete situations (Palestine, South Africa, Latin America, etc.). There have also been, or there will be in the future, other international conferences on the relationship between the Church and military dictatorships in Latin America; on various problems (juridical, social, etc.) regarding Latin American exiles; on the present forms of technological dependence of the Third World countries; and on the role of women in national liberation movements and in the making of a new society.

G. CONCLUDING REMARKS

The activity of the transnational groups which I have discussed here does not oppose the activity of the UN in the field of human rights. Nor, naturally, does it pretend – for it would be absurd to do so – to substitute or replace that action, if for no other reason because these groups are aware of the fact (which I pointed out above, in para. 2) that they have come into being in part *because of* the greater awareness of human dignity diffused from 1948 to the present by the United Nations. It is their intent to act in a way that is *supplementary* and *complementary* with respect to the activity of the United Nations. They start from the assumption that it is necessary to fight on more than one front and more than one level in order to effectively carry human rights and the rights of peoples into effect. The groups in question therefore intend to support and help the United Nations in fields in which the latter cannot explicate an effective action because of the governmental conditioning to which it is subjected. At the same time, however, the transnational groups under discussion try to strengthen and enhance the more progressive United Nations member States, in order to stimulate a more incisive action for human rights, mainly by investigating more deeply the socio-economic causes of situations which deviate from the respect of human rights and by seeking to abandon nationalistic or group outlooks.

APPENDIX

UNIVERSAL DECLARATION OF HUMAN RIGHTS*

ADOPTED AND PROCLAIMED BY GENERAL ASSEMBLY RESOLUTION 217
A (III) OF 10 DECEMBER 1948

Preamble

Whereas recognition of the inherent dignity and of the equal and inalienable rights of all members of the human family is the foundation of freedom, justice and peace in the world.

Whereas disregard and contempt for human rights have resulted in barbarous acts which have outraged the conscience of mankind, and the advent of a world in which human beings shall enjoy freedom of speech and belief and freedom from fear and want has been proclaimed as the highest aspiration of the common people,

Whereas it is essential, if man is not to be compelled to have recourse, as a last resort, to rebellion against tyranny and oppression, that human rights should be protected by the rule of law,

Whereas it is essential to promote the development of friendly relations between nations,

Whereas the peoples of the United Nations have in the Charter reaffirmed their faith in fundamental human rights, in the dignity and worth of the human person and in the equal rights of men and women and have determined to promote social progress and better standards of life in larger freedom,

Whereas Member States have pledged themselves to achieve, in cooperation with the United Nations, the promotion of universal respect for and observance of human rights and fundamental freedoms,

Whereas a common understanding of these rights and freedoms is of the greatest importance for the full realization of this pledge,

* Text taken from "Human Rights: A Compilation of International Instruments of the United Nations", United Nations publication, Sales No. E.73.XIV.2.

Now, Therefore,

The General Assembly

Proclaims this Universal Declaration of Human Rights as a common standard of achievement for all peoples and all nations, to the end that every individual and every organ of society, keeping this Declaration constantly in mind, shall strive by teaching and education to promote respect for these rights and freedoms and by progressive measures, national and international to secure their universal and effective recognition and observance, both among the peoples of Member States themselves and among the peoples of territories under their jurisdiction.

Article 1

All human beings are born free and equal in dignity and rights. They are endowed with reason and conscience and should act towards one another in a spirit of brotherhood.

Article 2

Everyone is entitled to all the rights and freedoms set forth in this Declaration, without distinction of any kind, such as race, colour, sex, language, religion, political or other opinion, national or social origin, property, birth or other status.

Furthermore, no distinction shall be made on the basis of the political, jurisdictional or international status of the country or territory to which a person belongs, whether it be independent, trust, non-self-governing or under any other limitation of sovereignty.

Article 3

Everyone has the right to life, liberty and the security of person.

Article 4

No one shall be held in slavery or servitude; slavery and the slave trade shall be prohibited in all their forms.

Article 5

No one shall be subjected to torture or to cruel, inhuman or degrading treatment or punishment.

Article 6

Everyone has the right to recognition everywhere as a person before the law.

Article 7

All are equal before the law are entitled without any discrimination to equal protection of the law. All are entitled to equal protection against any discrimination in violation of this Declaration and against any incitement to such discrimination.

Article 8

Everyone has the right to an effective remedy by the competent national tribunals for acts violating the fundamental rights granted him by the constitution or by law.

Article 9

No one shall be subjected to arbitrary arrest, detention or exile.

Article 10

Everyone is entitled in full equality to a fair and public hearing by an independent and impartial tribunal, in the determination of his rights and obligations and of any criminal charge against him.

Article 11

1. Everyone charged with a penal offence has the right to be presumed innocent until proved guilty according to law in a public trial at which he has had all the guarantees necessary for his defence.
2. No one shall be held guilty of any penal offence on account of any act or omission which did not constitute a penal offence, under national or

international law, at the time when it was committed. Nor shall a heavier penalty be imposed than the one that was applicable at the time the penal offence was committed.

Article 12

No one shall be subjected to arbitrary interference with his privacy, family, home or correspondence, nor to attacks upon his honour and reputation. Everyone has the right to the protection of the law against such interference or attacks.

Article 13

1. Everyone has the right to freedom of movement and residence within the borders of each State.
2. Everyone has the right to leave any country, including his own, and to return to his country.

Article 14

1. Everyone has the right to seek and to enjoy in other countries asylum from persecution.
2. This right may not be invoked in the case of prosecutions genuinely arising from non-political crimes or from acts contrary to the purposes and principles of the United Nations.

Article 15

1. Everyone has the right to a nationality.
2. No one shall be arbitrarily deprived of his nationality nor denied the right to change his nationality.

Article 16

1. Men and women of full age, without any limitation due to race, nationality or religion, have the right to marry and to found a family. They are entitled to equal rights as to marriage, during marriage and at its dissolution.
2. Marriage shall be entered into only with the free and full consent of the intending spouses.
3. The family is the natural and fundamental group unit of society and

is entitled to protection by society and the State.

Article 17

1. Everyone has the right to own property alone as well as in association with others.
2. No one shall be arbitrarily deprived of his property.

Article 18

Everyone has the right to freedom of thought, conscience and religion; this right includes freedom to change his religion or belief, and freedom, either alone or in community with others and in public or private, to manifest his religion or belief in teaching, practice, worship and observance.

Article 19

Everyone has the right to freedom of opinion and expression; this right includes freedom to hold opinions without interference and to seek, receive and impart information and ideas through any media and regardless of frontiers.

Article 20

1. Everyone has the right to freedom of peaceful assembly and association.
2. No one may be compelled to belong to an association.

Article 21

1. Everyone has the right to take part in the government of his country, directly or through freely chosen representatives.
2. Everyone has the right of equal access to public service in his country.
3. The will of the people shall be the basis of the authority of government; this will shall be expressed in periodic and genuine elections which shall be by universal and equal suffrage and shall be held by secret vote or by equivalent free voting procedures.

Article 22

Everyone, as a member of society, has the right to social security and is entitled to realization, through national effort and international co-operation and in accordance with the organization and resources of each State, of the economic, social and cultural rights indispensable for his dignity and the free development of his personality.

Article 23

1. Everyone has the right to work, to free choice of employment, to just and favourable conditions of work and to protection against unemployment.

2. Everyone, without any discrimination, has the right to equal pay for equal work.

3. Everyone who works has the right to just and favourable remuneration ensuring for himself and his family an existence worthy of human dignity, and supplemented, if necessary, by other means of social protection.

4. Everyone has the right to form and to join trade unions for the protection of his interests.

Article 24

Everyone has the right to rest and leisure, including reasonable limitation of working hours and periodic holidays with pay.

Article 25

1. Everyone has the right to a standard of living adequate for the health and well-being of himself and of his family, including food, clothing, housing and medical care and necessary social services, and the right to security in the event of unemployment, sickness, disability, widowhood, old age or other lack of livelihood in circumstances beyond his control.

2. Motherhood and childhood are entitled to special care and assistance. All children, whether born in or out of wedlock, shall enjoy the same social protection.

Article 26

1. Everyone has the right to education. Education shall be free, at least in the elementary and fundamental stages. Elementary education shall be compulsory. Technical and professional education shall be made generally available and higher education shall be equally accessible to all on the basis of merit.

2. Education shall be directed to the full development of the human personality and to the strenghtening of respect for human rights and fundamental freedoms. It shall promote understanding, tolerance and friendship among all nations, racial or religious groups, and shall further the activities of the United Nations for the maintenance of peace.

3. Parents have a prior right to choose the kind of education that shall be given to their children.

Article 27

1. Everyone has the right freely to participate in the cultural life of the community, to enjoy the arts and to share in scientific advancement and its benefits.

2. Everyone has the right to the protection of the moral and material interests resulting from any scientific, literary or artistic production of which he is the author.

Article 28

Everyone is entitled to a social and international order in which the rights and freedoms set forth in this Declaration can be fully realized.

Article 29

1. Everyone has duties to the community in which alone the free and full development of his personality is possible.

2. In the exercise of his rights and freedoms, everyone shall be subject only to such limitations as are determined by law solely for the purpose of securing due recognition and respect for the rights and freedoms of others and of meeting the just requirements of morality, public order and the general welfare in a democratic society.

3. These rights and freedoms may in no case be exercised contrary to the purposes and principles of the United Nations.

Article 30

Nothing in this Declaration may be interpreted as implying for any State, group or person any right to engage in any activity or to perform any act aimed at the destruction of any of the rights and freedoms set forth herein.

INDEX